TECHNICAL REPORT

T0302974

Adolescent Romantic Relationships as Precursors of Healthy Adult Marriages

A Review of Theory, Research, and Programs

Benjamin R. Karney, Megan K. Beckett,
Rebecca L. Collins, Rebecca Shaw

Prepared for the Department of Health and Human Services

RAND LABOR AND POPULATION

The research described in this report was conducted by RAND Labor and Population. The views expressed herein are those of the authors and do not necessarily reflect the official position of the Department of Health and Human Services.

Library of Congress Cataloging-in-Publication Data

Adolescent romantic relationships as precursors of healthy adult marriages : a review of theory, research, and programs / Benjamin R. Karney ... [et al.].
p. cm.
Includes bibliographical references.
ISBN 978-0-8330-4178-4 (pbk. : alk. paper)
1. Interpersonal relations in adolescence—United States. 2. Interpersonal relations in adolesence—Research. 3. Teenagers—United States—Attitudes. 4. Teenagers with social disabilities—United States—Attitudes. 5. Marriage—United States. 6. Interpersonal relations—Study and teaching—United States. 7. Family life education—United States. 8. Developmental psychology. I. Karney, Benjamin R.

BF724.3.I58A36 2007
155.5'18—dc22

2007021574

The RAND Corporation is a nonprofit research organization providing objective analysis and effective solutions that address the challenges facing the public and private sectors around the world. RAND's publications do not necessarily reflect the opinions of its research clients and sponsors.

Published 2007 by the RAND Corporation
1776 Main Street, P.O. Box 2138, Santa Monica, CA 90407-2138
1200 South Hayes Street, Arlington, VA 22202-5050
4570 Fifth Avenue, Suite 600, Pittsburgh, PA 15213-2665
RAND URL: http://www.rand.org/
To order RAND documents or to obtain additional information, contact
Distribution Services: Telephone: (310) 451-7002;
Fax: (310) 451-6915; Email: order@rand.org

Preface

Policymakers are interested in promoting healthy marriages in adulthood by providing services to strengthen the adolescent precursors of healthy marriage, especially within low-income populations. The broad goal of this report is to inform these efforts by evaluating the current landscape of theory, research, and interventions addressing the role of adolescent romantic relationships in the development of healthy adult marriages. To this end, the analyses presented here draw upon a thorough review of the existing theoretical and empirical literature in this area, as well as interviews with practitioners directly involved with developing or administering relationship education to adolescents. By bringing together relevant research and theory from a wide range of disciplines that have examined these issues, the analyses presented here may be of use to several different audiences, including program developers and those working directly with adolescents, policymakers charged with developing polices to support healthy marriages, and researchers seeking to build upon the existing research and theory in this area.

This work was supported by a contract with the Administration for Children and Families within the Department of Health and Human Services, and conducted within the RAND Corporation Labor and Population program. RAND Labor and Population has built an international reputation for conducting objective, high-quality, empirical research to support and improve policies and organizations around the world. Its work focuses on labor markets, social welfare policy, demographic behavior, immigration, international development, and issues related to aging and retirement with a common aim of understanding how policy and social and economic forces affect individual decisionmaking and the well-being of children, adults, and families.

The views expressed in the report are those of the authors and do not necessarily reflect the official positions of the Administration for Children and Families or the Department of Health and Human Services.

For more information on RAND Labor and Population, contact Arie Kapteyn, Director, RAND Labor and Population, RAND Corporation, 1776 Main Street, P.O. Box 2138, Santa Monica, CA 90407-2138, (310) 393-0411 x7973, email: Arie_Kapteyn@rand.org.

Contents

Figures

Tables

Executive Summary

Introduction: Sowing the Seeds of Healthy Marriage in Adolescence

During the last half of the 20th century, divorce rates more than doubled, reaching a peak in the 1980s that has since declined only slightly. Over the same period, rates of cohabitation (i.e., unmarried couples sharing a household) have greatly increased and, perhaps as a consequence, the average age at which people are getting married has risen significantly. As much as these trends have affected all segments of society, they have been especially pronounced within low-income populations, suggesting that forming and sustaining a healthy marriage may be uniquely challenging in the context of economic disadvantage.

The Healthy Marriage Initiative. Concern about the potential social impact of these trends has motivated community leaders and policymakers to initiate programs and policies to encourage and support healthy marriages, especially among low-income populations. At the federal level, these efforts began in 1996 with the passage of the Personal Responsibility and Work Opportunity Reconciliation Act (PRWORA). Among the goals of the law were to "encourage the formation and maintenance of two-parent families" and to "end the dependence of needy parents on government benefits by promoting . . . marriage" (Personal Responsibility and Work Opportunity Reconciliation Act, 1996, Section 401). When this measure was renewed in 2006, the new legislation allocated $750 million to the Department of Health and Human Services (DHHS) for activities that promote and support healthy marriages and responsible fatherhood. Recent funding announcements for this initiative have targeted low-income populations. Thus, a substantial level of federal and state resources will soon be devoted to efforts to support and strengthen marriages in low-income communities.

The Case for Targeting Adolescents. Although most activities designed to promote and support healthy marriages are aimed at adults, an accumulating body of evidence suggests that, by the time members of low-income populations reach adulthood, some of the factors that place them at higher risk for unmarried parenthood and divorce may already be in place. In particular, a number of researchers and theorists have suggested that the building blocks of healthy adult marriages are formed during adolescence. Among the many elements of adolescents' lives that may provide a foundation for healthy marriages as adults (e.g., the quality of the education they receive, their available career opportunities, protection from violence and substance abuse), researchers and policymakers have devoted particular attention to adolescents' romantic relationships. Indeed, more than 80 percent of first romantic relationships occur during adolescence, and experiences in these relationships can have potentially life-altering consequences for adolescents' emotional health, social and academic competence, and self-esteem. The consequences may be even more significant within low-income populations, where rates of sexually transmitted diseases (STDs), intimate partner violence, and teen pregnancy are disproportionately high. Recognizing the importance of adolescent romantic relationships to healthy adult development suggests that targeting those relationships directly may lay the foundation for subsequent healthier marriages in adulthood. Consistent with this strategy, the recent legislation allocating funds for the Healthy Marriage Initiative describes relationship-focused education in high schools as one of eight activities eligible for support.

Goals of the Report. To inform current efforts to strengthen the adolescent precursors of healthy marriage, the overarching goal of this report is to synthesize and evaluate the existing basic and applied literature on adolescent romantic relationships, with particular emphasis on experiences in these relationships as precursors of adult marriages. By evaluating the accumulated products of this work to date, the analyses described in this report should provide a foundation for policies to promote healthy marriages through programs aimed at adolescents.

Organization and Methods. The report is organized around three major tasks:

1. *Review descriptions of what adolescent romantic relationships are like.* To accomplish this task, the report assembles and reviews research that describes what adolescents believe and value about romantic relationships and marriage in general and how adolescents behave in their own romantic relationships.
2. *Review explanations of the role adolescent romantic relationships may play in adult development.* To accomplish this task, the report integrates existing theories of adolescent romantic relationships and adult development and evaluates the degree to which existing theories have received support from the empirical literature on adolescent relationships to date.
3. *Assess interventions designed to make adolescents' relationships, and their subsequent marriages, better.* To accomplish this task, this report reviews a diverse sample of available relationship education curricula targeted at adolescents and describes interviews with practitioners directly involved in this area.

Drawing on the results of these tasks, the report concludes by identifying priorities for future research in this area and offering strategies and suggestions for developing programs and curricula to promote healthy adult marriages during adolescence.

Definitions. Several words and phrases that appear repeatedly throughout this report should be defined explicitly. For example, the World Health Organization defines *adolescence* as the period of life from 10 to 19 years of age (Goodburn and Ross, 1995). We adopt the same definition, although most research on adolescents has focused on the six years associated with secondary school, i.e., the ages of 13 to 18. A *low-income household* is one in which the household income is less than 200 percent of the federal poverty line, adjusted for the number of individuals in the household. A *romantic relationship,* for the purposes of this report, is one in which the individual perceives an ongoing, reciprocated, emotional, erotically charged connection with a partner. It is worth highlighting that, by this definition, romantic relationships need not involve sexual behavior. On the contrary, the report draws a clear distinction between romantic relationships, which are defined by an emotional connection, and sexual behaviors, which may or may not occur in the context of a relationship. Because heterosexual relationships are the focus of the bulk of the literature in this area, this report focuses primarily on them.

Description: How Do Adolescents Think About and Behave in Romantic Relationships?

The State of the Data. Although there has been considerable research describing adolescent sexuality, there has been far less that directly addresses the relationships in which most of that activity takes place. What data do exist often come from smaller studies that may not generalize to low-income populations. For nationally representative data describing romantic relationships among adolescents, research to date has relied almost exclusively on just five studies: the National Longitudinal Study of Adolescent Health, the Youth Risk Behavior Survey, the National Survey of Family Growth, the National Survey of Adolescent Males, and the National Longitudinal Survey of Youth.

How Adolescents Think and Feel About Dating and Romance. On average, adolescents of all ages value romantic relationships highly and seek them out for themselves. Even young children are aware of and generally preoccupied with romantic issues. Beliefs about the qualities that are important for successful romantic relationships evolve as youth move from middle school to high school and on to college, and this evolution in part reflects increasing clarity about the concept of "boy (girl) friend" across these years. In general, younger adolescents' ideas about romantic relationships emphasize physical attraction (e.g., infatuations or "crushes" predominate), but in the later teen years adolescents grow to value intimacy and commitment in their relationships as well. Although a majority of adolescents have engaged in sexual intercourse by the end of twelfth grade, most of them nevertheless endorse the view that sexual intercourse is not appropriate for high school teens. However, adolescents are most accepting of sexual behavior within the context of a romantic relationship.

Adolescents' Attitudes and Expectations Regarding Marriage. Across ethnic, racial, and gender categories, most adolescents view marriage as an important and desirable goal, and most expect to get married themselves. Males endorse marriage more strongly than females, and among males, Hispanics endorse marriage more strongly than whites, who endorse it more strongly than blacks. Unwed teen mothers also feel favorably toward marriage, but they themselves have lower expectations of marrying, perceiving that a lack of suitable partners and other obstacles prevent them from achieving this goal. A slight majority of adolescents disapproves of divorce, but many nevertheless expect to experience divorce in their own lives. Over the past few decades, positive attitudes toward marriage have remained relatively stable, but acceptance of delaying marriage and cohabiting increased substantially. Together, these results highlight the important differences between adolescents' attitudes toward marriage and relationships in the abstract, and their potentially quite different expectations for their own lives.

How Adolescents Conduct Their Own Romantic Relationships. Through the course of adolescence, adolescents generally progress from same-sex friendships, to mixed-gender friendships, to romantic and sexual relationships with the opposite sex. For example, a national study of adolescents (Carver et al., 2003) found that 68 percent of 18-year-olds had been in a romantic relationship, compared with 26 percent of 12-year-olds. Adolescents' behaviors in their romantic relationships generally correspond with their self-reported attitudes and values. For example, entry into a romantic relationship precedes the initiation of sexual behavior for most adolescents, although this sequence is less likely for females and blacks than for males and non-blacks. Data on the duration of romantic relationships during adolescence are rare, but what data exist suggest that the average romantic relationship during adolescence is not transient but rather lasts up to a year or more, with black adolescents reporting longer relationships than white, Hispanic, and Asian adolescents. Moreover, most adolescents report that their relationships are characterized by a great deal of emotional involvement, including expressions of love, appearing in public as a couple, and exchanging gifts. Among sexually active adolescents, most describe themselves as monogamous, reporting only one partner in the previous 12 months. Moreover, sexual activity is more likely to occur in romantic relationships than in any other context, although some evidence from smaller studies suggests that low-income adolescents may have greater than average numbers of sexual partners. About 10 percent of adolescent romantic relationships also involve physical violence, with rates higher among blacks and Hispanics than among whites. Overall, the existing literature suggests that the majority of adolescents endorse the goals of healthy marriage initiatives and seek to behave in ways that are consistent with those goals.

Explanation: The Role of Adolescent Romantic Relationships in Adult Development

Existing Theories. Developmental psychology suggests that adolescence is a crucial period when the individual develops the tools to function as an independent adult. Yet, beyond this broad assertion, this field contains only a few theories that detail how these effects may come about. *Attachment theory,* the leading theoretical approach in this area, highlights the way the relationship with a primary caregiver shapes an infant's ideas about what to expect from relationships, which in turn affects how the individual approaches relationships in later life. This approach suggests that adolescence is a period during which enduring ideas and beliefs about relationships may be reinforced or altered by new experiences in romantic relationships. The *lifespan developmental perspective* points out that the concrete consequences of relationship experiences in adolescence (e.g., pregnancy, STDs) may facilitate or constrain development in ways that affect marital outcomes in adulthood. The recently proposed *Development of Early Adult Romantic Relationships* (DEARR) model draws attention to ways in which the social and physical environment of the individual affects relationship outcomes in adolescence and adulthood. The implication of all these ideas is that adolescents can be significantly altered by their romantic experiences in ways that have long-term implications for their subsequent romantic relationships and marriages during adulthood.

An Integrative Framework. To describe how the existing theories might fit together to organize thinking about research and intervention in this area, we assembled components from all three theories within a single integrative framework (see Figure S.1). The framework divides the variables relevant to understanding adolescent romantic relationships into three broad groups: antecedent conditions, adolescence, and adulthood. Antecedent conditions are variables that are essentially in place before adolescence begins, including elements of the distal context (e.g., culture, socioeconomic status [SES], neighborhood), the immediate context (e.g., family structure, school, peer groups), and stable characteristics of the individual (e.g., personality, intelligence, self-esteem). Within adolescence, the framework highlights the connection between attitudes and beliefs about relationships and marriage, on one hand, and relationship behaviors (e.g., timing of entry, number of partners), on the other. Within adulthood, the framework distinguishes between relationship outcomes (e.g., marital status, relationship quality, parental status) and other outcomes—such as employment, educational attainment, and mental health—that shape the circumstances of adulthood.

Implications of the Integrative Framework. What the current framework highlights from existing theories is the idea that adolescent romantic relationships in particular represent a potential developmental turning point—a stage of life where patterns established in the family

Figure S.1
An Integrative Framework to Account for the Adolescent Precursors of Adult Romantic Relationships

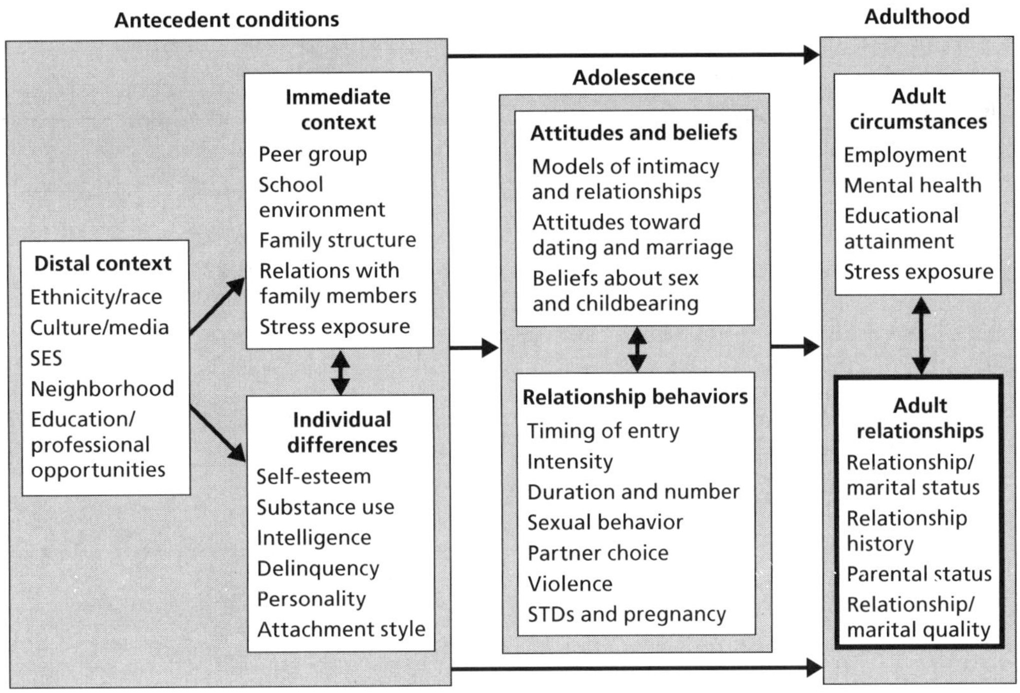

RAND *TR488-S.1*

of origin may be reinforced or substantially altered, depending upon specific choices, behaviors, and experiences. In arranging the three broad groupings of variables as shown in Figure S.1, the framework suggests that conditions in infancy and early adolescence set the stage for romantic experiences in adolescence and describes several possible paths through which these experiences may in turn affect romantic relationships and marital outcomes in adulthood. One possibility is that experiences in romantic relationships affect an adolescent's ideas about romantic attachments and attitudes toward marriage, which in turn affect choices and behaviors in adulthood. An alternative is that the concrete consequences of adolescent relationships (e.g., teen parenthood) affect the available options for forming and maintaining healthy marriages and relationships in adulthood by interfering with or facilitating educational attainment and identity development.

The framework also points out that such conditions as socioeconomic status or family structure may give rise to romantic relationships in both adolescence and adulthood, even if adolescent experiences in relationships exert no independent causal influence on adult outcomes. From this perspective, understanding the development of healthy adult relationships in low-income populations involves understanding how a low-income environment limits the options that an individual encounters at different stages of development.

Explanation: Reviewing Research on Adolescent Romantic Relationships

How This Review Was Conducted. No study has brought together all parts of the integrative framework in a single investigation. Instead, this review assembled research that has examined each of the three broad groups of variables identified within the framework. All studies reviewed here in some way address romantic relationships explicitly and make some attempt to explain or account for variability in individual outcomes.

Comments on Methods. Interpretations of the results of research on adolescent romantic relationships must necessarily be qualified by the limitations of the research methods used to obtain those results. Overall, research on adolescent romantic relationships has been limited in a number of ways that prevent the accumulated research in this area from supporting strong conclusions. These include

- lack of agreement on definitions of key terms
- lack of data from representative samples
- lack of longitudinal data
- failure to acknowledge age differences within adolescence
- reliance on data from individuals rather than couples
- reliance on self-report data
- inadequate controls for unmeasured variables that may account for the associations between measured variables.

Antecedents of Adolescent Relationships

Family of Origin. Across a wide range of methods and study designs, research indicates that when the early family environment of the child is relatively stable and when parents are warm and attentive, the child is more likely to experience more satisfying romantic relationships in adolescence and beyond. In contrast, when the early family environment is characterized by distress or disruption, the child is at greater risk for experiencing relationship problems. To account for these associations, some evidence suggests such that experiences with parents shape the ideas and beliefs about relationships that young people use to guide choices in their own romantic relationships. Behaviorally oriented work finds evidence that interactions with parents create habits of communicating that persist in subsequent interactions with romantic partners. Both lines of work imply that, absent interventions, adolescents with maladaptive patterns of belief and behavior grow into young adults with the same maladaptive patterns. These findings therefore support the idea that cognitive and behavioral interventions during adolescence may offer alternative models of thinking and behaving in romantic relationships to adolescents who might otherwise be at risk. However, such explanations have yet to be pitted against alternative explanations for these associations, such as genetic and contextual influences that may affect both family relationships and romantic relationships directly.

Individual Characteristics. Several enduring characteristics of children have been associated with continuities in their relationships across the life span. For example, personality in childhood has been associated with relationship outcomes in both adolescence and adulthood, and this effect appears to operate in part through the direct effects of personality on the timing of entry into dating and sexuality during adolescence. Individual variability in the timing of puberty and sexual maturation is also associated with variability in the timing of the initiation of sexual behavior, but this association is far weaker with respect to the initiation of dating behaviors.

Peer Groups. Across genders, having a larger peer network in late childhood predicts having closer romantic relationships in middle adolescence, and in turn more enduring romantic relationships in later adolescence. However, other data indicate that peer acceptance in early adolescence predicts both earlier entry into romantic relationships and greater use of alcohol. Thus, whereas having friends is a necessary first step toward the development of sexual and romantic relationships, what matters most may be not the size of the peer network but rather the composition of that network. Consistent with this idea, children whose friendships at ages 11–12 tend to be with preteens in the same grade are significantly less likely to report weekly dating at ages 13–14 and 15–16, compared with children who interact regularly with older peers. Peers also seem likely to shape the standards that adolescents apply toward those relationships. For example, boys who believe that aggression is more common in the relationships of their peers engage in more aggression in their own relationships.

Characteristics of the Partner. Very little is known about the ways that characteristics of adolescents' romantic partners affect the implications of adolescent romantic experiences. One exception is research on the effects of age differences between partners. As might be expected, several studies indicate that adolescents who are in relationships with partners more than two years older than themselves are vastly more likely to be sexually active, compared with adolescents whose partners are close to themselves in age.

Beliefs and Attitudes. Given the centrality of adolescents' beliefs and attitudes in current theories and current interventions, it is worth noting that very few studies have examined whether beliefs and attitudes are in fact associated with adolescents' experiences and behaviors in romantic relationships. Most studies that have examined this question have been focused on sexual behavior rather than romantic relationships. For example, religious affiliation and frequency of attendance at religious services, variables that may be proxies for more conservative attitudes toward sexual behavior, account for the timing of first intercourse among adolescents, such that stronger affiliation and more frequent attendance are associated with delays, even after controlling for demographic variables. Yet aside from sexual behaviors, little is known about how other behaviors and choices relevant to romantic relationships are associated with adolescents' beliefs and attitudes.

Implications for Adolescents

Psychological Well-Being. Relative to adolescents not involved in romantic relationships, adolescents in romantic relationships experience greater increases in depressive symptoms over one year, lower self-esteem, and higher risk for eating disorders. It appears that romantic relationships during adolescence provide an opportunity for emotional pain that puts young people at risk for experiencing depression and other emotional problems. However, this risk may be linked to unhealthy or unsuccessful relationships. Thus, the converse may also be true: Healthy relationships during adolescence may offer opportunities for growth and fulfillment that improve well-being and increase resilience.

Sexual Behavior. Experiencing a romantic relationship within the past 18 months is one of the most powerful predictors of sexual activity among adolescents. Yet existing research has been inconsistent about whether romantic relationships make safe sex and the use of contraception more or less likely among adolescents who are sexually active. For example, in one study, roughly half (52 percent) of female adolescents who had just met their sexual partner prior to having sexual intercourse used no method of contraception, compared with 24 percent of girls who reported that they were "going steady" with their partner. Another study found no difference in rates of self-reported condom use between those with a single partner and those who were sexually active with multiple partners. Still another indicates that, among sexually active adolescents in exclusive romantic relationships, condom use declines as the length of the relationship increases. How can we reconcile these contradictory sets of results? Some evidence from ethnographic and longitudinal research suggests that the predictors of condom use early in a relationship may differ from the predictors later in the same relationship. Early in a relationship, when adolescents are initiating sexual activity for the first time, they may be more comfortable discussing and enacting safe sex behaviors with partners that they feel closer to and trust. Over time, however, deepening trust in a partner may, ironically, encourage adolescent partners in lasting relationships to be less vigilant about condom use than partners in newer relationships.

Physical Aggression. The dominant theory of relationship violence among adolescents focuses on the idea of intergenerational transmission, i.e., the idea that antisocial behaviors in parents, including violence toward the child, lead to children who view aggression between intimates as acceptable, and in turn makes aggressive behavior toward romantic partners more likely. A number of longitudinal studies have found support for this general progression for males and females. Across a number of domains (e.g., socioeconomic resources, family relations, educational achievements, and problem behaviors), variables assessed during adolescence predict partner abuse at 21 more effectively than variables assessed prior to adolescence, suggesting that adolescence may be a crucial period in which the antecedents of partner violence take shape.

Substance Abuse and Academic Achievement. Although substance abuse and academic achievement are quite different outcomes, they have often been examined in the same studies. Much of the research on the implications of romantic relationships for these outcomes has focused on the effects of early or later entry into romantic relationships on substance abuse and academic achievement in girls. This work consistently shows that the earlier that girls become involved in romantic relationships, the higher their risks of later substance abuse and the lower their academic achievement. Yet, despite these results, it is not clear whether early entry into relationships causes problems for girls, or whether girls with preexisting problems are simply more likely to enter relationships early. Nor is it clear that the same effects hold true for boys. Late entry into romantic relationships, in contrast, is associated with higher intelligence, and those who do not date during adolescence have the highest grades and the lowest levels of delinquent behavior of all.

Implications for Adult Outcomes

Evaluating the effects of adolescent romantic relationships on adult outcomes, and adult marital outcomes in particular, requires, at minimum, long-term longitudinal research that follows adolescents into adulthood, assessing the nature of their romantic relationships at each stage of development. As many scholars in this area have noted, no research of this type has been published to date. The research that has attempted to link adolescent relationships to adult marital outcomes has so far been extremely limited in scope. For example, research focused specifically on the consequences of teen pregnancy has identified the economic and educational deficits that teen mothers experience relative to their peers who do not become pregnant, perhaps explaining the positive associations between premarital pregnancy and subsequent risk of divorce. But research in this vein does not account for the relational context in which those pregnancies occurred. To the extent that adolescents' experiences in romantic relationships have the immediate consequences reviewed in the previous section, it is reasonable to expect that evidence of long-term consequences may be found, because those immediate consequences have often been linked to adult marital outcomes. Yet without direct evidence that rules out alternative explanations of the obtained associations, conclusions about the role of adolescent relationships in adult marriages must remain tentative.

Conclusions

Although the existing research on adolescent romantic relationships is methodologically limited and incomplete, the results of this research offer some justification for efforts to target these relationships for intervention. Characteristics of children's family of origin and early environment are associated with their peer relationships. Peers do appear to influence timing of entry into romantic relationships. The immediate consequences of these relationships are the very ones that would be expected to influence adult marital outcomes. Moreover, studies that have followed individuals from early childhood through young adulthood do point to adolescence as a critical period during which significant antecedents of young adult outcomes take shape. Thus, the existing data are consistent with a model that views adolescent romantic relationships as a key period during which the foundations of healthy adult marriages may be strengthened. To the extent that further research confirms this emerging picture of adolescent relationships as a link in a causal chain leading from the early environment to adult marriages, then it would be warranted to intervene during adolescence, especially as a means of preventing the continuation of negative patterns in vulnerable youth.

Intervention: Review of Current Relationship Education Programs for Adolescents

How the Review Was Conducted. To evaluate the current state of relationship education aimed at adolescents, we spoke with decisionmakers, curricula developers and distributors, and practitioners who are delivering relationship curricula to low-income adolescents. Each informant was asked to nominate one or two highly regarded curricula in this area, and then the distributors of the most frequently nominated curricula agreed to send review copies for inclusion in the chapter on intervention. Thus, the specific curricula and programs reviewed cover the leading materials but do not represent a comprehensive list.

The Goals of Relationship Education for Adolescents. As with marriage education programs for couples, the broad goal of relationship education for adolescents is to impart some combination of knowledge, values, and skills believed necessary to establish healthy romantic relationships. Yet, in pursuit of that broad goal, programs differ in their specific objectives. For example, some programs explicitly seek to prepare adolescents for marriage in adulthood, whereas other programs are focused on promoting healthy relationships during adolescence. Some programs address romantic relationships specifically, whereas others address interpersonal relationships (e.g., with friends and family) more generally. Frequently, the stated objectives of available programs lack a clear connection to tangible outcomes, raising questions about how the effectiveness of these programs might be evaluated. An important step in refining existing programs would be to begin an explicit discussion of what their concrete objectives should be and how progress in meeting those objectives might be measured. It is not clear that such a discussion has taken place with regard to relationship education aimed at adolescents.

How Relationship Education Is Delivered to Adolescents. Relationship education is currently offered in a wide range of settings, including schools, the juvenile justice system, foster care, independent living facilities, programs for pregnant and parenting teens, camps, retreats, group homes, and after-school programs. Across these settings, the program developers and distributors that we spoke with identified five formats in which relationship education is typically delivered. The first of these, *relationship and marriage education* (RME), explicitly and more or less exclusively addresses interpersonal and romantic relationships and their implications. Typically, RME curricula contain some mix of intervention orientation and educational orientation. The other four formats include RME as a component of a broader curriculum.

For example, the national standards for *family and consumer sciences* (FACS) classes require that they include material on interpersonal relationships (i.e., understanding the impact of individual differences on interpersonal relationships, relationship skills, effective problem-solving). Because these classes are often a required part of the secondary school curriculum, they may be the program that routinely covers RME-related topics to which the largest number of low-income and other adolescents is exposed. *Character education* (CE) programs are defined as "teaching and learning for personal development" and may include "moral reasoning/cognitive development," "social and emotional learning," and "moral education/virtue" (Otten, 2000). Informants noted that they themselves were not clear about the standards to which adolescents were to be held and expressed some discomfort with the concept. *Abstinence education* (AE) programs have recently been called upon to address healthy relationships during adolescence and healthy marriages in adulthood. Indeed, incorporating RME curricula into abstinence education curricula may be an effective strategy for moving RME curricula into schools. Finally, *community-based initiatives* include efforts by national or community-based organizations to improve relationship outcomes as a primary or secondary objective of programs targeting at-risk youth.

Are These Programs Effective? There have been two obstacles to evaluating whether relationship education for adolescents is effective. First, as noted above, it has not been clear exactly what these programs are trying to achieve, and so the criteria for measuring effectiveness are not obvious. Second, conducting rigorous evaluation research requires the ability to randomly assign adolescents to treatment and comparison groups. Such research is costly, and not always possible (e.g., the law may prevent differential access to available programs). For both of these reasons, no rigorous evaluations of relationship education for adolescents have yet been completed. There have been quasi-experimental studies of three curricula—*The Art of Loving Well, Connections,* and *Love U2*—but the results of these evaluations are at most suggestive that relationship education curricula may improve relationship outcomes during adolescence. The Administration on Children and Families (ACF) is now supporting an experimental evaluation of the *Love U2: Relationship Smarts* curriculum that will test whether this program is effective when offered in schools with a high percentage minority and low-income student population. At present, however, the results of this evaluation are not available.

Does the Content of Existing Programs Map onto the Existing Research? When results from rigorous evaluations are lacking, an alternative way of evaluating the likely effectiveness of curricula is to assess how well the content of each curriculum aligns with what the research literature suggests is likely to be important. Comparing the content of the leading curricula to the integrative framework developed in this report suggests that these curricula have rarely covered the full range of content likely to be relevant to adolescents' relationships and eventual marriages. For example, all the leading curricula reviewed here seek to shape attitudes and beliefs regarding romantic relationships and marriage, and all of them address specific behaviors and choices in relationships, like commitment, whether or not to have sex, and how to choose a partner. In contrast, the existing programs are far less consistent in their coverage of how individual differences affect relationships. Most discuss self-esteem, but few examine the connections between romantic relationships and substance abuse or delinquency. The existing programs are least consistent in their coverage of issues external to the couple. For example, although most programs discuss how romantic relationships can be affected by each partner's peer groups, most do not acknowledge the role that families may play in shaping each partner's approach to a relationship, despite the fact that this is one of the strongest associations in the existing literature in this area.

Practical Concerns in Delivering Relationship Education to Low-Income Adolescents. Among the organizations we spoke with that have experience encouraging healthy adolescent relationships, there is uniform agreement that need for this programming is vital and that additional funds would help them better address the needs of the adolescents they work with. Moreover, there is also consensus that youth who participate in these efforts are highly receptive to them. Nevertheless, our informants also identified six practical concerns that have yet to be addressed:

1. *A need for more culturally appropriate curricula.* This ranged from a concern that the curricula are too explicit for the youth that are served (and their parents) to a concern that the curricula do not accurately reflect youth culture (such as hip-hop).
2. *Problems with curricula that overlook adolescent parents.* Program developers and administrators said that existing curricula largely ignore young mothers and fathers and pregnant women, and they would value efforts to tailor programs specifically for these groups.
3. *A need for assistance or guidelines for adapting curricula.* In cases where it is necessary to shorten existing curricula, program administrators would appreciate some guidance about which curriculum components are essential and which can be considered optional. In the absence of such guidelines, most administrators we spoke with simply used their best judgment when adapting curricula.
4. *Questions about the age-appropriateness of some curriculum components.* Many in the marriage education field believe that existing marital education programs should be adapted for and distributed to youth, but some informants with a background in adolescence (rather than in marriage education) expressed concerns about whether research supports the use of such curricula for all adolescents.
5. *A need for training in the logistics of serving at-risk youth.* For example, there is need for guidance on how to arrange childcare for adolescent parents, when to separate males and females in classes, and whether to offer incentives for participation. These are logistical questions that most people with experience interacting with low-income youth have faced before.
6. *Assistance in marketing relationship education to adult decisionmakers.* Given that some of those with whom we spoke have encountered resistance to relationship education among parents and community leaders, there may be a need to reach out to decisionmakers who are not involved in the relationship and marriage education movement to educate them about the need for and potential benefits of these efforts.

Future Directions for Research and Intervention

Immediate Priorities for Research. If programs and curricula targeting adolescent romantic relationships are to be effective, they must be grounded in an accurate understanding of how these relationships function and the role that they play in the development of healthy adult marriages. Promising directions for the next generation of research on adolescent romantic relationships include the following:

- Exploit nationally representative data sets to expand descriptions of low-income adolescents.
- Address diversity across cultures, ethnicities, and sexual orientations.
- Continue longitudinal studies that examine the consequences of adolescent experiences for adult outcomes.
- Conduct analyses that test genetic and economic explanations for links between adolescence and adulthood.
- Describe processes within adolescent relationships, such as conflict resolution and social support.

Research that pursues these directions would strengthen the empirical base of current programs and substantially advance efforts to promote healthy adult marriages.

Strategies for Programs and Curricula

General Organization. The accumulated and evolving research on adolescent romantic relationships offers ways to strengthen existing programs targeting those relationships as precursors of adult outcomes. The integrative framework described here, by mapping the range of possible content that relationship education curricula may contain, suggests organizing that content into three broad topics: *antecedent conditions*, issues relating to *adolescence,* and issues relating to *adulthood.* The research reviewed in this report suggests specific strategies for addressing each of these domains and the way they affect each other. Some of these strategies are already being used in existing programs.

Antecedent Conditions. Relationship education curricula may seek to directly affect the sources of adolescents' thoughts and behaviors in romantic relationships, or, to the extent that some antecedent conditions are impossible for individuals to change (e.g., family history), these curricula might help adolescents to recognize the impact that their backgrounds and personal histories have on their current relationships. For example, programs should

- help adolescents identify and express their own feelings and beliefs about romantic relationships
- explore the sources of their feelings and beliefs about relationships
- include training in interacting effectively with parents, siblings, and friends.

Adolescence. In addition to its focus on adolescents' attitudes, beliefs, and behaviors, the current framework also suggests that relationship education should acknowledge how the context external to a romantic relationship (e.g., the stresses that each partner faces, the resources and opportunities available to the couple, the physical environment) may affect how partners behave within the relationship. To accomplish these ends, programs should

- help adolescents understand how their models of relationships affect their behavior in their current and future relationships
- encourage adolescents to explore how their own behaviors affect the way other people respond to them
- help adolescents appreciate ways that their own or a partner's behavior might be changed or constrained in different kinds of environments
- offer relationship education in conjunction with or alongside programs aimed at improving adolescents' lives in other ways (e.g., substance abuse prevention, job training)
- in curricula that address safe sex and contraception, emphasize that using condoms does not indicate a lack of trust in a partner
- directly address beliefs about intimate partner violence.

Adulthood. Programs aimed at adolescents obviously cannot target adult outcomes directly. However, they can address the consequences of adolescent romantic relationships that are likely to have the greatest impact on adult outcomes, either by encouraging adolescents to consider the possible consequences of their choices and behaviors more carefully, or by teaching skills that help adolescents to manage possible negative consequences of their relationships more effectively. To accomplish these ends, programs should

- help adolescents to understand the ways that their behaviors and decisions in adolescence can affect their options in later life
- emphasize that successful marriages are an achievable goal for adults
- offer assistance in preventing or managing negative consequences of adolescent relationships.

Conclusion

None of the alternative intervention strategies described here are mutually exclusive or incompatible with current programs and curricula aimed at promoting positive outcomes experiences and outcomes for adolescents in romantic relationships. On the contrary, it seems likely that the programs most effective at promoting healthy adult marriages will be multifaceted, acknowledging that adolescents' experiences in romantic relationships, and the long-term consequences of those experiences, are woven into the broader fabric of their lives. Relationship education is likely to be one element in a repertoire of approaches. Reviewing the theory and evidence on the links between adolescence and later healthy marriage yields a number of ways that approaches to serving adolescents could be strengthened.

Acknowledgments

The analyses described in this report were made possible by generous contributions of time and support from a number of individuals.

First, the authors were fortunate to be able to call upon the expertise of an outstanding panel of consultants, each of whom contributed insights and direction that greatly improved the final report. The consultant panel for this project consisted of Rebekah Levine Coley, Ph.D. (Boston College), W. Andrew Collins, Ph.D. (University of Minnesota), Waldo Johnson, Ph.D. (University of Chicago), Marline Pearson (*Love U2* program), Marcela Raffaelli, Ph.D. (University of Nebraska–Lincoln), and Kay Reed (Dibble Fund for Marriage Education).

Second, the authors thank all the program developers, distributors, ACF grantees, and FACS state representatives for sharing their time, expertise, and materials, including Nancy McLaren, and from ACF, Stanley Koutstaal, William Coffin, and Diann Dawson.

Third, the authors thank Chalandra Bryant, Ph.D. (Penn State University), Joanne Davila, Ph. D. (SUNY Stony Brook), and Jennifer Kerpelman, Ph.D. (Auburn University), all of whom took the time to contribute additional insights and comments.

Finally, the authors are grateful to the outstanding team at ACF—project officer Nancye Campbell, Naomi Goldstein, and Allison Deschamps (now at Lewin Group)—for their stewardship of this project over the past year.

Abbreviations

ACF	Administration on Children and Families
Add Health	National Longitudinal Study of Adolescent Health
AE	abstinence education
BSF	Building Strong Families (program)
CDC	Centers for Disease Control and Prevention
CE	character education
D.A.R.E.	Drug Abuse Resistance Education
DEARR	Development of Early Adult Romantic Relationships
DHHS	Department of Health and Human Services
DRA	divorce-registration area
FACS	Family and Consumer Sciences
HIV	human immunodeficiency virus
MRA	marriage-registration area
MTF	Monitoring the Future
NLSY	National Longitudinal Survey of Youth
NSAM	National Survey of Adolescent Males
NSFG	National Survey of Family Growth
NSFH	National Survey of Families and Households
PREP	Prevention and Relationship Enhancement Program
PRWORA	Personal Responsibility and Work Opportunity Reconciliation Act
RME	Relationship and Marriage Education
SHM	Supporting Healthy Marriages
STDs	sexually transmitted diseases
TANF	Temporary Assistance for Needy Families
YRBS	Youth Risk Behavior Survey

CHAPTER ONE

Introduction

Trends in Marriage, Cohabitation, and Child-Bearing

The last half of the 20th century witnessed substantial changes in the practice of marriage in the United States (Cherlin, 2004, 2005). During this period, divorce rates more than doubled, reaching a peak in the 1980s that has since declined only slightly (Singh et al., 1995). Currently, nearly 50 percent of first marriages are expected to end in divorce or permanent separation (Bramlett and Mosher, 2002). Over 80 percent of those who experience divorce remarry, but their marriages are even more likely to end (Cherlin, 1992).

Figure 1.1
U.S. Divorce Rates over Time

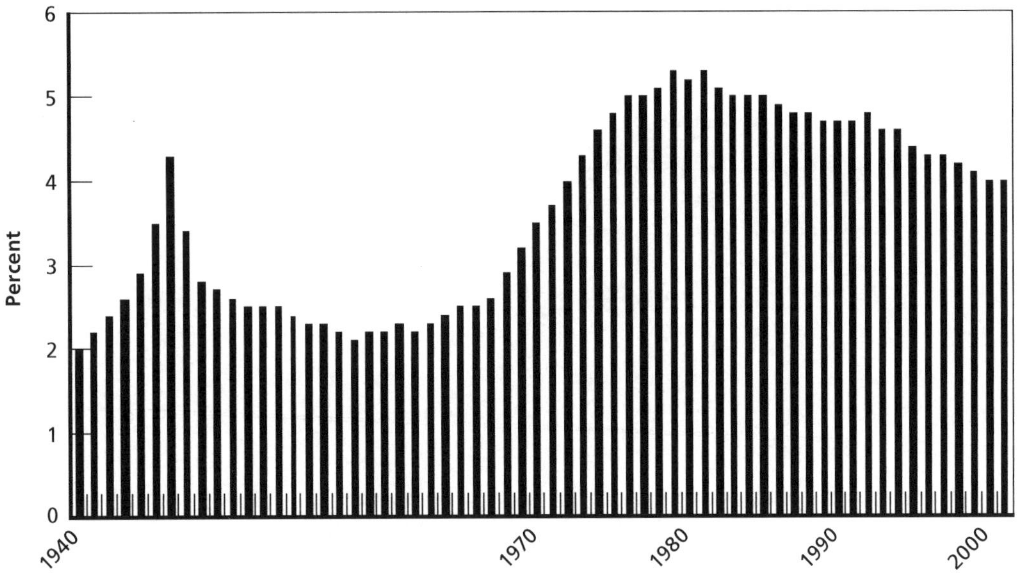

SOURCE: National Center for Health Statistics.
NOTE: Rates represent divorces per capita per year.
RAND *TR488-1.1*

Despite the increased risk of marital disruption, rates of marriage have remained relatively stable over time (Schoen and Standish, 2001), and over 95 percent of people get married at some point in their lives (Kreider and Fields, 2001). Yet, although the number of people getting married has not changed, rates of cohabitation (i.e., unmarried couples sharing a household) have greatly increased (Bramlett and Mosher, 2002; Bumpass and Lu, 2000; Seltzer, 2004). Perhaps as a consequence, the average age at which people are getting married has risen since the middle of the past century, indicating that people are delaying their entry into marriage (Schoen and Standish, 2001). As rates of marital disruption and cohabitation were rising during the 1980s, rates of unmarried births in the United States were increasing dramatically—from 18 percent of all live births in 1980 to 30 percent of all live births by 1992. From 1992 to the present, the rate of increase in unmarried birth leveled off substantially, reaching 33.2 percent in 2000 (Martin et al., 2002).

As notable as these general trends are, they are even more pronounced within low-income populations (Fein, 2004; McLanahan, 2004). For example, rates of divorce for low-income women are substantially higher than they are for middle- and high-income women and nearly twice as high for women who live in low-income neighborhoods compared with those who live in high-income neighborhoods (Bramlett and Mosher, 2002; Raley and Bumpass, 2003). Compared with more affluent couples, low-income couples are four times more likely to have their first child before getting married, and they have additional children more rapidly after marriage as well (Elwood and Jencks, 2004). Even among couples that marry and remain married, low-income spouses report significantly higher levels of marital distress than do middle- or high-income spouses (Amato et al., 2003; Karney, Garvan, and Thomas, 2003). Together, these trends suggest that forming and sustaining a healthy marriage, while a significant challenge for all segments of society, may be uniquely challenging in the context of economic disadvantage (Hernandez, 1997; Martin, 2004).

Supporting Healthy Marriages: Where to Intervene?

Concerned about the potential social impact of these trends, community leaders and policymakers at the local, state, and federal level have initiated programs and policies designed to encourage and support healthy marriages, especially among low-income populations. At the federal level, these efforts began in 1996 with the passage of the Personal Responsibility and Work Opportunity Reconciliation Act (PRWORA), legislation that allowed states new flexibility in administering aid to their poorest residents. The law explained its goals explicitly, which included to "encourage the formation and maintenance of two-parent families" and to "end the dependence of needy parents on government benefits by promoting . . . marriage" (Personal Responsibility and Work Opportunity Reconciliation Act of 1996, Section 401).

By the time this measure was up for reauthorization in 2002, promoting marriage had moved to the forefront of welfare reform, with President Bush announcing that "stable families should be the central goal of American welfare policy" (CNN, February 27, 2002). In support of this goal, the Bush administration requested, as part of the reauthorization of the Temporary Assistance for Needy Families (TANF) program, that funds be appropriated to the

Department of Health and Human Services (DHHS) over five fiscal years for activities that promote and support healthy marriages. Congress passed this legislation in February 2006, appropriating $150 million annually for activities to support healthy marriage and responsible fatherhood. Thus, a substantial level of federal and state resources will soon be devoted to efforts to support and strengthen marriages in low-income communities.

How should these newly available resources be allocated? What sorts of programs and interventions are likely to be most effective? As many observers have noted, the existing research on marriage and intimacy within low-income populations is sparse by any standard (e.g., Fein et al., 2003; Seefeldt and Smock, 2004). Reviews of the marriage education literature in particular have noted again and again that research on the causes and correlates of healthy marriage has to date examined samples composed almost exclusively of white, middle-class, college-educated couples (e.g., Carroll and Doherty, 2003; Fein et al., 2003; Halford et al., 2003; Jakubowski et al., 2004; Karney and Bradbury, 1995; Sayers, Kohn, and Heavey, 1998).

To address the limitations of the existing research, two ongoing studies funded through the Administration on Children and Families (ACF)—the Building Strong Families (BSF) project and the Supporting Healthy Marriages (SHM) study—are currently evaluating the effectiveness of different educational programs aimed at (1) helping low-income unmarried parents form healthy marriages and (2) helping low-income married parents maintain their relationships. Both projects seek to provide adult couples that have expressed an intention to marry or have already married with tools for achieving their aims.

Until more data on marriage and relationships in low-income populations can be accumulated, it is too early to speculate about the effectiveness of interventions aimed at low-income adults. Yet there is reason to expect that, by the time members of low-income populations reach adulthood, the seeds of marital disruption may already have been sown. For example, compared with members of middle- and upper-income populations, they are more likely to have been raised in single-parent homes (McLanahan and Sandefur, 1994) and to have been exposed to physical and sexual abuse during childhood and adolescence (Cherlin et al., 2004). As noted earlier, members of this population are far more likely to become parents before considering marriage (Elwood and Jencks, 2004). Research has shown that all these experiences are associated with a lower rate of subsequent marriage (Lichter, Graefe, and Brown, 2003) and a higher risk of subsequent marital disruption among those who do marry (Amato and Booth, 2001; Furstenberg, 1979).

Are the Seeds of Healthy Marriages Sown in Adolescence?

Recognizing that low-income young adults may have already accumulated a number of risk factors for experiencing marital disruptions or unmarried parenthood, programs focused on preventing marital disruption and supporting healthy marriages have begun to target individuals and couples earlier in their development. Specifically, a number of researchers and theorists have suggested that the building blocks of healthy adult marriages are formed during adolescence (e.g., Collins and Sroufe, 1999; Collins and Van Dulmen, 2006; Furman and Shaffer,

2003; Furman and Simon, 1999; Giordano, Manning, and Longmore, 2006; Tallman, Burke, and Gecas, 1998). Among the many elements of adolescents' lives that may provide a foundation for healthy marriages as adults (e.g., the quality of the education they receive, the available career opportunities, protection from violence and substance abuse), researchers and policymakers have devoted particular attention to adolescents' romantic relationships.

Indeed, by the time they reach the age of 18, more than 80 percent of adolescents have experienced their first romantic relationship (Carver, Joyner, and Udry, 2003). Although these relationships tend to be shorter than the relationships of adults and involve relatively low levels of interdependence (for example, adolescents rarely live together), adolescents' experiences in romantic relationships nevertheless have potentially life-altering consequences for their emotional health (e.g., Monroe et al., 1999), social and academic competence (e.g., Neemann, Hubbard, and Masten, 1995), and self-esteem (e.g., Connolly and Konarski, 1994; Masten et al., 1995). These relationships also provide the primary backdrop for intimate partner violence, decisions about whether and when to engage in sexual behavior, contraceptive use, exposure to sexually transmitted diseases (STDs), and pregnancy (e.g., Capaldi and Gorman-Smith, 2003; Ford, Sohn, and Lepkowski, 2001; Manlove et al., 2006). The risks and benefits associated with romantic relationships may be especially relevant to low-income populations, where relationships may compensate for limited educational and employment opportunities as a means of achieving adult status, possibly contributing to disproportionately high rates of STDs, intimate partner violence, and teen pregnancy among low-income teens (e.g., Coates, 1999; Doljanac and Zimmerman, 1998; Edin and Reed, 2005; Eyre et al., 1998; Raffaelli, 2005).

In light of the potential consequences of romantic relationships during adolescence, these relationships have been assigned an important role in theories of healthy adult development (e.g., Erikson, 1968; Sullivan, 1953). Erikson (1968), for example, suggested that forming intimate relationships outside the family of origin is a crucial step toward developing an independent identity. More recently, developmental psychologists have picked up on this theme, highlighting the role of adolescent romantic experiences in setting the stage for the formation of stable relationships during young adulthood (e.g., Collins, 2003; Furman and Shaffer, 2003; Giordano, 2003). Reaching the same conclusion, marital researchers have suggested that understanding healthy adult relationships requires an understanding of the early relationship experiences of each partner (Parke, 1998; Story et al., 2004).

Reflecting a growing consensus, policymakers and educators have become increasingly invested in interventions and educational curricula that directly target the romantic relationships of youth and young adults (e.g., Eccles and Gootman, 2002). For example, Florida's Marriage Preparation and Preservation Act of 1998 mandated that ninth and tenth grade high school students be required to take a course in life management skills that includes material on marriage and relationships. The legislation reauthorizing TANF describes education in high schools about the value of healthy marriages and healthy relationship skills as one of eight activities eligible for support within the Healthy Marriage Initiative (Deficit Reduction Act, 2006). To address the call for new curricula, programs have been developed that seek to promote effective functioning in the romantic relationships of adolescents and teens, and elementary and secondary schools are beginning to adopt these materials.

In sum, substantial attention and resources are now being directed toward adolescent romantic relationships, based on the assumption that these relationships represent an important window of opportunity for improving relationship outcomes among adults.

Adolescent Romantic Relationships: The State of the Field

Current efforts to direct relationship education toward adolescents will be most successful at promoting healthy adult marriages to the extent that (1) relationship-relevant beliefs and behaviors during adolescence are, in fact, important precursors of adult marriages and (2) interventions target the specific beliefs and behaviors that have the greatest impact on adult outcomes. Research on the role of adolescence in adult development has not settled either of these issues. As several recent reviews of this area have noted (e.g., Crouter and Booth, 2006; Florsheim, 2003b; Furman, Feiring, and Brown, 1999; Giordano, 2003), the empirical literature on romantic relationships among adolescents is still in its early stages.

Despite repeated calls for research that examines the effect of adolescent relationships on development (Collins and Van Dulmen, 2006; Furman and Shaffer, 2003; Zani, 1993), research on intimacy among adolescents has instead focused almost exclusively on the causes and consequences of sexual behavior (Whitehead and Pearson, 2006). One result of this focus is that "we know more about the individual, family, peer, and even community effects on sexual behavior than about the relationship context(s) within which these behaviors unfold" (Giordano, 2003, p. 268). Efforts to evaluate the role that adolescent romantic relationships play in adult development have been even more limited (e.g., Collins and Van Dulmen, 2006; Kan and Cares, 2006), leaving a serious gap in understanding adolescent romantic relationships (Florsheim, 2003b). As some have concluded, "In many ways, romantic and sexual partnerships can be considered the 'last frontier' in the study of adolescent relationships" (Giordano, 2003, p. 258).

The lack of basic research in this area mirrors a similar lack of data on programs and interventions. Although specific curricula that address relationships and relationship skills among adolescents have become available across the country, to date there has been no systematic research on how these curricula are being implemented across states and regions, the elements that available curricula include or leave out, or their effectiveness in general and within specific populations (e.g., low-income groups).

Objectives and Scope of This Report

A crucial step toward advancing current efforts to promote later healthy marriages among young people by promoting healthy relationships during adolescence is to assemble, review, and synthesize the existing basic and applied literature on adolescent romantic relationships, with particular emphasis on these experiences as precursors of adult marriages. The overarching goal of this report is to evaluate the accumulated research in these areas, and in so doing to provide a solid foundation for future research and policy.

Two limitations of this report are worth noting at the outset. First, although the explicit goal of the project was to evaluate research on the adolescent precursors of healthy marriages within low-income populations, there are scant data that address this issue directly. As has already been noted, few existing studies have addressed adult marriage in low-income populations, and few existing studies have addressed romantic relationships among adolescents. The research ideally suited for the purposes of this report lies in the intersection of these two sparsely populated sets. As a consequence, for many of the issues that are directly relevant to programs targeting the relationships of low-income adolescents, there simply has not been any research. Where there has been work that explicitly focuses on low-income populations, that work has been emphasized in this report. Where such work does not exist (the more frequent case), the text describes work with other populations, including appropriate caveats about how well or poorly the results of this work may generalize to low-income groups.

Second, despite an explicit interest in the precursors of healthy adult marriages and romantic relationships, this report does not attempt to define what makes a marriage or a romantic relationship healthy. As other reviewers of this literature have observed, determining whether a specific experience in relationships is healthy or dysfunctional may lie outside the realm of empirical research. Psychologist Paul Florsheim, in an important edited volume on romantic relationships in adolescence (Florsheim, 2003b), identified several obstacles to addressing this issue definitively (Florsheim, 2003a). First, particularly within adolescence, experiences that are painful or distressing in the short term may be adaptive or educational over the lifespan. Most adolescents, for example, would not describe the breakup of their first relationship as a positive experience, but it may nevertheless be an important step toward the development of a mature sense of self (e.g., Barber, 2006). Thus, "it is very difficult to tease apart negative emotions associated with a normal adolescent romance from psychological symptoms associated with a dysfunctional relationship, except in the extreme" (Florsheim, 2003a, p. 373).

In addition, behaviors that may be functional for a relationship (e.g., commitment, spending time together) may be dysfunctional for the individual, and vice versa. In other words, the meaning of healthy behaviors may depend on the specific outcome in question.

Finally, the standards by which a relationship is judged as healthy vary according to historical era and cultural context. For example, over time, the stigmas once attached to divorce and premarital sex have greatly diminished. Even within a single era, different cultures vary in the extent to which they emphasize romantic love as a critical element of a successful marriage. Thus, what is considered healthy in a particular place and time may not be considered healthy in other contexts. The current report sidesteps these issues, instead focusing on how specific beliefs and behaviors have been associated with specific outcomes during adolescence and adulthood.

Organization of the Report

This report is organized around three central tasks. To provide a foundation for the rest of this report, the first task—which is the focus of Chapter Two—is to *review descriptions of what adolescent romantic relationships are like.* What do adolescents think and value about romantic relationships, and what are their expectations and attitudes toward marriage? What is the prevalence of different kinds of romantic experiences across adolescence and within specific subgroups of interest (e.g., low-income populations)? How have relationship-relevant attitudes and behaviors been changing over time? Chapter Two reviews the available literature on these questions, establishing what is known and what remains to be described.

The second task—the focus of Chapters Three and Four—is to *review explanations of how adolescent romantic relationships function*. How can we account for the range of romantic relationships that adolescents experience? What role do these relationships play in developing healthy adult marriages? Chapter Three reviews existing theories that have attempted to explain the causes, correlates, and consequences of adolescent romantic relationships and concludes by assembling elements from prior theories into a single integrative framework. This integrative framework then provides the organization for Chapter Four, which reviews the empirical literature that has examined precursors of adolescents' romantic relationships, and the implications of those relationships for outcomes during adolescence and later adulthood. This literature review attempts to be comprehensive but places emphasis on research that draws links between adolescent experiences and adult marital outcomes.

The third task—and the focus of Chapter Five—is to assess interventions designed to make adolescents' relationships, and their subsequent marriages, better. What programs exist that target romantic relationships in adolescence? What are the features of existing programs, and how do these features map on to the variables that the empirical research suggests may be important? What is the evidence for the effectiveness of these programs at affecting outcomes during adolescence and subsequent adulthood? To address these questions, Chapter Five reviews existing curricula that provide relationship education to adolescents, highlighting areas of convergence and divergence between these curricula and the empirical literature, and describes the results of interviews with practitioners who consented to share their experiences and concerns.

Chapter Six concludes the report by identifying priorities for future research in this area and drawing from the existing research to offer guidelines for developing programs and curricula that target adolescent relationships.

Defining Terms

To clarify the discussion in the chapters that follow, it is worth being explicit about how we use several words and phrases that appear repeatedly throughout this report.

Adolescence. The World Health Organization defines adolescence as the period of life from 10 to 19 years of age (Goodburn and Ross, 1995). We adopt the same definition. In practice, most research on adolescents has focused on the six years associated with secondary school, i.e., the ages of 13 to 18. When used in this report, the word *youth* is meant to be a more general term, encompassing adolescence and childhood.

Low-income. The U.S. Census Bureau defines a low-income household as one in which the household income is less than 200 percent of the federal poverty line, adjusted for the number of individuals in the household (e.g., Bramlett and Mosher, 2002). In practice, research and programs that seek to address low-income populations are far less precise, because data on the household income of research participants are rarely available. Instead, individuals' level of income is usually inferred on the basis of their neighborhood, or the fact that they or their families are receiving public assistance. The current report adopts this more inclusive stance as well.

Romantic/intimate relationship. In this report, we use the terms romantic relationship and intimate relationship interchangeably. Defining these terms precisely has been an ongoing challenge for many disciplines because different cultures, and even different individuals within a culture, often disagree on the behaviors and commitments that characterize romantic relationships. As will be discussed in subsequent chapters, adolescents themselves disagree with their partners more than 50 percent of the time about whether or not they are even in a romantic relationship (Carver and Udry, 1997; Kennedy, 2005). Rather than define romantic relationships, the most common approach within research on this topic is to simply ask the adolescent whether he or she has experienced a romantic relationship, leaving the respondent to determine what a romantic relationship actually is. For the purposes of the current report, *a romantic or intimate relationship is one in which the individual perceives an ongoing, reciprocated, emotional, erotically charged connection with a partner* (e.g., Brehm, 1985). Two aspects of this definition are worth highlighting. First, as defined in this report, romantic relationships need not involve sexual behavior. On the contrary, we draw a clear distinction between romantic relationships, which are defined by an emotional connection, and sexual behaviors, which may or may not occur in the context of a relationship. The definition includes the idea of erotic feelings to distinguish romantic relationships from friendships, but it does not require erotic or sexual behaviors. Second, the definition used here does not require that the feelings about the relationship or the partner be positive. A distressing or abusive relationship can still be a romantic relationship by this definition. Finally, because heterosexual relationships are the focus of the bulk of the literature in this area, this report focuses primarily on them.

CHAPTER TWO

Describing Adolescents' Beliefs, Attitudes, and Behaviors with Respect to Romantic Relationships

The legislation that reauthorized the TANF program allocates money for eight different activities to promote healthy marriages (Deficit Reduction Act, 2006). Of these, two activities directly affect adolescents: public service campaigns to promote the value of marriage, and high school curricula that teach the value of marriage and healthy relationship skills. The decision to specify these activities presumably rests on an implicit theory about the needs of adolescents. Specifically, these activities assume that the beliefs, attitudes, and behaviors of adolescents need changing and that potentially dysfunctional patterns among adolescents need to be fixed. Is this true? How much do we know about what adolescent romantic relationships are like? What do adolescents believe about marriage, divorce, and cohabitation and what do they value about their own current and future relationships? How do adolescents' beliefs and values translate into behaviors with respect to romantic relationships?

Programs that target adolescent romantic relationships are likely to be most effective to the extent that they are informed by accurate answers to these questions. Thus, the goal of this chapter is to assemble and review the existing research that describes adolescent romantic relationships. In particular, the research reviewed in this section examines what adolescents believe is true about romantic relationships, what they value in their own relationships and what they hope for in their future relationships, and how they actually conduct their relationships during adolescence. Unless otherwise noted, all between-group differences described here are statistically significant.

Data Sources

Accurately and comprehensively describing current patterns and trends in adolescent relationships is challenging for several reasons. First, as noted in Chapter One, there simply has not been much research that directly addresses issues related to adolescent romantic relationships. Second, results from large-scale, nationally representative surveys of youth have focused primarily on sexual behavior and other health risk behaviors, often to the exclusion of the romantic relationships in which those behaviors take place. Third, studies that provide a broader window into adolescent romantic relationships, including research that links adolescent dating to psychological and behavioral outcomes, tend to have limited generalizability because of small sample sizes or unique study settings (Carver, Joyner, and Udry, 2003).

For nationally representative data on romantic relationships among adolescents and young adults, research to date has relied almost exclusively on just five studies: the National Longitudinal Study of Adolescent Health (Add Health), the Youth Risk Behavior Survey (YRBS), the National Survey of Family Growth (NSFG), the National Survey of Adolescent Males (NSAM), and the National Longitudinal Survey of Youth (NLSY). Each of these surveys covers a range of topics, with some covering a wide range of health risk and health-related behaviors, and others focusing somewhat more narrowly on sexual behavior and romantic relationships. All sampled through multistage, stratified, clustered sampling, usually including over-samples of certain underrepresented racial or ethnic groups. Because these five studies provide the basis for so much of what is known about adolescent relationships, each study is worth describing in more detail.

National Longitudinal Study of Adolescent Health (Add Health)

Designed primarily to examine the precursors of health-related behaviors among adolescents, Add Health has collected three waves of data to date (Harris et al., 1997). Wave I assembled a school-based sample of youth in grades 7–12 during the 1994–1995 school year. Wave II assessed the same respondents one year later, and Wave III contacted them approximately seven years later, when respondents were in young adulthood. The survey was conducted through written self-administered questionnaires, and data on sexual behavior specifically were collected through in-home interviews using audio-enhanced, computer-assisted, self-interviewing methods. With respect to understanding adolescent behaviors in romantic relationships, a unique feature of Add Health is that respondents were asked to identify up to three romantic relationships that they had experienced in the previous 18 months and to answer questions about those relationships. The survey also includes comprehensive information about sexual activity and sexual risk taking, although it includes very few items assessing relationship attitudes. A single chapter describing the relationship data from Add Health (Carver, Joyner, and Udry, 2003) is currently one of the most frequently cited sources of data on adolescent experiences in romantic relationships.

Youth Risk Behavior Survey (YRBS)

The YRBS refers to a national survey conducted by the Centers for Disease Control and Prevention (CDC) involving a school-based nationally representative sample of adolescents in grades 9–12. The YRBS has been conducted every two years, beginning in 1991, and data collection occurs through written self-administered questionnaires. The YRBSS (note the additional S) refers to the national school-based survey plus state and local school-based surveys conducted by state and local education and health agencies. The YRBS monitors six categories of priority health-risk behaviors among youth and young adults: (1) behaviors that contribute to unintentional injuries and violence; (2) tobacco use; (3) alcohol and other drug use; (4) sexual behaviors that contribute to unintended pregnancy and sexually transmitted diseases (STDs); including human immunodeficiency virus (HIV) infections; (5) unhealthy dietary behaviors; and (6) physical inactivity. In addition, the YRBSS monitors general health status and the prevalence of obesity and asthma. Our report primarily describes data from the national YRBS surveys (e.g., Garofalo et al., 1998; Garofalo et al., 1999; Silverman et al., 2001).

National Survey of Family Growth (NSFG)

Designed primarily to assess fertility and fertility-related behaviors, the NSFG collects data through in-person interviews and self-administered questionnaires of people ages 15–44 living in U.S. households. The survey has been conducted multiple times, on a different cohort of respondents each time. Cycles 1–5 were conducted in 1973, 1976, 1982, 1988, and 1995. They included only women and focused on marriage, divorce, contraception, infertility, and the health of women and infants in the United States. Cycle 6 was conducted in 2002 and included both men and women. Of the five national data sets emphasized here, the NSFG is the only one that does not limit its sample to teenagers.

National Survey of Adolescent Males (NSAM)

Designed as a counterpart to the NSFG, the NSAM includes only male teenagers ages 15–21 from nationally representative U.S. households. There are two cohorts within the NSAM. The original, longitudinal cohort was surveyed in 1988 (males ages 15–19), 1990–1991 (males ages 16–21), and 1995 (males ages 21–27). The new cohort was surveyed in 1995 and included males ages 15–19. The study was conducted through face-to-face interviews and self-administered questionnaires.

National Longitudinal Survey of Youth (NLSY)

The NLSY is one of the oldest survey initiatives. The survey was first administered in 1979 (NLSY79) and included a nationally representative sample of 12,686 young men and women who were 14–22 years old when they were first surveyed in 1979. These individuals were interviewed annually through 1994 and are currently interviewed on a biennial basis. NLSY97 was launched in 1997 and contains a nationally representative sample of about 9,000 youths who were 12 to 16 years old as of December 31, 1996. Data collection has been conducted via interviews and questionnaires. The NLSY surveys are focused more on educational and workforce-related issues, but they do contain some data on adolescent relationships and romantic and sexual behavior.

In addition to these five data sets, other data on specific aspects of adolescent relationships are available. For example, Monitoring the Future (MTF), a survey focusing on drug use that includes high school student respondents from across the country, asks about marital expectations and values (Johnston et al., 1995). The National Survey of Families and Households (NSFH) measures marital attitudes and beliefs, focusing on the views of young adults (ages 19–34). We include some references to the NSFH where no data on younger individuals are available. Data on birth statistics come from the National Center for Health Statistics, based on birth certificate data for every child born in the United States. Abortion rates are from the CDC's National Center for Chronic Disease Prevention and Health Promotion, primarily based on data on women having abortions from most state health departments. Abortion data are also available from the Alan Guttmacher Institute's annual survey of abortion providers.

Teenage marriage and divorce rates are based on samples of records of states that participate in the marriage-registration area (MRA) and divorce-registration area (DRA).

Limitations of the Available Data

The data sources described above provide most of the information reviewed in the rest of this chapter. Although they are nationally representative, these studies also tend to be limited in several ways. First, the data in the surveys are generated entirely by the self-reports of the respondents. As has been well documented (Singer and Presser, 1989), self-reports, especially about sensitive topics like romantic relationships, are highly vulnerable to memory biases and distortions. For example, partners are often poor at recalling their behaviors in romantic relationships (e.g., Jacobson and Moore, 1981) and rely instead on their general feelings about the relationship to guess what their behaviors were likely to have been (e.g., Weiss, 1984). Respondents may also distort their responses deliberately to create a favorable impression for the researcher, e.g., by neglecting to admit to illegal or undesirable attitudes and behaviors. Because self-reports are susceptible to these biases, data generated by self-reports are likely to underestimate the prevalence of negative behaviors and attitudes.

Second, most of the national data sets include only a small set of items relevant for understanding intimate relationships. Thus, only a narrow range of attitudes and behaviors have been addressed, even within the studies that have examined these issues directly.

Third, for surveys with school-based samples, results may not generalize to out-of-school youth. This is a particularly noteworthy limitation when considering low-income youth. These youth may be at greater risk for engaging in high-risk behaviors and their potentially negative consequences, and yet may be most likely to be underrepresented in surveys drawing upon school-based samples.

Fourth, although some of these surveys are longitudinal (i.e., the same individuals provided data at several assessments over time), analyses of most of these data have tended to be cross-sectional (i.e., examining associations among variables assessed at a single assessment). Cross-sectional analyses can estimate associations among variables but do not support conclusions about causal relationships between variables.

Fifth, because the questions asked and the samples addressed vary across studies, the existing literature offers little basis for comparing results across different studies. Because most of this research has been cross-sectional, this means that there are scant data that allow descriptions of trends in adolescent romantic relationships over time, and all inferences about trends over time should be considered tentative.

Sixth, although analyses of data from these surveys usually contain breakdowns by race and ethnicity, they very rarely contain breakdowns by household income or by variables—such as poverty status, neighborhood quality, or urban versus rural—that may serve as proxies for household income. Because race and ethnicity in themselves are poor proxies for income (e.g., most blacks and Hispanics are not low-income; see Bachrach, 1998), this limits what existing analyses of these data sets can say about the population currently being targeted by healthy marriage initiatives.

The studies that have addressed youth relationships in low-income or urban populations have tended to be far smaller in scale (e.g., Connolly et al., 2004; Hogan, Astone, and Kitagawa, 1985; Hogan and Kitagawa, 1985; Miller, Forehand, and Kotchick, 2000; O'Donnell, O'Donnell, and Stueve, 2001; Silver and Bauman, 2006; VanOss Marín et al., 2006; Whitaker, Miller, and Clark, 2000). Many of the studies are qualitative and thus provide a richer picture of youth perceptions than might be possible with prevalence estimates and average responses to quantitative measures. Yet, whereas small-scale studies provide valuable insight into adolescent subgroups of particular interest to the current project, they suffer from their own limitations. First, they also tend to be cross-sectional, limiting their ability to support causal inferences. Second, they are also based primarily on self-report data. Third, the studies' smaller sample sizes limit their statistical power to identify significant relationships among variables. Finally, the characteristics of the respondents and the settings in which the studies take place impose limits on the generalizability of the study results, even when comparing across studies involving similar subgroups of adolescents. Despite these limitations, we describe results from several small-scale studies, especially when these studies address gaps in the results from national surveys.

Adolescents' Attitudes and Beliefs Regarding Dating and Romance

The fact that adolescents' experiences in romantic relationships are significantly associated with such outcomes as violence and depression (e.g., Capaldi and Gorman-Smith, 2003; Monroe et al., 1999; Wekerle and Avgoustis, 2003) suggests that these relationships play an important role in adolescents' lives. Small-scale studies suggest that even young children are aware of (Connolly et al., 1999) and generally preoccupied with (Simon, Elder, and Evans, 1992) romantic issues. By age 9, children express clearly distinct conceptions of romantic relationships versus opposite-sex friendships, with their descriptions of romance uniquely characterized by longing, physical attraction, and commitment (Connolly et al., 1999). Opposite-sex friendships, in contrast, are perceived to be less intimate (i.e., involving less self-disclosure and less closeness) than same-sex friendships (Lempers and Clark-Lempers, 1993; O'Donnell, 1979), suggesting a continuum of intimacy from opposite-sex friendships at the low end, to romantic relationships at the high end.

In general, adolescents value romantic relationships highly and seek them out for themselves. One study of sixth through eighth graders observed high levels of interest in having a boyfriend or girlfriend across all grade levels, indicating that interest in a romantic relationship is already established by grade 6 (Darling et al., 1999). However, in a large ethnically diverse sample of Canadian youth in grades 5 through 8, interest in having a boyfriend or girlfriend in the near future was higher for those in grades 7 and 8 than for those in grades 5 and 6 (Connolly et al., 2004). The difference in findings may have to do with differences in the ethnic makeup or dating experience of the populations represented by these two samples. In the Canadian study, it was also shown that interest in having a boy- or girlfriend was greater among youth from European or Caribbean backgrounds than among Asian-Canadians and among youth who had recent experience with dating. Interest was not higher among youth who had participated in mixed-gender group activities but had not been out on a date, and there were no differences in romantic interest among boys versus girls (Connolly et al., 2004). Another factor that may play a role in dating interest, and that is closely linked to age, is pubertal development. Youth become more interested in romantic relationships during puberty (Harris et al., 1997; Miller and Benson, 1999).

Beliefs about the qualities that are important for successful romantic relationships evolve as youth move from middle school to high school and on to college, and this evolution in part reflects increasing clarity about the concept of "boy(girl) friend" across these years. In grade 6, youth are more likely to ask what "counts" as a date or as a girlfriend or boyfriend; but by grade 8, youth understand questions about romantic relationships immediately (Darling et al., 1999). Descriptions of romantic relationships at age 15 commonly include self-disclosure and support, in addition to physical attraction and commitment (Feiring, 1999b). Physical attraction is most likely to be part of boys' descriptions, whereas self-disclosure and support are more prevalent in girls' descriptions (Feiring, 1996, 1999a). Older teenagers' conceptions of what it means to have a boyfriend or girlfriend also include both self-disclosure and companionship but are less likely to include physical attractiveness or passion (Connolly and Johnson, 1996; Furman and Buhrmester, 1992; Furman and Wehner, 1994). When asked to supply reasons for dating particular individuals, middle school youth place greater emphasis on superficial characteristics of potential partners, whereas college students focus more on partners' future plans and mutuality of feelings (Galotti, Kozberg, and Appleman, 1990; Roscoe, Diana, and Brooks, 1987). In general, Connolly and Goldberg (1999) argue that younger adolescents' romantic relationships are primarily characterized by physical attraction (e.g., infatuations or "crushes" predominate), and that this emphasis becomes moderated in the later teen years as teens grow to value intimacy and commitment. Waldinger and colleagues (2002), in research on ideas about relationships generally (not just romantic relationships) found that the same themes appear in the narratives of youth at ages 14 to 16 as at age 25, but that the young adults' narratives were more complex than the adolescents' narratives, possibly as a result of more experience with relationships. We speculate that, as youth achieve more independence from their parents, the future implications of a romantic relationship become more salient, accounting for the some of the change in relationship beliefs and values as they get older.

When describing dating and romance, young teens in a non-random sample of high-school-age youth or younger focused on positive aspects of relationships (Feiring, 1996). During early adolescence, a majority of females believe that romantic relationships should be important but not everything in life, that romance should be heterosexual, and that a girl should not have feelings for a boy who is already attached to another girl (Simon, Elder, and Evans, 1992). By age 18, in contrast, descriptions of romantic relationships frequently describe jealousy and concerns about compatibility as part of romantic relationships, with girls more likely than boys to mention compatibility, reciprocity, and jealousy in their descriptions (Feiring, 1999a). Qualitative research has identified jealousy and infidelity as especially salient themes in African-American adolescents' descriptions of committed sexual relationships (Eyre et al., 1998).

Several studies have directly examined adolescents' beliefs about the role of sexual behavior within various types of relationships. As noted earlier, romantic relationships are the primary contexts for sexual behavior among adolescents (Collins and Sroufe, 1999; Sprecher, Barbee, and Schwartz, 1995). Consistent with this observation, within a multiethnic sample of 452 18- to 25-year-olds, initiation of new sexual activities is considered more appropriate when it occurs within a serious romantic relationship (Feldman, Turner, and Araujo, 1999). According to a national survey of 12- to 19-year-olds, approximately two-thirds "strongly agree" that sex should occur only within such a relationship (Albert, 2004). Indeed, the majority of adolescents have their first sexual intercourse with someone they are going steady with or know well and like a lot (Abma et al., 2004). Consistent with this fact, the modal reason reported for first intercourse is "to have the partner love them more" (Rodgers, 1996). Although adolescents are most accepting of sexual behavior within the context of a romantic relationship, it is worth noting that the majority of respondents also endorse the view that intercourse is not appropriate for high school teens, with rates of disapproval at 63 percent among boys, and 76 percent among girls (Albert, 2004). Sexual activity may be less strongly linked to relationship commitment and emotional intimacy among gay, lesbian, or bisexual youth (Herdt and Boxer, 1993), for whom a romance or dating may be too public while sex is more private (Diamond, Savin-Williams, and Dubé, 1999). These youth, especially lesbians, may also develop passionate, asexual same-sex friendships (Diamond, Savin-Williams, and Dubé, 1999).

Adolescents' Expectations and Attitudes About Marriage, Cohabitation, and Divorce

A decade ago, most high school students in the MTF study expected to marry, and reported that having a happy marriage was important to them (Johnston et al., 1995). In these data, 72 percent of boys and 82 percent of girls expected to get married at some point. According to a recent analysis of the 2002 NSFG (Flanigan, Huffman, and Smith, 2005), most teens continue to feel favorably about marriage, although there are differences in the strength of support for marriage across genders and racial and ethnic groups. With respect to gender differences, among boys ages 15–19, a strong majority (69 percent) agree that "it is better for a person to get married than to go through life being single." Among girls ages 15–19, a majority (54 percent) feel this way, but many girls (42 percent) disagree.

According to the 2002 NSFG data, girls' attitudes toward marriage do not differ by race/ethnicity, but boys' attitudes do (Flanigan, Huffman, and Smith, 2005). Although a majority across all ethnic groups favor marriage, endorsement of marriage over remaining single ranges from 60 percent among black males to 75 percent among Hispanic males, with white males falling in between. Closer examination of these patterns reveals that boys have more favorable marriage attitudes than girls among Hispanics and whites, but there are no similar gender differences among black teens—black teens of both genders are less favorable toward marriage than white teens. It is not clear whether or not these differences persist into adulthood. For example, among the 19- to 34-year-old respondents in the NSFH, blacks, Hispanics, and whites were all equally likely to say that they planned to marry (Brown, 2000; Bulcroft and Bulcroft, 1993; Bumpass, Sweet, and Cherlin, 1991). The differences between the studies may be the result of developmental changes in attitudes toward marriage, or they may result from the fact that the NSFG measured attitudes toward marriage whereas the NSFH tapped plans to marry. Although adolescent attitudes toward marriage differ by gender and race/ethnicity, they do not appear to differ by age. For example, attitudes toward marriage are similarly positive among younger (ages 15–17) and older (ages 18–19) teens (Flanigan, Huffman, and Smith, 2005).

Of particular interest to policymakers seeking to promote marriage are the marital attitudes of young unwed parents. Four percent of girls ages 15–19 gave birth in 2004, and most teens who give birth are unmarried (Hamilton et al., 2005). Studies focusing on unwed teen parents suggest that they may view marriage differently from other youth, if not less favorably. For example, two small studies of teenage mothers indicate that they believe men are unreliable and likely to be unfaithful, suggesting that their expectations for a stable marriage are low (Furstenberg, 1995; Maynard, 1995). Although many young mothers are in a relationship with the father of their child (Furstenberg, Brooks-Gunn, and Morgan, 1987), in one sample of more than 100 low-income black teen mothers and their partners, most of the respondents nonetheless believed they would not get married (Burton, 1995). These young mothers believed that the fathers of their children would be unable to support the child, suggesting that they remained unmarried in part for this reason. An ethnographic study of 292 low-income single mothers also identified mistrust for men as a salient obstacle to marriage for this subgroup (Edin, 2000). Perhaps as a result, one study of a population with high rates of teen pregnancy—black low-income girls—found that fertility and marriage are only loosely linked in the minds of this group (East, 1998).

Just as adolescents generally feel positively toward marriage and expect to get married themselves, they generally disapprove of divorce. Just under half of teens from the 2002 NSFG sample (48 percent of girls and 42 percent of boys) agree "divorce is usually the best solution when a couple can't seem to work out their marriage problems." There are no substantial differences in these attitudes based on gender, sexual experience, or age. As with attitudes toward marriage, however, there are differences by race/ethnicity among boys. Hispanic (51 percent) and black (53 percent) males are more likely then white males (38 percent) to endorse divorce in the face of marital problems (Flanigan, Huffman, and Smith, 2005). It is worth noting that, even though youth generally do not approve of divorce, many nevertheless expect to experience divorce themselves. In the MTF, where 72 percent of boys and 82 percent of girls expected to get married, only 59 percent of respondents believed that they would stay married (Johnston et al., 1995). This finding points out the important differences between adolescents' attitudes toward marriage and relationships in the abstract, and their potentially quite different expectations for their own experiences (Cherlin, 1988).

Most young people are accepting of cohabitation, according to the same NSFG analysis. Only about a third of boys (32 percent) and girls (36 percent) agree, "A young couple should not live together unless they are married." There are no differences by race/ethnicity among boys, but white (34 percent) girls are less likely to disapprove of cohabitation than Hispanic (40 percent) or black (39 percent) girls. Younger boys are more likely to disapprove of cohabitation than older boys, but there are no age differences among girls (Flanigan, Huffman, and Smith, 2005).

As noted earlier, only limited data suggest how adolescents' attitudes toward marriage, divorce, and cohabitation have changed over time. The best of these data come from the MTF survey, which has been conducted annually for three decades (Schulenberg et al., 1995). Data from the years 1976 to 1992 indicate that adolescents' attitudes toward marriage became slightly less positive during that time, with fewer indicating that they agree or mostly agree that people have fuller and happier lives if they marry. During the same period, however, the percentage indicating that it is extremely or quite important to them to have a good marriage and family life remained stable, again pointing out the different results obtained when questions are asked about relationships in the abstract or about the individual's own experiences. In 1992, more youth agreed or mostly agreed that it was a good idea for a couple to live together before marriage than they had in 1976—this increase was relatively dramatic, a shift from 40 percent to 54 percent. As the authors note, this constitutes a change toward normative acceptance of cohabitation. During the same period, adolescents' predictions about their age at marriage increased by approximately four years, especially among girls. This may reflect the increasing importance of college education for women during the time frame covered by the assessments. Overall, these data suggest shifts in how adolescents understand the normative path toward marriage but do not indicate changes in their expectations of marrying at some time in the future.

Correlates of Adolescents' Attitudes and Beliefs Regarding Romantic Relationships

The average trends described thus far in this chapter mask considerable diversity in the attitudes of adolescents toward intimate relationships and marriage. Research in this area is only beginning to examine variables that may account for this diversity. This section reviews several variables that have been examined in more than one study.

Sexual Experience

One survey of first-year college students (approximately age 19) indicates that virgins feel more favorable toward marriage than those with multiple sex partners (those with one partner fell in between; see Salts et al., 1994). However, the more recent and generalizable NSFG data do not fully corroborate this finding. Among female respondents in the 2002 NSFG, there were no differences in marriage attitudes depending on sexual experience; among boys the difference fell just short of statistical significance (71.5 percent of virgin males were pro-marriage compared to 66 percent of nonvirgins; see Flanigan, Huffman, and Smith, 2005). An association between marital attitudes and adolescent sexual activity could underlie the association between teen childbearing and attitudes toward marriage, to the extent that teens who are more sexually active are also more likely to become pregnant. However, there are no published studies providing evidence of such a link.

Parents and Peers

Adolescents may develop their ideas about romantic relationships through their observation of and interaction with parents and peers (Rose and Frieze, 1989). In support of this idea, Simon and colleagues (Simon, Elder, and Evans, 1992) observed that adolescents' normative beliefs about how one should feel and behave in a romantic relationship develop through repeated discussions with their peers. Other studies also suggest that peers reinforce the importance of romantic relationships, especially among girls (Douvan and Adelson, 1966).

Media

Adolescents are major consumers of mass media, on average spending about eight hours each day with television, music, movies, video games, magazines, and the Internet (Roberts, Foehr, and Rideout, 2005). Connolly and Goldberg (1999) speculate that the media influence adolescents' attitudes and beliefs about romantic relationships. Most research that has examined media effects on youth has focused on television, since it is the medium that adolescents spend the most time using (Roberts, Foehr, and Rideout, 2005).

Television often portrays dating relationships as adversarial. These depictions may affect young viewers' beliefs about what is typical in relations between real men and women (Bandura, 1994; Gerbner et al., 1994). Indeed, Ward (1995) has argued that television distorts adolescents' beliefs about intimate relationships by promoting a view of dating in which dating is a competition—women are objects that men aggressively strive to obtain, and both genders play a strategic and manipulative game to obtain the partner they desire. In various laboratory studies with high school students from diverse ethnic and racial backgrounds, Ward has found support for this view (e.g., Ward and Friedman, 2006; Ward, Hansbrough, and Walker, 2005). In a recent study of undergraduate women, more frequent viewing of reality dating television programs was correlated with the belief that dating is a game, and that men and women are adversaries (Zubriggen and Moregan, 2006). Taking the notion of conflictual relationships a step further, Johnson et al. (1995) described an experimental study showing that black adolescent girls exposed to rap videos expressed greater acceptance of teen dating violence than those not exposed.

A notable exception to television's portrayal of intimate relationships as adversarial is the depiction of married couples. For example, few television programs portray serious conflict between spouses (Heintz, 1992), and when conflict is depicted, it is typically resolved easily and with appropriate communication (Comstock and Strzyzewski, 1990). This may promote positive views of marital relationships among adolescents. In fact, television viewing is positively associated with high school students' reports that they want to get married, stay married to the same person for life, and have children (Signorielli, 1982). However, the same study found that television viewing was correlated with the opinion that people see so few good or happy marriages in the real world that they question marriage as a way of life. The latter finding is consistent with the concern expressed by some theorists (e.g., Cantor, 1990) that exposure to media portraying marriage in an overly positive light might lead to idealized beliefs about what marriage and relationships entail, leaving youth unprepared for the hard work of relationship maintenance. It may also lead them to judge the real-life marriages that they encounter more harshly.

Television may also influence adolescents' beliefs about the role of sex in intimate relationships. Sexual behavior is common in a variety of television programming, and when it is depicted, it is typically between unmarried individuals (Greenberg and Busselle, 1996) and often involves individuals who have little or no prior relationship (Kunkel et al., 2005). Exposure to television portrayals of nonmarital sex has been shown in laboratory studies to produce greater acceptance of sexual indiscretions among teen viewers (Greenberg, 1994). Correlational research suggests that regular exposure to sex on TV may also lead to teens' dissatisfaction with their own relationships, particularly the sexual aspects of them (Greenberg, 1994). Similar work also indicates that exposure to sexual content on television and in other media may lead to initiation of intercourse earlier in adolescence (Brown et al., 2006; Collins et al., 2004; Martino et al., 2006).

Of course, sexual content is most prevalent in pornographic material, which is not typically shown on television but is now readily available in many homes via the Internet. Rates of exposure to pornography through magazines, films, and the Internet range from 48 percent to 92 percent among teens, depending on the medium and the sample studied (Bryant, 1985; Malamuth and Impett, 2001). Zillman (1994) argues that the values instilled by pornography are antithetical to those necessary to forming and maintaining traditional families, undermining commitment and moral behavior. Kubey and Donovan (2001) suggest that spouses and monogamy can be devalued as a result of exposure. There has been very little empirical research examining such effects, and nothing addressing young viewers. Studies of young adults, however, provide preliminary support for their contentions. Men who regularly view pornography are more dissatisfied with their spouses (Zillman and Weaver, 1989) and see their girlfriends as less attractive (Weaver, Masland, and Zillman, 1984). Men and women exposed to pornography in an experimental setting report less interest in having children than do controls (Zillman, 1994). To the extent that adolescents are still developing their conceptions of romantic relationships, the effects of exposure to pornography may be stronger and longer lasting for adolescents, although no experimental research has addressed this possibility directly.

Adolescents' Behaviors in Romantic Relationships

Do adolescents' beliefs and attitudes regarding romantic relationships correspond to how they actually conduct their relationships? This section describes current trends in adolescent relationship behaviors and discusses changes over time if such data are available. Included in this review is research on timing of entry into romantic and sexual relationships, the number and duration of relationships, degree of involvement between partners, characteristics of partners (i.e., observed preferences in partner selection), the use of contraception, and dating violence.

Through the course of adolescence, adolescents' peer relationships generally progress from same-sex friendships, to mixed-gender friendships, to romantic and sexual relationships with the opposite sex. Dating activities over this stage of life tend to progress from outings in mixed-sex groups, to opposite-sex friendships, to dating (Feiring, 1996).

Data from several studies support this progression. For example, among children ages 11–12 in the NLSY79, the vast majority (92 percent) had never or rarely dated; if they had, they had done so sporadically. In contrast, fewer adolescents ages 13–14 and 15–16 reported never or almost never dating (71 percent and 46 percent, respectively) (Cooksey, Mott, and Neubauer, 2002). In a noteworthy racial difference, blacks ages 13–14 and 15–16 in this sample were more likely than their nonblack peers to report never or almost never having dated (79 percent versus 69 percent and 59 percent versus 43 percent, respectively); (Cooksey, Mott, and Neubauer, 2002). Using data from the Add Health study, Carver, Joyner, and Udry (2003) found a similar pattern, showing that, in the 18 months prior to the survey, 26 percent of 12-year-olds had been in a romantic relationship, whereas 68 percent of 18-year-olds had been in a romantic relationship. A Canadian study paints the same picture, noting that, once in a romantic relationship, adolescents were less likely to return to a previous stage of dating or affiliative relationships (Connolly et al., 2004).

One reason that the age at which adolescents enter into romantic relationships is important is that the timing of initiation of dating is closely associated with sexual initiation. For example, in the aforementioned study of the teenagers of the NLSY79 sample, 50 percent of those who reported having sex for the first time between ages 11–12 and 15–16 indicated that they had begun dating first. This general tendency masks significant variance by gender and race; females and blacks were less likely than males and nonblacks to have initiated dating prior to initiating sex (Cooksey, Mott, and Neubauer, 2002).

In sum, nationally representative samples indicate that most people experience their first romantic relationships during adolescence and these romantic relationships usually precede adolescents' first sexual experiences. The specific timing of entry into these experiences is associated with gender and race/ethnicity. Although the data exist to compare patterns in low-income and upper-income groups, such comparisons have not yet been conducted.

Duration of Adolescent Romantic Relationships

Reporting on the timing of when adolescents typically enter adolescent romantic relationships is challenging because adolescents do not always know exactly when their relationships began, particularly if partners were friends before they were romantic partners. Younger boys and black adolescent males have the most difficulty identifying when their relationship began, and older girls and white adolescent females have the least difficulty (Carver, Joyner, and Udry, 2003). Without reliable reports of when relationships begin, estimating the duration of adolescent relationships is also a challenge, even though adolescents are very aware of the date that their relationships end because breakups are usually associated with a specific event.

Estimating the duration of adolescent romantic relationships is further complicated by the methods used to study the relationships. For example, the Add Health study asked adolescents who had been in a relationship in the last 18 months to provide information about up to three of their romantic relationships. Data analyses only included data on the relationship that was listed first, which was likely to be the most important and/or the longest relationship, thereby underreporting the frequency and duration of short-term relationships (Carver, Joyner, and Udry, 2003). Keeping this bias in mind, the Add Health study observed a median duration of adolescent romantic relationships of 16 months for girls and 12 months for boys. Older adolescents in the Add Health study reported having longer relationships. The median duration was 5 months for adolescents under age 14, 8 months for adolescents between 15 and

16, and 21 months for adolescents over age 16. Substantial differences in median relationship duration were observed across racial and ethnic groups—black adolescents reported a median duration of more than 24 months (Giordano, Manning, and Longmore, 2005), whereas white, Hispanic, and Asian adolescents reported median durations of 12 months, 15 months, and 11 months, respectively.

In sum, whereas data on the duration of adolescent relationships remain incomplete, the data that exist suggest that the average romantic relationship during adolescence is not transient but rather lasts up to a year or more. It is not clear whether the same patterns would be observed within low-income populations specifically.

Degree of Involvement Between Partners

Involvement in romantic relationships during adolescence can be defined in terms of how adolescents describe their own relationships and feelings about their partners, as well as the type, amount, and frequency of activities or behaviors that occur within the relationship.

The Add Health study is a valuable source of information about these issues. To assess the level of social connectedness in adolescent romantic relationships, the Add Health study asked adolescents a variety of questions about one of their recent relationships. Within the Add Health Wave II data (Carver, Joyner, and Udry, 2003), 81 percent of adolescents in romantic relationships considered themselves to be a "couple," 67 percent went out together with no one else present, 68 percent told their partners that they loved them, 62 percent gave each other gifts, and 49 percent spent less time with their friends in order to spend more time with their partner. Overall, boys and girls tended to provide similar reports of spending less time with friends in order to spend time with their partner; however, girls tended more often than boys to report engaging in other acts expressing intimacy or commitment, such as thinking of themselves as a couple (86 percent versus 76 percent), giving each other gifts (66 percent versus 57 percent), saying that they love the other person (71 percent versus 75 percent) and going out together with their partner alone (71 percent versus 67 percent). Older adolescents reported engaging in these behaviors more frequently than younger adolescents, and, in separate analyses of the same data set, white adolescents report these behaviors more frequently than adolescents of other races and ethnicities (Giordano, Manning, and Longmore, 2005).

Because Add Health allows the respondent to choose a relationship to describe, it may be biased toward assessing more serious relationships. Yet the NLSY study also asked adolescents about dating habits and going steady, and found, consistent with the results from Add Heath, that as adolescents got older, they described their relationships as more involved. Among the youth in the NLSY79 sample, 27 percent of those ages 15–16 went on more than one date per week, compared with 10 percent of those ages 13–14 (Cooksey, Mott, and Neubauer, 2002). A convenience sample of 493 youth ages 12 to 24 recruited from youth organizations, public schools, and private schools also found that, compared with younger adolescents, older adolescents had more dating experiences; had been in love more times; scored higher on measures of passion, intimacy, and commitment-related romantic beliefs; and scored lower on measures of romantic idealization (Montgomery, 2005). Consistent with the results from Add Health, females scored higher than males on measures of intimacy and self-consciousness, although they reported being in love fewer times than males and were less likely to believe in love at first sight. An independent small-scale study of adolescents describes their typical dating activities as including going out to dinner and hanging out at school, the mall, or each other's homes (Feiring et al., 2002).

Multivariate analyses of the NLSY data described above suggest that the degree of involvement between partners is associated with sexual activity among adolescents. Specifically, these data indicate that sexual activity is more closely associated with how adolescents define their relationships generally (e.g., "going steady" versus casual dating) than with the self-reported frequency of specific behaviors like going on dates (Cooksey, Mott, and Neubauer, 2002). Other studies also find that, although sexual activity is prevalent across a range of types of relationships, it most frequently occurs in relationships described as close and committed. For example, among males 15–19 years old in the 2002 NSFG who had had sexual intercourse in the past three months, 62 percent describe themselves as "going steady," 14 percent considered themselves to be "just friends" with their female partner, 10 percent are cohabiting, 9 percent reported that they go out once in a while with the sexual partner, and 1 percent are married (Martinez et al., 2006). For females under age 20 in the 2002 NSFG study who had ever had sexual intercourse, 75 percent described themselves as "going steady," 14 percent described their first sexual partner as someone they had "just met or were just friends with," 7 percent went out with the partner once in a while, and 4 percent were cohabiting or married (Abma et al., 2004). The younger a female's age at sexual initiation, the more likely she is to describe the partner as someone whom she had just met or was just friends with. Thirty-three percent of female teenagers who first had sexual intercourse at age 14 or younger fit in this category, compared with only 11 percent of female teenagers who were ages 17–19 at the time they first had sexual intercourse (Abma et al., 2004). It is worth noting that these analyses examine the proportion of sexual activity among adolescents that takes place within romantic relationships. There have been no comparable analyses of the proportion of romantic relationships that include sexual activity, an independent and relevant question.

In sum, although data on the degree of involvement between partners in adolescent romantic relationships remain sparse, the best existing data suggest that romantic relationships among adolescents are most frequently characterized by a relatively well-defined bond between the members of a couple, and the likelihood of experiencing this bond increases throughout adolescence. It is not known how the intensity of romantic relationships varies across income groups.

Number of Romantic and Sexual Relationships in Adolescence

Over the past few decades, some evidence indicates a downward trend in the prevalence of adolescent dating. Based on data from the Monitoring the Future study from 1975 to 2004, dating appears to be becoming less common. Since the early 1990s, data for students in eighth, tenth, and twelfth grade show that the percentage of students who do not date at all is increasing. From 1992 to 2004, the percentage of eighth graders who did not date at all increased from 48 to 51 percent; the increase for tenth graders was 28 to 37 percent; and for twelfth graders, the increase was from 14 to 27 percent. Using the same data, from 1991 to 2004, the percentage of twelfth graders who date frequently, defined as going on one or more dates per week, declined from 34 percent to 27 percent. In 2004, eighth grade females were more likely to report never dating than male eighth graders (57 percent compared with 46 percent). The differences between genders for having never dated shrink as they age: 38 percent of tenth grade girls and 36 percent of tenth grade boys never date and the difference between twelfth grade girls and boys was not statistically significant (Child Trends, 2006). The problem with interpreting these data is that the term dating is defined only vaguely across these studies. It is not clear how declines in dating may be associated with trends in other kinds of involvements among adolescents.

In a cross-sectional look at Add Health Wave I data, 55 percent of all adolescents in the sample (ages 12–18) experienced a romantic relationship in the 18 months preceding the study. Another 10 percent of adolescents were involved in a "liked" relationship, where the adolescents did not report that they were in a romantic relationship but reported involvement in behavior indicative of romantic relationships, such as holding hands, kissing, or telling someone they loved or liked them. Thirty-five percent of adolescents in the sample had not been involved in any romantic relationship in the past 18 months. The prevalence of involvement in romantic relationships followed a consistent increasing pattern in older ages compared to younger. With the exception of Asian adolescents, who had consistently low rates of romantic relationships, white, black, Hispanic, and Native American adolescents all had similar rates of relationship experience (Carver, Joyner, and Udry, 2003).

The NSFG study provides nationally representative estimates of the number of sexual partners adolescents have had. Although reports of sexual partners do not map perfectly onto number of relationship partners, the fact that most sexual activity among adolescents takes place within romantic relationships suggests that these estimates may be close approximations of the number of romantic relationships that adolescents experience. Indeed, consistent with the data from other studies, the 2002 NSFG data (Abma et al., 2004) indicate that 61 percent of sexually active female teens and 47 percent of sexually active male teens had only one sexual partner in the last 12 months. Sexually active male teens are more likely than their female counterparts to report having had two to three partners in the previous year (32 percent versus 22 percent, respectively), and also more likely to have had no partners in the previous year (14 percent versus 9 percent, respectively). Gender differences do not emerge for teens reporting four or more partners in the previous year (8 percent for both genders).

Some evidence suggests that low-income adolescents may have a greater than average number of sexual partners. For example, one study of 1,287 urban, minority youth living in economically disadvantaged neighborhoods showed that, by tenth grade, 54 percent of males and 18 percent of females had had four or more lifetime sexual partners, with no significant differences for ethnicity within gender (O'Donnell, O'Donnell, and Stueve, 2001). It is worth exploring whether this pattern holds true among the low-income segments of national data sets.

In sum, consistent with the finding that most romantic relationships among adolescents last more than one year, most adolescents are not experiencing romantic and sexual relationships with multiple partners. At the same time, there is substantial variability across adolescents. The fact that low-income adolescents may report higher numbers of sexual partners at earlier ages may indicate higher numbers of romantic relationships as well, but this possibility remains to be explored directly.

Characteristics of Romantic Partners in Adolescence

Research on adolescent romantic relationships tends to focus on the individual respondent, rarely asking questions about the partner. The data that do exist generally suggest that adolescents tend to be in relationships with partners who are similar to themselves in age, race, socioeconomic background, academic interests, and likelihood of engaging in risk-taking behavior.

With respect to age, although adolescents in the Add Health study did have relationships with older and younger partners, most adolescents had partners whose age was within a few years of their own (Carver, Joyner, and Udry, 2003). Adolescent boys tend to have older romantic partners until they reach late adolescence (17–18), and then they tend to select partners who are younger than themselves. Across ages and across racial and ethnic groups, more than two-thirds of adolescent boys in the Add Health study described relationships with partners who were within a year of their own age. In contrast, most female respondents in the Add Health study described relationships with partners older than themselves, and this holds true for all ages. Among females of all ages, the mean age of partners was oldest for blacks and Hispanics (two years older in both groups), and youngest for whites (1.68 years older).

The Add Health data also reveal that adolescents tend to enter romantic relationships with others of the same race and ethnicity. However, the prevalence of interracial relationships appears to be negatively affected by the racial composition of the school environment (i.e., the higher the proportion of students of the same race, the fewer interracial relationships reported) (Carver, Joyner, and Udry, 2003).

Regarding other characteristics of partners, a study involving a subset of Add Health data collected within one midsize, close-knit, predominantly working-class Midwestern U.S. town showed that adolescents tended to select partners similar with respect to: socioeconomic status, grade point average, college plans, attachment to school, trouble in school, drinking behavior, IQ, and grade (Bearman, Moody, and Stovel, 2004). The same adolescents also tended to select partners similar with respect to sexual experience, suspension from school, smoking, and age, though females showed a slight preference for male partners in a higher grade (Bearman, Moody, and Stovel, 2004). Within the range of denominations available in this sample, a partner's religious denomination did not appear to be an important aspect of partners' characteristics.

Characteristics of adolescents' partners are also related to the likelihood of relationships being sexual in nature. Data from Wave II of the Add Health study found that, for both genders, being friends with a partner before the relationship became romantic decreased the odds that the couple was having sexual intercourse, compared with being acquaintances prior to the romantic relationship (Kaestle and Halpern, 2005a). The likelihood of a couple in a romantic relationship being sexually active increased with relationships that were longer in duration, involved older partners, and involved partners who did not live in a family with two biological parents (Kaestle and Halpern, 2005a). A different study found that adolescents are likely to have their first sexual experiences with partners who have already been sexually active (Rodgers, 1996).

Another noteworthy aspect of partner preference is the preference for partners of the same or opposite sex. Some researchers have estimated that 10 percent of U.S. youth identify as gay, lesbian, or bisexual at some point in their lives (D'Augelli, 1988). Wave I Add Health data found that, for respondents who reported having a relationship in the last 18 months, 2 percent of boys and 4 percent of girls reported a romantic relationship with someone of the same sex (Carver, Joyner, and Udry, 2003). Although individuals in same-sex romantic relationships during adolescence may or may not end up getting married to someone of the opposite sex as adults, studies have found that, among this group of teens, romantic difficulties are significantly associated with risk for depression, substance abuse, and truancy (e.g., Anderson, 1993; Diamond, 2003; Savin-Williams, 1994).

In sum, adolescent romantic relationships are generally characterized by similarity between partners, but the degree of similarity, at least in terms of race and ethnicity, is affected by the composition of the pool of available partners.

Intimate Partner Violence in Adolescence

A final element relevant to describing romantic relationships among adolescents is the prevalence of dating violence. In Wave I of the Add Health study (conducted during 1994–1995), 12 percent of respondents had been the victim of physical dating violence and 20 percent had been the victim of psychological dating violence at some point in the previous 18 months (Halpern et al., 2001). Within the window between Wave I and II of the Add Health study, 12 percent of male adolescents and 14 percent of female adolescents reported being abused by an intimate partner (Roberts, Klein, and Fisher, 2003). In Wave II data from the Add Health study, a history of any abuse by an intimate partner was reported by 21 percent of male respondents and 22 percent of females. Specifically, 19 percent of adolescents reported that their partner had sworn at them, 13 percent reported that their partner had insulted them in front of others, 8 percent reported that their partner had pushed or shoved them, 3 percent had been threatened with violence by their partners, and 3 percent reported that their partner threw something at them. Prevalence of abusive behavior was similar for both genders. Abusive behavior appears to increase as adolescents' age, but begins to decline at around age 18 (Carver et al., 2003).

In the YRBS studies, the prevalence of dating violence has been quite stable over time. Of boys in the 1999 YRBS study, the prevalence of physical dating violence was 9 percent over the past 12 months (Howard and Wang, 2003). Of students in the 2003 YRBS study, again 9 percent reported being victims of physical dating violence in the past 12 months (Black et al., 2006). Of students included in the 2005 YRBS study, another 9 percent reported that they had been "hit, slapped, or physically hurt on purpose by their boyfriend or girlfriend (i.e., dating violence)" at some point in the 12 months preceding the survey. Dating violence was more prevalent among black and Hispanic students compared with white students (12 percent, 10 percent, and 8 percent, respectively), and more prevalent among older students compared with younger students (11 percent of twelfth graders, 10 percent of eleventh graders, 9 percent of tenth graders, and 7 percent of ninth graders) (Eaton et al., 2006).

To examine conflict within adolescent romantic relationships in more detail, a study of 869 high school students in the San Francisco Bay area asked those who had been involved in romantic relationships to rate the frequency with which they used specific conflict resolution tactics to resolve disagreements with their partners. In decreasing order of use, respondents indicated that they used compromise, distraction, avoidance, overt anger, seeking social support, and violence. Gender, age, and racial/ethnic differences in the use of the six tactics included the following: Girls reported using compromise and overt anger more frequently than boys, whereas boys described using distraction more frequently than girls; older teens described using compromise more frequently than younger ones; blacks described using violence more frequently than whites, whereas whites described using compromise more frequently than blacks (Feldman and Gowen, 1998).

Summary and Conclusions

The data on adolescents' attitudes and values with respect to romantic relationships, while sparse, come together to form a consistent picture. From an early age, adolescents understand that romantic relationships are distinct from other kinds of relationships they experience (e.g., family relationships or friendships). Moreover, by middle school, most adolescents desire a satisfying romantic relationship for themselves. How youth define romantic relationships appears to develop over the course of adolescence—from an emphasis on the positive aspects of romance, such as physical attraction and companionship, during the middle-school years, to an acknowledgement of more complex issues like jealousy and infidelity among older adolescents. They express disapproval of sexual intercourse among teens, but also believe that sex, when it occurs, is most appropriate within the context of a committed romantic relationship. The apparent tension between these two views may reflect the limits of the self-report method (i.e., respondents may be attempting to respond as they believe researchers would like them to respond) as opposed to any real conflict in adolescents' views about sex and relationships. In general, when asked to describe their attitudes and values regarding romantic relationships, most adolescents endorse values consistent with prevailing societal standards.

With respect to the future, data from a number of different sources converge to suggest that most adolescents view a healthy and happy marriage as an important life goal and expect to marry eventually. The value of marriage for adolescents does not vary much by age, but males are more likely than females, and Hispanic males more likely than white and black males, to endorse being married over being single. Consistent with their positive attitudes toward marriage, most adolescents disapprove of divorce. Attitudes toward divorce do not vary by age or gender, but do vary by race/ethnicity, such that Hispanic and black males view divorce as more acceptable than white males do. The limited data on historical trends suggest that these attitudes have been relatively stable over the past few decades.

Yet, despite their favorable views toward marriage as an institution, most adolescents also believe that marriage is a risky proposition. This is especially true among samples of adolescent unwed parents, who value marriage but nevertheless perceive obstacles to achieving a satisfying marriage for themselves. Even within the general population, significant proportions of adolescents who expect to marry also expect to experience divorce. Thus, adolescents appear to recognize that situational constraints may prevent them from achieving the life-long marriages that they desire. Perhaps as a consequence, recent decades have seen a substantial rise in adolescents' acceptance of cohabitation.

The gap between adolescents' aspirations and their expectations suggests a potentially important avenue for relationship education directed toward adolescents' beliefs and values regarding marriage. Specifically, curriculum developers may wish to emphasize healthy adult marriage as not only desirable, but possible and achievable as well. In conjunction with programs to address real barriers to marriage (e.g., employability, substance abuse, lack of financial stability), such a curriculum could benefit adolescents by teaching specific steps that adolescents can take to maximize their chances of reaching their goals.

Adolescents' romantic and sexual behaviors generally correspond with their self-reported attitudes and values. For example, adolescents' strong desires for romantic relationships are consistent with the observation that most young people experience their first romantic relationships during adolescence. Just as adolescents generally endorse the idea that sexual behaviors are most appropriate in the context of a close, romantic relationship, so do the majority of adolescents engage in sexual behaviors within the context of exclusive romantic relationships. Moreover, these relationships are described, on average, as relatively long-lasting (i.e., enduring for more than a year) and characterized by a relatively high degree of intimacy, with couples exchanging expressions of love, expecting each other to be sexually exclusive, and appearing as a couple in public.

Yet these mean trends clearly mask considerable variability associated with gender, ethnicity, and level of income, and this variability remains to be explored in detail. In particular, data from small samples suggest that low-income adolescents, especially low-income males, may be experiencing a higher number of shorter and less intimate relationships than members of other groups. More generally, the existing literature suggests that the majority of adolescents already endorses the goals of healthy marriage initiatives and seeks to behave in ways that are consistent with those goals.

The research reviewed in this chapter describes a picture in broad strokes, but that picture can be refined and elaborated in important ways. For example, only a handful of smaller studies explicitly explored the romantic representations and experiences of gay and lesbian youth. Whereas there is some suggestion that income influences perceived marital prospects, the existing literature provides insufficient evidence to determine whether the relationship attitudes and values of low-income youth are contributors to the low likelihood of successful marriage in this group. Finally, because measurement of these variables has been inconsistent across studies, it is difficult to assess trends in adolescents' attitudes and behaviors over time. As Florsheim (2003a, p. 372) has observed, "The changing face of adolescent romance only underscores the importance (and the urgency) of collecting data that will allow us to track trends and fluctuations and determine their meaning and direction."

CHAPTER THREE

Theoretical Perspectives on Adolescent Relationships and Adult Development

The majority of research on intimate relationships among youths and adolescents begins and ends with description. By itself, this is no mean feat, because adolescents' beliefs, attitudes, and behaviors with respect to romantic relationships are often in flux and vaguely defined. Yet informing current policy and interventions requires moving beyond describing these experiences and toward explaining the role that they may play in the development of healthy adults and healthy adult marriages. That adolescents' experiences with romantic relationships do play some role in adult development is a point of agreement among developmental psychologists. Sullivan (1953), for example, was one of the first to suggest that a major task of adolescence is to develop intimate relationships outside the family unit. Erikson (1968) elaborated on this idea, describing these first intimate relationships as the route through which the adolescent forms an independent identity. The implication of these ideas is that adolescents can be significantly altered by their romantic experiences in ways that have long-term implications for their subsequent romantic relationships during adulthood. Many others have echoed and elaborated upon this general theme (e.g., Feinstein and Ardon, 1973; Gray and Steinberg, 1999; Sullivan, 1953; Thorbecke and Grotevant, 1982; White et al., 1987; Zani, 1993).

Yet, beyond the broad assertion that adolescents' romantic experiences are likely to affect their adult outcomes, there has been little theory that details how these effects may come about. In light of ongoing efforts to develop programs and curricula targeting adolescent romantic relationships, an analysis of the models available to guide these efforts seems especially timely. The effectiveness of current and future interventions is likely to depend heavily on the extent to which those interventions in fact address elements that theory suggests are important to the development of healthy relationships in adolescence and healthy marriages in adulthood.

Thus, the goal of the current chapter is to identify and integrate theoretical perspectives on how adolescents' experiences affect their adult outcomes, with emphasis on the theories that have been most influential in guiding empirical research. After describing the most prominent perspectives, the chapter concludes by presenting an integrative framework that assembles elements from each perspective and may serve to identify priorities for future research and intervention in this area. At the outset, it is worth noting that this report cannot do justice to the richness and complexity of all the theoretical perspectives that have been applied toward understanding the role of adolescence in adult development. This chapter is of necessity selective, outlining only the central premises of each theory reviewed. More detailed discussions are cited where appropriate.

Attachment Theory

Summary of the Theory

Attachment theory, the perspective described and subsequently elaborated by Bowlby (1969; 1973; 1980), has been called "the most prominent theoretical position within the existing relationships literature" (Giordano, 2003, p. 259). The heart of the theory is Bowlby's observation that the survival of human beings, in contrast to that of many other species, depends on a capacity to form close relationships. In particular, the survival of human infants requires a bond with a caregiver (usually the parent) strong enough to motivate considerable self-sacrifice on the caregiver's part. So crucial is this bond for survival that Bowlby postulated an evolved attachment system designed to maintain and regulate close relationships across the lifespan.

Over the three volumes expanding on this perspective, Bowlby offered two premises with direct relevance for explaining the role of adolescent romantic experiences in adult development. First, infants and young children internalize their experiences with their primary caregivers to form enduring models of what intimacy and intimate relationships are generally like. Different experiences with caregiving are likely to result in different models, and Ainsworth and her students (e.g., Ainsworth, 1989) were instrumental in describing specific types of models that may arise. For example, to the extent that the primary caregiver (usually the mother) is attentive and available, the infant learns to expect care from others and trust that it will be provided, i.e., develops a secure model of attachment. In contrast, to the extent that the primary caregiver is unreliable or distant, the infant learns not to trust others and to rely on indirect techniques of soliciting attention, such as whining, crying, or withdrawal. These patterns have been described as reflecting an insecure model of attachment, which in turn has been divided into anxious/ambivalent or avoidant models (e.g., Ainsworth et al., 1978).

Second, an infant's generalized models of relationships can be self-perpetuating. That is, beliefs and expectations about relationships with others affect an individual's behavior toward others, who tend to respond in kind, validating the original beliefs and expectations. In this way, models of relationships developed in infancy and early childhood are played out and supported in relationships during adolescence, which in turn give rise to continuity between those relationships and relationships formed in adulthood (e.g., Hazan and Shaver, 1987; Waters et al., 2000).

Derivations of the attachment perspective have focused heavily on the idea of continuity across different sorts of relationships throughout adolescence. For example, Furman and his colleagues (Furman and Flanagan, 1997; Furman and Wehner, 1994, 1997) have suggested that, in early childhood, children begin to form friendships that echo the themes and patterns they experienced in their family of origin. As the child begins to mature sexually during adolescence, supportive and companionate relationships with peers evolve into romantic attachments that continue the same themes and patterns. Collins and his colleagues (Collins, 1997; Collins and Sroufe, 1999; Collins and Van Dulmen, 2006) have offered a similar view on the continuity across this period. Their descriptions of adolescence explicitly refer to models and beliefs about relationships as mechanisms that preserve the individual's habits of interacting across relationships with parents, peers, and romantic partners. Indeed, this sort of continuity and change has been supported by longitudinal research that follows infants through later adolescence (Carlson, Sroufe, and Egeland, 2004). Marital researchers have offered similar models to explain the role that early experiences with parents and friends may play in the outcomes of adult marriages (Story, Rothman, and Bradbury, 2002; Tallman, Burke, and Gecas, 1998).

Yet despite the prevailing emphasis on continuity, the attachment perspective acknowledges that models of relationships are responsive to experience, and so are susceptible to change (e.g., Waters et al., 2000). To the extent that romantic relationships represent a new variety of close relationship and one that fulfills new functions for the individual relative to relationships with parents and friends (Collins, 1997; Erikson, 1968), adolescence represents a unique period during which models of relationships formed in infancy may be reshaped by new experiences into models that will carry the individual through adulthood (Sroufe et al., 2005). Even the most secure models of intimacy can be shattered by a negative romantic experience, just as an anxious or avoidant model may be soothed by a positive experience. Thus, adolescent romantic relationships, although grounded in earlier experience, may nevertheless be viewed as playing an independent causal role in later adult development, and this is why developmental psychologists have begun to focus attention on adolescence to explain subsequent adult relationships (e.g., Collins and Sroufe, 1999; Collins and Van Dulmen, 2006; Furman and Simon, 1999; Tallman, Burke, and Gecas, 1998).

Evaluating the Theory

The broad influence of attachment theory has served to connect within a common framework research on infancy, childhood, and adult relationships that had previously been considered separate domains. Whereas the work of Sullivan (1953) and Erikson (1968) had predicted links between adolescence and adulthood, attachment theory offers mechanisms, e.g., individual models of relationships, that plausibly explain how those links might come about. The richness of this perspective connects it to biological, evolutionary, and developmental approaches to understanding human development, and justifies the enthusiastic interest that it has received from researchers and practitioners.

Yet attachment theory has not been without its critics, who have noted at least two ways that this perspective has yet to be elaborated (Giordano, 2003). First, by emphasizing continuity across relationships, attachment theory tends to underemphasize what may be unique about different types of relationships or what may be unique about different specific relationships experienced by an individual. For example, an individual may experience many romantic relationships over time, and recent evidence from young adults suggests that they develop distinct models for each relationship (La Guardia et al., 2000).

Second, by emphasizing individual cognitions and interpersonal interactions, research guided by attachment theory often overlooks broader social influences on experiences in relationships. Socioeconomic variables, characteristics of the partner, and the cultural context all seem likely to affect adolescents' choices with respect to romantic relationships and thereby affect their adult outcomes. Research derived from attachment theory does not generally address these sources of influence.

Implications for Intervention

In general, by assuming that experiences during adolescence play a causal role in the development of adult models of romantic relationships, attachment theory justifies programs and interventions that target adolescent relationships as a way of improving subsequent outcomes for adults. More specifically, the theory suggests that addressing adolescents' models of romantic relationships may be a way of altering the course of their romantic trajectories. In particular, it highlights three promising directions for promoting healthy romantic relationships in adolescence and healthy marriages in adulthood.

First, to the extent that adolescents' behaviors in their romantic relationships are likely to be affected by their personal models of what relationships are like and what they can expect from them, adolescents may benefit from the opportunity to express and examine their models explicitly. Many adolescents may take for granted that their own expectations for romantic relationships are the same as those of their peers. Through free writing, or group discussions, adolescents might be encouraged to articulate their assumptions about relationships and compare their assumptions with each other.

Second, adolescents might be encouraged to examine the sources of their models of relationships. When asked to consider where their ideas about relationships come from, many adolescents may spontaneously look to their families of origin, or relationships with peers, or the media. Those who have already had experiences in romantic relationships may look to those. A facilitator might help adolescents to explore sources of continuity and discontinuity in their own lives and to identify patterns that they wish to continue and relationship habits they may wish to break.

Third, program facilitators can help adolescents understand how their beliefs and assumptions about romantic relationships may affect their behavior in their relationships. This need not be tied directly into dry presentations of research findings, nor must it necessarily involve self-disclosure. For example, a facilitator might use a series of vignettes that describe individuals with different styles of attachment (e.g., "Tasha has never felt she could trust her partners completely"; "Sanjay feels he can do pretty well on his own without romantic relationships") and then ask participants to discuss how those different individuals might respond to common interpersonal scenarios (e.g., "A friend made a date to have lunch with you at noon, but was 30 minutes late"). By examining how general ideas about relationships might affect specific behaviors in these scenarios, adolescents may come to see how their own behavior in specific relationships, and possible continuities between their experiences of relationships in different contexts, might be affected by their own assumptions and beliefs.

The Lifespan Development Perspective

Summary of the Theory

The question of how adolescent romantic relationships may affect adult outcomes is really a question of development over the lifespan of the individual. Theories of lifespan development therefore offer a number of insights into these issues. Although there have been many different theories within research on lifespan development (e.g., Baltes, 1987; Ceci and Hembrooke, 1995; Zoccolillo et al., 1992), in this chapter we review one perspective developed by Caspi, Elder, and their colleagues (e.g., Caspi, 1987; Elder, Pavalko, and Hastings, 1991) that has been especially prominent in research on adult relationships.

These researchers had access to longitudinal data sets that assessed individuals multiple times over the course of their entire lives, from shortly after birth or during childhood in the 1920s and 1930s, through their adulthoods during the 1940s and 1950s, on through later life at the end of the 20th century. By examining ratings of these individuals' personalities across their lives, and by comparing these ratings with the experiences of these individuals at different stages of their lives, the researchers identified and described two distinct mechanisms to account for continuity and change in personalities across time (Caspi, Bem, and Elder, 1989). The first, echoing similar ideas in attachment theory, is *interactional continuity*—the idea that a child's personality affects the way the child interacts with others, who respond in kind and tend to reinforce the child's personality. Thus, bullies are reinforced for bullying, and shy children are reinforced for being shy, and as a result both types of children persist in their accustomed ways of interacting with others (Caspi, Elder, and Bem, 1987, 1988).

Attachment theory and interactional continuity both highlight the ways that experiences in specific interactions with specific individuals can have lasting consequences for the way a person subsequently interacts with other individuals. Whereas research guided by attachment theory has tended to focus on the cognitive aspects of this process, interactional continuity returns to Bowlby's original focus on behavioral habits and tendencies as the source of links between relationships during infancy and later childhood. The two approaches make similar predictions about how relationship experiences at different stages of life are associated with each other.

A second mechanism described by the lifespan development perspective, and one that differs from anything described by attachment theory, is *cumulative continuity*. Cumulative continuity is the idea that behaviors and choices at different developmental stages have consequences that accumulate to shape and constrain an individual's options at subsequent stages of life. Whereas interactional continuity focuses on interpersonal relationships and their consequences for the individual, cumulative continuity emphasizes the interaction between individuals and their social structures. For example, individuals who are aggressive and uncontrolled as children suffer academically and socially. As they progress through school, the consequences of their behavior accumulate, limiting their options for higher education and thereby their opportunities for adult employment. Thus constrained economically, their options for meeting potential romantic partners and forming a family are similarly limited (Caspi, Elder, and Bem, 1987).

Applied specifically to intimate relationships, the lifespan developmental perspective suggests that romantic relationships formed in adolescence may affect adult relationships in two ways: by supporting or altering the way an individual interacts with potential romantic partners and by giving rise to concrete outcomes (e.g., depression, pregnancy, STDs, educational attainment, marriage) that have implications for the choices available to the individual as an adult.

Evaluating the Theory

By offering two mechanisms to explain the continuity of relationships across different stages of development, the lifespan development perspective echoes and expands on themes raised by attachment theory. Whereas research derived from attachment theory has tended to focus on processes within and between individuals, the lifespan development perspective, as elaborated by Caspi, Bem, and Elder (1989), more directly acknowledges interactions between individuals and their environments. Thus, the lifespan perspective highlights not only the interpersonal consequences of adolescent romantic relationships but also the potential implications of these experiences for subsequent employment and educational opportunities. This directly ties thinking about adolescent romantic relationships to economic and sociological models.

Yet because this approach has been used mostly to describe links between young children's experiences and their adult outcomes, it remains incompletely developed with regard to explaining adolescent romantic relationships directly. For example, the approach emphasizes continuity over the lifespan, and in so doing neglects potential sources of discontinuity. Romantic relationships in particular may be a particularly important source of discontinuity for some adolescents because characteristics of romantic partners (e.g., their levels of achievement versus their levels of delinquency) and events within relationships (e.g., violence, pregnancy) can affect individual opportunities independent of the individual's personality.

Implications for Intervention

Interactional and cumulative continuity may be powerful concepts for program developers seeking to attune adolescents to the long-term implications of their romantic relationships. Each of them suggests specific exercises that could be employed in relationship education that targets adolescents.

For example, participants in these programs might be introduced to the idea of interactional continuity and encouraged to explore how it operates in their daily lives. This need not involve personal disclosure. For example, adolescents might be encouraged to adopt a persona and then role-play an interaction with someone who does not know the persona that they have adopted. How does the naïve participant interact with someone who has adopted a shy persona? How are the same person's behaviors different when interacting with an aggressive persona? How do the reactions of the naïve participant reinforce the personas that adolescents have adopted? By examining these questions in a neutral environment, adolescents may gain a clearer understanding of the sources of interactional continuity in their own lives.

Understanding the implications of cumulative continuity might call for a different strategy. After the concept is defined, adolescents might be guided in thinking about all the potential outcomes of their decisions regarding romantic relationships, and about the sequence of consequences that might follow from those outcomes, on into adulthood. For example, a group of participants might consider the possible immediate consequences of deciding not to enter into a relationship at all, and then the consequences of different sorts of decisions within relationships. It would be important to include the broadest possible range of potential outcomes in this sort of discussion—both positive and negative—so that all participants might identify with the possible paths being outlined. By drawing out these sequences, adolescents may come to appreciate the range of effects that their decisions about romantic relationships can have on their lives.

A second implication of cumulative continuity for programs that target adolescents as a means of promoting healthy adult marriages is that it is possible to educate adolescents in ways that prevent or minimize the adverse cumulative consequences of negative events in their own lives. Programs that effectively prevent teen pregnancy, substance abuse, or truancy, for example, should have the cumulative effect of promoting more favorable trajectories into adulthood, and thus more favorable circumstances for eventual healthy marriages. Programs that support adolescents who have experienced negative events should have the same potential for long-term benefits. To the extent that adolescents who have experienced teen pregnancy, problems with criminal behavior, or substance abuse can be assisted in gaining access to opportunities for recovery and advancement, these adolescents may have a better chance of maintaining a healthy marriage in adulthood than they otherwise would have.

The Development of Early Adult Romantic Relationships (DEARR) Model

Summary of the Theory

The Development of Early Adult Romantic Relationships (DEARR) model is a framework developed by Bryant and Conger (Bryant and Conger, 2002; Bryant, 2006) to address the sources of relationship behaviors in early adulthood. In contrast to attachment theory and the lifespan development perspective, both of which are broad approaches to understanding human relationships and interactions, the DEARR model is specifically designed to address romantic relationships. Because it has been proposed only recently, there is at present very little empirical research that has examined the premises of the model directly. Yet it nevertheless warrants mention here because it highlights some links that are not emphasized in prior theories of romantic relationships over the lifespan.

The DEARR model initially echoes attachment theory by suggesting that early experiences in the family of origin shape an individual's orientation toward romantic relationships. Whereas attachment theory identifies this influence as operating mostly through the individual's interactions with others, the DEARR model takes a broader view, suggesting that early experiences affect the developing individual in three ways.

First, like attachment theory, the DEARR model suggests that the developing child learns through experiences in the family of origin what relationships are like, and these models go on to shape the individual's expectations for relationships outside of the family. Thus, children accustomed to receiving support are likely to be more trusting that support will be provided by romantic partners when needed, whereas children raised in less supportive families will learn not to expect support in their romantic relationships.

Second, consistent with the idea of interactional continuity, the DEARR model explicitly suggests that patterns of interaction developed among family members give rise to similar patterns played out with romantic partners. Thus, children accustomed to hostility and manipulation in their families are likely to express hostility and engage in manipulative behavior in their own relationships as young adults, whereas children accustomed to warm and supportive interactions are more likely to possess the skills to behave in a warm and supportive way toward their own romantic partners.

Third, the model acknowledges the role that the social structure (e.g., socioeconomic status [SES], acute and chronic stressors, peer relationships) plays in romantic relationships, and suggests that the circumstances of the family of origin largely determine these features as well. In other words, individuals born into privileged families will have access to educational opportunities, resources, and social circles that individuals born into underprivileged families will lack. Those opportunities, resources, and social circles form the environment within which the individual's early experiences in romantic relationships play out. To the extent that the environment is supportive, it facilitates successful relationships, and to the extent that the environment is demanding, it hinders successful relationships. Thus, the DEARR model draws attention to the links between the family of origin and the context of young adult relationships in a way that the other two perspectives reviewed here do not.

The final proposition of the DEARR model is that early experiences in the family of origin (e.g., ideas about relationships, behavioral habits, and environmental supports and demands) directly affect the individual's thoughts and behaviors within young adult relationships and thus affect the success or failure of those relationships. In other words, the elements of the model are presumed to contribute to whether or not young adults are able to do such things as resolve conflict, provide support, and place trust in their romantic partners. These specific behaviors are then described as directly accounting for the outcomes of young adult relationships.

Evaluating the Theory

The DEARR model expands upon prior views of the precursors of healthy adult relationships and marriages in two important ways. First, the model acknowledges multiple and simultaneous sources of continuity between relationships across the lifespan, including enduring models of relationships, behavioral tendencies, and stable environments. Second, the model describes causal paths among these elements, drawing direct and indirect links between experiences in the family of origin, aspects of the broader social structure, and the success of romantic relationships in young adulthood. Especially innovative is the idea that families not only teach children how relationships operate but also place children in environments that constrain or facilitate how those lessons get expressed.

Yet, the DEARR model is new and still awaits development and elaboration. Most notably, the model does not mention adolescent relationships directly. Although adolescent experiences with romantic relationships would seem to be a crucial intermediate stage between childhood and early adulthood, the DEARR model skips over this stage, describing only direct associations between early experiences and young adult relationship processes and outcomes. This is an important oversight, leaving the DEARR model unable to acknowledge the possibility that adolescents may learn from their experiences with romantic relationships in ways that contribute independently to their young adult outcomes.

Implications for Intervention

Two elements of the DEARR model are especially noteworthy for programs and interventions targeting adolescent relationships. The first is the idea that what partners do in their relationships—how they express affection, how they communicate, how they resolve conflicts—is what directly accounts for the success or failure of their relationships. Thus, the DEARR model supports the idea of teaching relationship and interpersonal skills as a way of improving relationship outcomes among adolescents and adults. In particular, the DEARR model suggests that teaching relationship skills during adolescence may be a way of severing negative patterns that might otherwise persist from childhood through young adulthood.

The second is the idea that the nature of a couple's environment affects how their relationship skills are expressed. This is a subtle idea that may not be immediately intuitive to adolescents. As extensive research in social psychology has demonstrated, a common tendency is to attribute other people's behavior to their own skills and dispositions, underestimating the ways that the environment can change how people behave (e.g., Gilbert and Malone, 1995; Jones and Harris, 1967). Adolescents may appreciate the opportunity to consider ways that their own or a partner's behavior might be changed or constrained in different kinds of environments. For example, adolescents might be asked to consider a couple trying to resolve a disagreement about money. Would it change the nature of their discussion if they were relatively affluent and discussing whether to remodel a room in the house, compared to if they were low-income and discussing how to pay the bills? Would it matter if the conversation took place on a weekday or a weekend? Whether or not young children are around? How would these scenarios play out differently in the context of a marriage versus other relationships? By drawing out the links between what happens inside relationships and what is going on outside relationships, adolescents may better appreciate the broader forces that affect their experiences within their own relationships.

By highlighting the interplay between processes within romantic relationships and the environment of the couple, the DEARR model also suggests ways of packaging and delivering relationship skills education that may make these programs more effective. To the extent that a supportive environment, i.e., an environment free from stress and rich in support and resources, facilitates the expression of relationship skills, programs that teach relationship skills may be most effective if they are provided in conjunction with or alongside programs that target adolescents' environments directly. For example, relationship skills classes might be offered in connection with programs on job training or substance abuse prevention. Any efforts to provide adolescents with greater opportunities for healthy development may provide a suitable arena for promoting healthy relationships as well.

Integration: Assembling a Model of the Precursors of Adult Romantic Relationships

Thus far, we have reviewed and drawn out the practical implications of three existing theoretical perspectives relevant to understanding the role of adolescent romantic relationships in adult development. The key points of this review are summarized in Table 3.1.

As Table 3.1 makes clear, despite some overlap among the theories, each highlights different ideas, all of which appear to be crucial for a comprehensive understanding of the role adolescent relationships may play in adult development. The goal of the rest of this chapter is to integrate the key ideas of the existing theories into a single framework. Doing so offers several potential benefits for researchers and policymakers focused on adolescent relationships as precursors of healthy adult marriages (e.g., Bouchey and Furman, 2003; Kan and Cares, 2006). First, an integrative framework brings the insights of multiple perspectives together within a single source. Second, assembling the components of existing theories into a single structure may highlight important questions or avenues for intervention that have been underexamined over overlooked entirely. Third, to the extent that it is as broad and comprehensive as possible, an integrative framework should be a useful tool for organizing the existing research and practice literature in this area. The integrative framework is presented in Figure 3.1.

Figure 3.1
An Integrative Framework to Account for the Adolescent Precursors of Adult Romantic Relationships

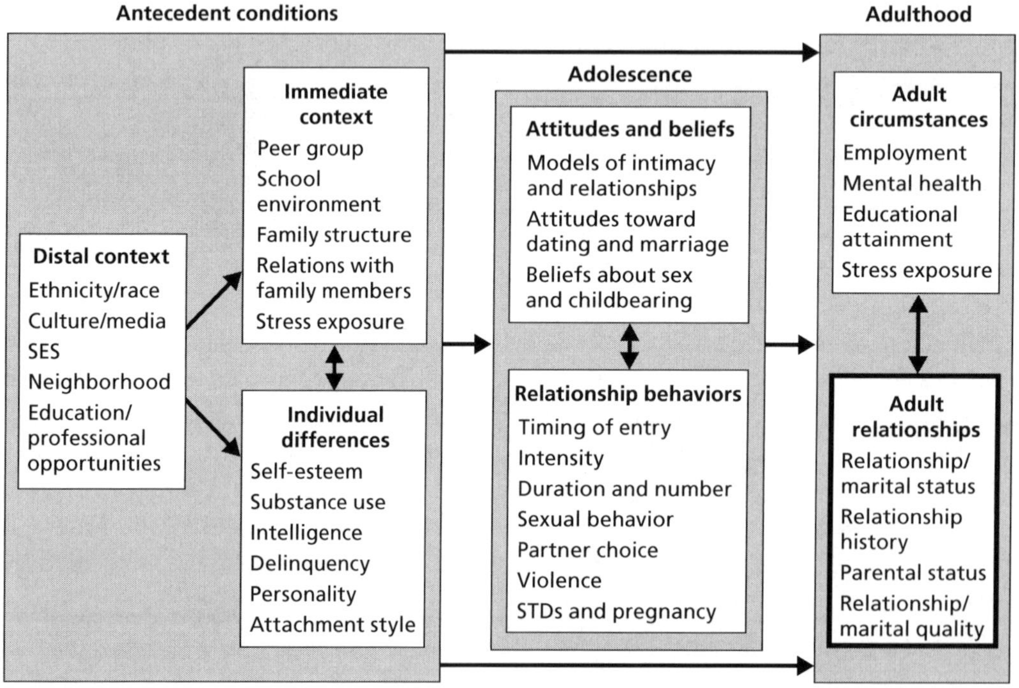

RAND *TR488-3.1*

Table 3.1
Summary of Theories

Theory	Main Premises	Evaluation	Implications for Intervention
Attachment theory	Infants develop general models of relationships based on their experiences with their primary caregivers. These models shape expectations and behaviors in subsequent relationships, and are thus reinforced.	Provides a mechanism (i.e., models of relationships) to explain continuity in relationships across the lifespan. Highlights first romantic experiences as a potential source of change in these models.	Identify the models that adolescents use to understand their own relationships. Examine sources of relationship models. Understand how models of relationships affect behavior in relationships.
Lifespan development perspective	Interactions with others tend to reinforce a child's personality (interactional continuity). Choices and behaviors early in life have consequences that shape options available later in life (cumulative continuity).	Acknowledges ways that the social structure (e.g., resources, employment, social networks) affects relationships. Explains multiple ways that adolescent relationships can affect adult outcomes, including marriage.	Explore how personality can be reinforced through interactions with others. Trace the cumulative consequences of different decisions about romantic relationships. Learn to prevent or minimize negative outcomes that may have cumulative consequences for adolescents.
DEARR model	Early experiences in family of origin affect capacity for successful relationships in three ways. Child develops models from observing family. Child develops habits from interacting with family. Family shapes the environments where the child forms subsequent relationships.	Explains that behaviors within relationships directly account for the success and failure of those relationships. Suggests how environments may facilitate or constrain effective processes within relationships.	Teach adolescents skills for effective relationships maintenance. Explain how specific environments (e.g., stress vs. support) may affect the expression and practice of relationship skills. Associate relationship education with programs that improve environments for adolescents directly.

The integrative framework depicted in Figure 3.1 describes how aspects of adolescent experiences, and adolescents' romantic relationships in particular, may account for outcomes, especially marital outcomes, during adulthood. To this end, the framework divides relevant variables into three broad groups represented by the three gray rectangles in the figure: antecedent conditions, adolescence, and adulthood. Each of these three categories helps to organize several broad constructs represented by the smaller white rectangles in the figure. Listed within each rectangle are examples of specific variables that might be measured to assess each construct. By grouping variables in this way, the framework suggests that those variables may have similar sorts of associations with variables grouped within other constructs. The specific variables listed are meant to be suggestive rather than exhaustive.

Antecedent Conditions

Many variables that existing theories suggest are important for understanding relationships across the lifespan are essentially in place before adolescence begins—certainly before adolescents experience their first romantic relationships. The integrative framework presented here describes these variables as *antecedent conditions*. Within this grouping, the framework further subdivides these variables into three broad constructs. Most removed from the individual are elements of the *distal context* (e.g., ethnicity/race, SES, the media environment, and the neighborhood environment) that shape the environments within which individuals grow up and within which their initial ideas about romantic relationships are formed. In general, these variables are stable, or at least more stable than other elements of the model, so the arrows describing paths of influence from these variables to other elements in the model are depicted as unidirectional.

Consistent with the DEARR model, the framework suggests that elements of the distal context affect adolescent and adult romantic relationships only indirectly, through their direct effects on the more proximal conditions of adolescence. One of these is the *immediate context* of the adolescent, including family structure, relations with family members and peers, the school environment, and the experience of chronic and acute stress. The second of these are the *individual differences* that adolescents bring to their first romantic experiences (e.g., self-esteem, substance use, academic achievement).

Both of these sets of conditions are shaped by the distal context of the individual. For example, substance use (an individual difference) and family structure (an element of the immediate context) both vary significantly with socioeconomic status (an element of the distal context). The immediate context and individual differences also affect each other. For example, peer groups affect the likelihood of substance abuse, and relationships with parents and peers affect self-esteem. Together, elements of the distal context, the immediate context, and the individual interact to provide the foundation from which the individual's first experiences with romantic relationships arise.

Adolescence

Regarding experiences with romantic relationships during adolescence, the framework describes two sets of variables as directly affected by antecedent conditions. The first of these are the adolescent's *attitudes and beliefs* about romantic relationships, sex, and marriage. Included here are the individual's models of what intimate relationships are like, presumably developed through early interactions with parents, as attachment theory suggests. Yet the framework also accounts for the possibility that other factors, such as the media or interactions with peers, may also contribute to relationship-relevant attitudes and beliefs during adolescence.

The second set of variables that can be examined during adolescence is *relationship behaviors,* i.e., the individual's specific choices and experiences in romantic relationships during this stage of life. This set of variables includes partner choice and so accounts for characteristics of the partner as well as of the individual. It also includes the timing of entry into the first romantic relationship and so allows the framework to be applied to those who enter romantic relationships early, late, or not at all. These variables also include specific outcomes of relationship behaviors, such as STDs and pregnancy, that may have long-term implications for individual development. Relationship behaviors and attitudes and beliefs are portrayed as influencing each other: Attitudes and beliefs presumably affect the choices that adolescents make with regard to their romantic relationships; at the same time, their experiences in those relationships may reinforce or alter their attitudes and beliefs.

Adulthood

The framework presented here brings together antecedent conditions and adolescent experiences to account for individual outcomes experienced during adulthood. Because this framework has been designed as a tool for promoting healthy marriages in particular, the framework gives special emphasis to variables relevant to understanding *adult relationships*. These include not only marital status and marital quality but also the quality and stability of other types of relationships, the individual's relationship history (many relationships or few, longer relationships or shorter), and whether the individual has become a parent.

Having highlighted adult relationship and marital outcomes, the framework groups all other outcomes as *adult circumstances*, analogous to the immediate context of adolescent relationships. Although employment, mental health, and educational attainment may all be affected by an individual's experiences in early life and in adolescence, these outcomes also form the context for the adult relationships that are the particular focus of this framework. The framework groups these outcomes together to reflect this emphasis.

In arranging the three broad groupings of variables in this way, the framework adopts a straightforward logic. Specifically, it suggests, consistent with existing models of adult development, that conditions in infancy and early adolescence set the stage for romantic experiences in adolescence and that these experiences may in turn affect romantic relationships and marital outcomes in adulthood. Integrating prior theoretical approaches, the model offers several paths through which adolescent experiences may affect adult outcomes.

Consistent with attachment theory, one path operates through cognitions (i.e., relationship behaviors → attitudes and beliefs → adult relationships). The idea here is that experiences in romantic relationships may affect an adolescent's ideas about romantic attachments and attitudes toward marriage, which in turn affect choices and behaviors in adulthood. Thus, secure, trusting relationships in adolescence may make the prospect of adult marriage more appealing and attainable, whereas unstable or violent relationships in adolescence may lead to reluctance to risk deeper emotional connections.

An alternative path operates through the concrete consequences of adolescent relationships (i.e., relationship behaviors → adult circumstances → adult relationships). For example, teen parenthood, one of the most severe potential consequences of adolescent romantic relationships, has been shown to interfere with subsequent educational attainment and identity development (Coley and Chase-Lansdale, 1998; Furstenberg, 1980), limiting the available options for forming and maintaining healthy marriages and relationships in adulthood. In general, the current framework suggests that, by facilitating or impeding development during adolescence, experiences in adolescent romantic relationships may contribute to more or less favorable conditions for romantic relationships in adulthood.

At the same time, the model acknowledges that the antecedent conditions that shape adolescent relationships may continue to have direct implications for adult relationships (i.e., direct paths of influence between antecedent conditions and adult outcomes). That is, conditions such as socioeconomic status or family structure may affect romantic relationships in adolescence and adulthood, whether or not adolescent experiences in relationships exert any independent causal influence on adult outcomes.

Research on the effects of early entry into romantic relationships has raised this possibility directly. For example, a number of studies have noted that, especially for girls, early entry into romantic relationships is associated with greater risk for later substance abuse and delinquency (Aro and Taipale, 1987; Furstenberg, Brooks-Gunn, and Chase-Lansdale, 1989; Grinder, 1966; Pawlby, Mills, and Quinton, 1997). These studies have also noted that early entry into romantic relationships is itself predicted by other risk factors (e.g., Connolly, Furman, and Konarski, 2000), leaving the independent effects of the relationship behaviors unclear. These findings raise the possibility that adolescent relationships are expressions of antecedent conditions and, as such, are precursors of adult relationship outcomes but may not be independent causes. Support for this view would not imply that adolescent relationships are unimportant, only that they may be better treated as markers of risk than as targets of intervention themselves.

Evaluating the Model

To explain the development of healthy adult marriages and relationships, the integrative framework presented here assembles and elaborates upon the theoretical perspectives that have preceded it. Like attachment theory, the model assigns a prominent place to early experiences and beliefs about relationships. Like the lifespan developmental perspective, the model acknowledges that the concrete consequences of early relationship experiences may impact subsequent adult outcomes. Like Bryant and Conger's (2002) DEARR model, the current model draws both direct and indirect paths between individuals' early environment and their adult outcomes.

What the current framework adds to the existing work is the idea that adolescent romantic relationships in particular represent a potential turning point in development, a stage of life during which patterns established in the family of origin may be reinforced or substantially altered, depending upon specific choices, behaviors, and experiences. Furthermore, the framework draws paths that help explain the role that socioeconomic status may play in the development of healthy adult relationships. Specifically, the framework suggests that socioeconomic status directly affects the immediate context of adolescent relationships and the circumstances of adult relationships. From this perspective, the task for understanding the development of healthy adult relationships in low-income populations involves understanding how a low-income environment limits the options that an individual encounters at different stages of development.

Yet, although the framework brings together a wide range of thinking, it nevertheless leaves several important questions about the role of adolescent experiences in adult outcomes awaiting further specification. First, because it focuses on individual development, the framework underemphasizes dyadic processes. Those processes are recognized in the model (as part of relationship behaviors and adult relationships), but the specific role that interactions between partners may play in adult development deserves further elaboration. Second, the framework does not address gender differences directly, although it is likely that specific paths in the model differ for males and females. Third, the framework fails to distinguish among what are likely to be very different sorts of relationship outcomes in adulthood. For example, the precursors of parenthood, enduring marriages, and satisfying relationships (marital or not), may each be distinct, so that different early experiences lead to different patterns of adult outcomes. Drawing these distinctions remains a task for future research and theory.

Despite these limitations, however, the framework as described here may be useful for organizing the existing literature on the role of adolescent romantic experiences in adult development. By locating existing research within the model, it should be possible to identify propositions that have been investigated and supported, those that have failed to receive support, and those that have yet to be examined empirically. The next chapter adopts this approach to review and evaluate the existing empirical research on these issues.

Implications for Intervention

In addition to providing an organization for empirical research, the framework presented here may be used to organize intervention strategies aimed at promoting healthy marriages as well. Different activities supported by the Healthy Marriage Initiative (HMI) may be viewed as targeting different specific elements of the framework. For example, many programs supported by HMI directly address adult relationships without regard to possible precursors of those relationships. Other programs, such as those currently being evaluated by the Supporting Healthy Marriage and Building Strong Families projects, target adult relationships but also aim to improve adult circumstances through referrals to needed services. The framework presented here supports programs that adopt this broader approach, suggesting that any efforts to improve adult circumstances should facilitate healthier adult marriages as well.

The programs of central interest to the current report, those aimed at adolescents and their relationships, target experiences and choices believed to be precursors of adult marriages. The framework suggests the range of content that these programs might include. For example, curricula developed for younger adolescents may emphasize attitudes and beliefs more than relationship behaviors because younger adolescents may have fewer experiences with romantic relationships from which to draw. Curricula targeting older teens may be broader, including instruction in specific behaviors that have been associated with effective conflict resolution. Broader still would be programs that include material to address consequences of romantic experiences, such as pregnancy and STDs. The framework presented here serves to describe the dimensions along which different curricula might vary and to specify how different elements within each program might enhance each other.

The framework also highlights potential targets of intervention that may not be considered central to adolescent romantic relationships per se but might nevertheless be important for setting the stage for healthy adult marriages. For example, the framework suggests that programs targeting adolescents should address the sources of their attitudes and beliefs about romantic relationships and marriage. The framework invites program developers to consider how distal factors, such as culture and race, as well as more proximal factors, such as neighborhoods and peer groups, affect adolescents' experiences. It seems likely that a broad-based approach to intervention and education will be most effective in providing adolescents with a foundation for healthy marriages in adulthood. The integrative framework identifies the elements that might be included in such an approach and suggests how they might be organized. Chapter Five of this report draws upon this framework to structure a review and analysis of current curricula targeting adolescents and to identify possible gaps in the content currently being offered.

In addition to providing a way for thinking broadly about interventions and programs, the framework described here also raises important questions for policymakers and program developers to consider. As the framework makes clear, there are several different ways to consider the role of adolescent romantic relationships in the development of healthy marriages. To the extent that the way adolescents conduct their romantic relationships independently accounts for the outcomes of their adult marriages, these relationships are an appropriate target for interventions. Evidence to this effect would justify developing and supporting programs that target adolescent relationships in order to improve adult outcomes. However, to the extent that adolescents' experiences in their romantic relationships are symptoms of broader risk factors rather than risk factors in themselves, relationship experiences may be viewed as markers of vulnerability and resilience rather than as causes. Evidence supporting this view would suggest allocating additional resources toward programs that directly target such antecedent conditions as socioeconomic status and family structure. The framework presented here recognizes that these perspectives on the role of adolescent romantic relationships in adult development are not mutually exclusive. Indeed, the framework describes these alternative paths of influence as operating simultaneously.

Summary

Efforts at promoting healthy adult marriages through programs targeting adolescents are likely to be most effective to the extent that they are guided by clear theories of the role that adolescents' experiences in romantic relationships play in adult development. This chapter reviewed three established theoretical perspectives that address this issue: attachment theory, the life-span development perspective, and the DEARR model. As summarized in Table 3.1, each of these perspectives highlights different elements of adolescent experience that appear crucial for a comprehensive understanding of the role that these experiences may play in the development of healthy marriages.

To facilitate efforts to draw upon theory in developing new research and new programs, components from each of the three perspectives were assembled within the integrative framework presented in Figure 3.1. As depicted by the figure, the precursors of healthy adult marriages may be grouped roughly into three broad categories: antecedent conditions (i.e., relatively stable elements of adolescents' lives that may be in place before they experience romantic relationships); attitudes, beliefs, and behaviors during adolescence; and circumstances and relationship outcomes during adulthood. Placing adolescence in the center of the framework suggests that adolescence may be a key turning point, a time when patterns established in early childhood may be reinforced or permanently altered. Yet the framework also acknowledges that such antecedent conditions as family history and SES may have direct affects on adult marital outcomes, leaving the precise causal role of adolescent relationships in adult development unclear.

Assembling this integrative framework offers a structure for organizing research on adolescent romantic relationships and programs that target these relationships as precursors of healthy marriages. The next two chapters draw upon the framework to structure reviews of each of these domains.

CHAPTER FOUR

Review of Research on the Causes, Correlates, and Consequences of Romantic Relationships in Adolescence

Despite theoretical interest in the role of adolescent romantic experiences in adult development, up to now, research on adolescent experiences of intimacy has focused primarily on sexual behavior, often to the exclusion of the relationships in which those behaviors take place (Brown, Feiring, and Furman, 1999; Furman and Shaffer, 2003; Giordano, 2003). Over the past few years, several important edited volumes (Crouter and Booth, 2006; Florsheim, 2003b; Furman, Brown, and Feiring, 1999) have drawn attention to the need for research on adolescent relationships per se, and their role in adult development in particular. Even the most recent of these volumes, however, ends with the observation that claims about the continuity of romantic experiences between adolescence and adulthood continue to rest more on speculation than on empirical evidence (Kan and Cares, 2006).

Yet research on the causes, correlates, and consequences of adolescent romantic relationships does exist, albeit scattered across a wide range of academic disciplines and publishing outlets. The goal of this chapter is to assemble this literature in a single place and to take stock of the accomplishments of work in this area to date. In so doing, the chapter offers three potential benefits for efforts to understand the role of adolescent romantic experiences in adult development. First, establishing a common base of knowledge on adolescent romantic relationships will assist researchers in designing new studies that build upon and refine what has already been established. Second, by organizing the existing research within a single framework, this review highlights directions for future research on propositions and associations that have been understudied or overlooked entirely. Third, a review of the field to date allows interventions targeting adolescent romantic relationships to proceed from the firmest possible empirical foundation and promotes the accumulation of future empirical research in ways that maximally inform policies and programs.

The Scope and Procedures of This Review

In general, the review was designed to examine research relevant to understanding the role of adolescent romantic relationships in adult development. This broad aim directed our attention toward studies addressing the integrative framework described in Chapter Three. It should be noted at the outset that no study has brought together all parts of the framework in a single investigation. Instead, this review assembles research that has examined each of the three broad groups of variables identified within the framework. First, we identified studies linking relationship behaviors and experiences during adolescence to antecedent conditions, e.g., variables assessed in the family of origin and aspects of the social context. Second, we identified studies examining variables likely to be associated with relationship experiences during adolescence, e.g., attitudes and beliefs, peer group membership, physical development. Third, we identified studies examining the consequences of experiences in adolescent romantic relationships for outcomes assessed during adolescence and later adulthood.

For each of these categories of research, we identified relevant studies in three ways. First, we consulted prior reviews of research on adolescent dating and romantic relationships (e.g., Bouchey and Furman, 2003; Collins and Madsen, 2006; Furman and Shaffer, 2003; Giordano, 2003). Although each of these reviews identified important studies in this area, none attempted to be systematic or comprehensive and none was specifically designed to understand adolescent romantic relationships as precursors of adult marriages. Second, to identify studies not included in prior reviews, we conducted literature searches through Internet-based databases (i.e., Web of Science, PsychInfo, Social Science Abstracts) using a wide range of keywords (e.g., adolescence, adolescent, romance, intimacy, relationships, etc.). Abstracts for new studies identified in this way were scanned for their relevance to the goals of the current project. Third, we consulted with colleagues in this area and solicited recommendations of additional relevant research from them. This combination of procedures offers confidence that the studies assembled here are reasonably comprehensive of the existing work in the area to date.

Once we had identified a potentially relevant study, we based the decision to include it in the review on several considerations. First, all studies included here in some way address romantic relationships explicitly. As has been noted, a vast array of research on adolescence has examined sexual behaviors in this population without addressing the relational context of those behaviors directly. That research has been the topic of several reviews of its own (e.g., Bissell, 2000; Bonell, 2004; Brooks-Gunn and Paikoff, 1997; Card, 1999; DiIorio, Pluhar, and Belcher, 2003; Herold and Marshall, 1996; Santelli et al., 2006) and so was not included here. However, we did include research on sexuality and sexual behaviors that also included analyses of relationships per se.

Second, the studies included in the review had to make some attempt to explain or account for variability in individual outcomes. Studies that simply described adolescent relationships were reviewed in Chapter Two of this report and are not reviewed again here. Case studies, ethnographies, and studies of very small samples were generally excluded by this criterion. However, studies that offer descriptive data and also attempt to account for variability in outcomes are reviewed in both chapters.

Third, this review defined adolescence as the period of life from 10 to 19 years of age, consistent with the definition of adolescence put forth by the World Health Organization. As a result, research on romantic relationships among college students was, for the most part, excluded from the review. The only exceptions to this rule were cases in which the only available study on a topic was one that addressed college students or when the study explicitly stated that all relationships were assessed among respondents under age 19. These exceptions are noted in the text.

Fourth, the studies included in the review come from peer-reviewed journals, edited book chapters, or reports from reputable research organizations. Unpublished doctoral dissertations were not included.

Fifth, our inclusion criteria did not include any restrictions on the age of the study, but the text emphasizes more recent work over older work.

Sixth, our inclusion criteria allowed research on same-sex relationships, but research in this area is so underdeveloped (Diamond, 2003; Savin-Williams, 2001) that the final pool of studies included very few that addressed same-sex relationships.

An important consideration throughout the conduct of this review was whether the studies addressed low-income populations specifically. It bears repeating that the broad goal of this report is to examine research relevant to promoting healthy marriages within low-income populations specifically. Yet, as has also been mentioned previously, there is almost no research that directly addresses the precursors of healthy marriages in low-income populations—and even less research on adolescent relationships in low-income populations. For these reasons, the income level of the sample was not a criterion for inclusion in this review. Instead, the review addresses research from a broad range of samples, from sample of convenience to nationally representative samples, with studies of nationally representative samples receiving more emphasis in the text. Throughout, the analyses of the research speculate on the extent to which the results of existing research are likely to generalize to low-income populations.

Comments on Methodological Issues

Interpretations of the results of research on adolescent romantic relationships must necessarily be qualified by the limitations of the research methods used to obtain those results. Thus, it makes sense to begin the literature review by commenting on methodological issues that pertain to the majority of the studies reviewed here. These methodological issues then provide a context for the analyses of the substantive findings that follow.

Lack of Agreement on Definitions of Key Terms

In Chapter One, we noted that researchers have yet to reach a consensus on what makes an intimate relationship healthy, let alone what makes intimate relationships healthy among adolescents. The challenge of defining relevant terms concretely affects other areas of this field as well (Kan and Cares, 2006). For example, research on adolescent romantic relationships has yet to provide a concrete definition of what a romantic relationship is and what it is not. As noted in Chapter One, researchers tend to leave the task of definition to study participants, who are free to decide for themselves whether and when they are in romantic relationships. Analyses of data from the Add Health study reveal the potential consequences of this practice. In Add Health, respondents were asked to nominate up to three individuals with whom they had experienced a romantic relationship. Because Add Health examines school-based samples, many of the individuals so nominated were also respondents, allowing analyses of the extent to which nominations were reciprocated. In fact, a large percentage of the nominations were not reciprocated, i.e., the two individuals did not agree on whether or not they had ever been in a romantic relationship (Carver and Udry, 1997; Kennedy, 2005). If the definition of a relationship is so vague that two individuals so frequently disagree on whether they had one, the looseness of existing definitions of terms, such as dating, going steady, falling in love, etc., raise serious questions about what research on these phenomena is actually studying.

Lack of Data from Representative Samples

As noted in Chapter Two, at least five studies of nationally representative samples include assessments of variables relevant to understanding adolescent experiences in romantic relationships. Yet, as also pointed out in Chapter Two, to date analyses of these data have generally been descriptive. Theory-testing within these data sets—and even analyses that compare youth across levels of SES, race, and ethnicity—is possible, but so far it has not been conducted. Thus, research that tests hypotheses about the causes and consequences of adolescent romantic experiences has tended to rely on data from smaller samples and samples of convenience. This limitation particularly affects the ability of existing research to comment on low-income youth.

Lack of Longitudinal Data

To best understand how specific relationship experiences during adolescence may account for outcomes during later life, researchers have been unanimous in calling for a longitudinal approach (e.g., Collins and Van Dulmen, 2006; Eccles and Gootman, 2002; Furman and Shaffer, 2003; Giordano, 2003; Kan and Cares, 2006). Yet longitudinal data on adolescents' romantic relationships have accumulated slowly. Even within theory-based research on small samples, most research on the correlates and consequences of adolescent relationships to date has drawn from cross-sectional or retrospective data collected at a single assessment, with the Add Health study being a notable exception. The weaknesses of cross-sectional designs for drawing inferences about causal influence have been well documented (e.g., Brewin, Andrews, and Gotlib, 1993; Karney and Bradbury, 1995).

In addition to the Add Health study, longitudinal research that has assessed adolescents' relationship experiences directly include the Toledo Adolescent Relationships Study (e.g., Giordano, Longmore, and Manning, 2006; Giordano, Manning, and Longmore, 2005), the Minnesota Longitudinal Study of Parents and Children (e.g., Carlson, Sroufe, and Egeland, 2004; Sroufe et al., 2005), a study of 103 German middle-school children (Seiffge-Krenke, Shulman, and Klessinger, 2001), and the Oregon Youth Study (e.g., Capaldi and Clark, 1998). These studies offer suggestive evidence for the continuity between adolescent and adult romantic experiences, but all three studies have sampled predominately white, middle-class families, leaving the generalizability of their results to other populations (e.g., low-income populations) an open question.

Failure to Acknowledge Age Differences Within Adolescence

Researchers commonly define adolescence as a stage of life spanning from approximately the ages of 10 to 19. This time is of particular interest to those studying romantic relationships because, as many have noted, the capacity for relationships changes drastically during this period (e.g., Brooks-Gunn, Petersen, and Eichorn, 1985; Brown, 1999, 2006; Collins and

Madsen, 2006; Erikson, 1968; Laursen and Collins, 1994; Sroufe et al., 2005; Sullivan, 1953). For example, the cognitive skills that permit an individual to feel empathy and understand the perspective of another person do not mature until later in adolescence (e.g., Hill and Palmquist, 1978). Older teens use different strategies to resolve interpersonal conflicts than do younger teens (Feldman and Gowen, 1998). The meanings ascribed to love and intimacy change significantly over this period as well (e.g., Bouchey and Furman, 2003; Connolly et al., 1999; Waldinger et al., 2002).

To the extent that adolescents of different ages are differentially prepared for romantic relationships, the same experiences occurring at different ages may have different associations with later young adult outcomes. Experiences that may have positive consequences for development when they occur later in adolescence (e.g., falling in love, exclusivity, commitment, spending significant amounts of time together) may have negative consequences when they occur too early. Existing research on these issues has rarely acknowledged this possibility. Instead, most longitudinal work comparing different stages of development either groups respondents within a stage regardless of age or treats age as a control variable. As a consequence, the way that age may affect the links between adolescent romantic experiences and adult outcomes remains an open question.

Reliance on Data from Individuals Rather Than Couples

An irony of research on romantic relationships is that the great majority of it gathers data solely from individuals (Furman, 1984; Karney and Bradbury, 1995). A reliance on individual reports similarly characterizes research on romantic relationships among adolescents (Collins and Madsen, 2006; Furman and Hand, 2006). As a result, several important questions about these relationships have been overlooked within this literature. Although it is hard to imagine that adolescent relationships are not affected in significant ways by characteristics of partners, "In the study of adolescent romantic relationships, no published findings have yet addressed questions of the partner's identity or the impact of the partner's characteristics on relationship quality" (Collins and Van Dulmen, 2006, p. 80). Without such data, it remains possible that the consequences of relationship experiences during adolescence stem entirely from attributes of the partner (e.g., age difference, substance use, religiosity), rather than from relationship behaviors per se (Collins and Madsen, 2006).

Reliance on Self-Report Data

Virtually all research on adolescent romantic relationships and development relies exclusively on self-report data. Thus, most of what is known about adolescents' experiences and outcomes comes from their own descriptions. As has been widely discussed in the survey literature (e.g., Schwarz, 1999; Singer and Presser, 1989), self-reports can provide a limited or even distorted picture of a phenomenon, for several reasons. First, self-reports are subject to distortions because of failures of recall (i.e., individuals do not always remember their experiences accurately and so resort to educated guesses when responding to surveys) and deliberate bias (e.g., respondents may alter their answers to create a favorable impression for the researcher). Second, when an independent variable (e.g., relationship experiences) and a dependent variable (e.g., depression) are both assessed via self-reports, the association between them can be inflated by the fact that the measurements share a common method (e.g., Fincham and Bradbury, 1987). Third, there may be important aspects of adolescents' lives that they simply do not have access to (e.g., their parents' mental health history). There are several ways of broadening the range of research methods to overcome the limitations of self-report data, including collecting reports from multiple observers and collecting observational data, but these approaches have not been widely adopted.

Inadequate Controls for Exogenous Variables

Perhaps the most significant limitation of the existing literature on the long-term consequences of adolescent relationship experiences is the neglect of third-variable influences (Collins and Madsen, 2006; Halpern, 2003). Current interventions targeting the romantic relationships of adolescents assume not only that more successful adolescent relationships are associated with more successful adult relationships but also that experiences during adolescence are contributing causes of adult experiences. Evaluating the support for this assumption requires research that recognizes and carefully accounts for third-variable threats to causal validity (e.g., Shadish, Cook, and Campbell, 2002). The term *third variable* refers to a variable that has not been measured in a study but that may account for the association between two variables that have been measured. For example, early initiation of sexual intercourse may be associated with depression and behavior problems during adolescence (e.g., Aro and Taipale, 1987). One possible explanation for this association is that early initiation of sexual intercourse causes depression and behavior problems. However, it is also possible that the association between these two variables comes about only because they are both caused by an unmeasured third variable, such as socioeconomic status or level of parental supervision. The third variable therefore threatens causal inferences.

If associations between adolescent experiences and later young adult outcomes are products of third variables—or at least are in part due to such influences, whether genetic or environmental—then interventions that enhance adolescent relationships are much less certain to improve relationships in young adulthood. In contrast, if the associations between adolescent experiences and young adult outcomes can be observed even after controlling for genetic and environmental influences that affect both outcomes directly, then interventions that target adolescent relationships are more likely to achieve the desired improvements in adult outcomes. To the extent that research has ignored third-variable threats to causal validity, resulting estimates of adolescent experiences' influence on later young adult outcomes may be inflated.

Conclusions

In general, research on the role of adolescent romantic relationships in adult development still awaits the rigor and methodological sophistication that could support strong conclusions. Lack of data does not appear to be the limiting factor in this area. For example, within such nationally representative, longitudinal data sets as Add Health and the NLSY lie data that could be used to examine central premises of current models. To date, however, definitive analyses of these data have not been conducted, leaving the existing research to rely primarily on studies of limited scope and generalizability. Keeping these limitations in mind, the following review evaluates the accumulated results of these studies, organized according to the specific paths suggested by the integrative framework presented in the previous chapter.

Antecedents of Adolescent Romantic Relationships

The integrative framework presented in Chapter Three suggests that adolescents' early environments affect adult development through their direct effects on adolescent romantic relationships. Support for these models requires, as a preliminary step, evidence that adolescent experiences in romantic relationships are associated with their early environments. The emergent research on adolescent romantic relationships has examined these associations. Although, as noted above, much of this research relies on retrospective data, the results from cross-sectional and longitudinal studies of this question consistently point to strong associations between early environments and experiences and romantic relationships during adolescence.

Family of Origin

By far the most thoroughly studied antecedent of adolescent romantic relationships is the environment and structure of the adolescent's family of origin. The best of these studies assess family variables during infancy and early childhood and then use those assessments to account for romantic experiences when those children have grown into adolescents and young adults. Research using this design has found evidence for substantial continuity between several distinct aspects of infants' and children's experiences in the family of origin and their subsequent experiences in romantic relationships.

Of particular interest to policymakers are the implications of family structure, i.e., whether a child is raised by two married parents. In this regard, research examining the intergenerational transmission of divorce has shown that children of divorced parents are significantly more likely to experience divorce themselves as adults (Amato, 1996; Amato and DeBoer, 2001). To explain this association, developmental psychologists, guided by attachment theory, have explored whether the structure of parents' relationship is specifically associated with children's orientations toward romantic relationship during adolescence. For example, Summers et al. (1998) compared the attachment styles of young adults whose parents either divorced or remained married during adolescence, finding that children of divorced parents reported less secure romantic attachments, even after controlling for demographic differences between the two groups. Others have noted that children of divorced parents express less optimism about their own marital prospects (e.g., Sprague and Kinney, 1997) and more negative attitudes toward marriage during adolescence (e.g., Tasker and Richards, 1994). Such findings are consistent with models suggesting that parental divorce influences adult marital outcomes through its direct effects on adolescents' personal ideas and beliefs about relationships. However, as others have noted (e.g., Amato, 2001), there are several other, noncognitive paths through which parental divorce may affect the development of romantic relationships across the life course, including the cumulative effects of the reduced socioeconomic status and educational attainment that follow divorce (Tasker and Richards, 1994).

A relatively well-developed body of research has looked beyond family structure to examine how relationships among family members account for the development of romantic relationships in adolescents and adults. One especially rigorous demonstration of these associations involved recording interactions among family members in 99 families with adolescents and coding the quality of those relationships (Bell and Bell, 2005). The quality of the interactions accounted for significant variability in the well-being of the adolescents 25 years later. Similar research drawing from the British National Child Development Study also finds that good relationships with parents and siblings at age 16 is associated with more satisfying marriages at age 33 (Flouri and Buchanan, 2002). In other words, consistent with the integrative framework presented in Chapter Three, there is evidence of direct associations between relationships with parents during adolescence and well-being during adulthood.

Consistent with the idea that these associations operate through their direct effects on romantic relationships during adolescence, several studies have shown direct links between the quality of family relationships during infancy and early childhood and the quality of romantic relationships during adolescence and young adulthood. Some of this research has drawn upon cross-sectional and retrospective data that are subject to questions of bias and shared method variance (e.g., Benson et al., 1993; Feeney, Noller, and Patty, 1993; Furman et al., 2002; Murry et al., 2006; Reese-Weber and Marchand, 2002). The best of this research, however, draws upon longitudinal studies of children and their families over time, and has often been guided, explicitly or implicitly, by an attachment theory perspective. For example, the Minnesota Longitudinal Study of Parents and Children has followed the children of 267 first-time mothers from 1975 to the present and includes self-report and observational assessments of mother-infant interactions during infancy, as well as assessments of dating experiences during adolescence and early adulthood. Analyses of the multiple waves of data available for each child reveal significant continuity in the nature of the interpersonal relationships that these children experienced across stages of development (e.g., Carlson, Sroufe, and Egeland, 2004; Sroufe et al., 2005). Specifically, children whose interactions with their mother were coded as more positive during infancy grew up to have more secure representations of peer and romantic relationships during adolescence and subsequently had more successful romantic relationships in young adulthood (see also Collins et al., 1997; Seiffge-Krenke, Shulman, and Kressinger, 2001). Research focused more specifically on attachment styles finds similar links between the observed interaction between mothers and their infants and the attachment representations of those infants up to 20 years later (Roisman et al., 2005; Waters et al., 2000).

Other longitudinal research in this vein assesses children's relationships with their parents during adolescence as predictors of their subsequent romantic experiences during young adulthood. For example, further analyses of data from the Minnesota Longitudinal Study of Parents and Children examined associations between videotaped interactions between parents and their 13-year-old children and those children's subsequent interactions with their romantic partners at ages 20–21 (Roisman et al., 2001). Results revealed that children who interacted more positively with their parents at age 13 also interacted more positively with their romantic partners at ages 20–21. Moreover, this association appeared to operate through attachment styles in later adolescence (age 19). In other words, adolescent interactions with parents predicted later models of relationships in adolescents, and those models in turn accounted for the way adolescents treated their partners as young adults.

Conger et al. (2000), in an independent eight-year longitudinal study that also drew upon observational data, showed that when adolescents' interactions with their parents were more involved and supportive, their later interactions with romantic partners were coded as more supportive and less hostile. These behaviors in turn accounted for the associations between relationships with parents and the quality of romantic relationships in young adulthood (Conger et al., 2000). In contrast, when higher levels of negativity were observed in parent-child interactions during adolescence, the later social relationships of those adolescents appear to suffer (Kim et al., 2001). A separate study that videotaped parent-child interactions when children were 13 years old found that children whose parents failed to respect boundaries were subsequently more vulnerable to experiencing intimate partner violence in young adulthood (Linder and Collins, 2005).

Although the general pattern of association between relationships with parents and relationships with romantic partners holds true for males and females, some studies have described gender differences in the specifics of these associations. For example, analyses of data from the Add Health study, while confirming that more positive feelings about parental relationships predict higher levels of satisfaction in romantic relationships seven years later, suggest that this association comes about through different mechanisms for males and females. For males, poor relationships with parents predict lower self-esteem, which in turn accounts for significant variance in their later romantic satisfaction. For females, self-esteem did not play a significant role in this relationship, but number of sexual partners did, so that girls reporting worse relationships with their parents had more partners, which helped to account for their lower romantic satisfaction in young adulthood (Joyner and Campa, 2006). An independent six-year study that followed 122 adolescents through early adulthood found stronger, but similar, associations between family variables and later romantic relationship variables for females than for males (Feldman, Gowen, and Fisher, 1998).

The general pattern of association between the early family environment and relationships with romantic partners is further confirmed by studies that have examined the implications of specific experiences within the family of origin. One that has received particular attention is the experience of physical or sexual abuse in childhood, both of which, not surprisingly, have been associated with less secure attachment styles in adolescence (Flanagan and Furman, 2000) and higher likelihood of experiencing and perpetrating aggression in later romantic relationships (Linder and Collins, 2005). Several studies further suggest that exposure to marital distress between parents also increases the child's risk of experiencing dating violence and poorer relationship outcomes in adolescence and adulthood (e.g., Amato and Booth, 2001; Capaldi and Clark, 1998; Kinsfogel and Grych, 2004; Simons, Lin, and Gordon, 1998; Steinberg, Davila, and Fincham, 2006). Finally, longitudinal data from the NSFH have been used to show that children whose parents monitor their activities prior to adolescence initiate dating and sexual behavior later during adolescence, compared with children whose activities were less closely monitored by their parents (Longmore, Manning, and Giordano, 2001).

It is hard to judge how well any of this work applies to low-income youth specifically. To the extent that instability and distress in the family of origin predict worse outcomes in later romantic relationships, children in low-income populations should be at greater risk for experiencing relationship problems, because these populations experience higher levels of family instability and distress. A rare study that examined these issues in low-income populations examined cross-sectional and retrospective data from a sample of 267 black female adolescents from impoverished neighborhoods (Adam and Chase-Lansdale, 2002). Among these young girls, reports of having been separated from their parents and reports of higher numbers of residential moves were associated with higher levels of adjustment problems, including sexual behavior problems, even after adjusting for demographic and economic variables. Although these are not the same variables that have been examined in general population samples and white samples, the results do paint a similar picture, suggesting that early experiences of instability in the family of origin have lasting consequences for the development of healthy relationships.

In sum, within a literature that is still in its early stages of development, no question has been studied more extensively than the implications of aspects of the family of origin. It is promising that, despite a wide range of operationalizations and methodologies, the results of this work are generally consistent across studies. When the early family environment of the child is relatively stable and when parents are warm and attentive, the child is more likely to experience more satisfying romantic relationships in adolescence and beyond. When the early family environment is characterized by distress or disruption, the child is at greater risk for experiencing relationship problems.

With these associations established, how these associations come about remains to be explored. Research guided by attachment theory finds evidence of cognitive mechanisms, such that experiences with parents shape the ideas and beliefs about relationships that young people use to guide choices in their own romantic relationships. Behaviorally oriented work finds evidence of skills-based mechanisms, such that interactions with parents form the basis for subsequent interactions with romantic partners. Both lines of work imply that, absent interventions, development through adolescence and into adulthood should be characterized by continuity, such that adolescents with maladaptive patterns of belief and behavior grow into young adults with the same maladaptive patterns. These findings therefore support the idea of cognitive and behavioral interventions during adolescence to sever these links and offer alternative models of thinking and behaving in romantic relationships to adolescents who might otherwise be at risk.

However, such explanations have yet to be pitted against third-variable explanations for these associations, such as genetic and contextual influences that may affect both family relationships and romantic relationships directly. Until alternative hypotheses have been ruled out definitively, causal statements about the effects of the family of origin on healthy adult relationships must be considered premature.

Individual Characteristics

In addition to the family of origin, enduring characteristics of the child have also been thought to account for continuities in relationships across the lifespan. For example, to the extent that personality is relatively stable over time, personality observed in infancy and early childhood may be associated with relationship outcomes in adolescence and young adulthood.

Caspi and his colleagues have been leaders in exploring this possibility, drawing upon studies that follow individuals across their lives to demonstrate the implications of childhood personality for adolescent and adult relationships. In a series of studies drawing from the Berkeley Longitudinal Study, Caspi and colleagues identified the paths through which different temperaments observed in early childhood gave rise to specific patterns of outcomes in later life (Caspi, 1987; Caspi, Bem, and Elder, 1989; Caspi, Elder, and Bem, 1987, 1988). Children judged by parents and teachers as explosive during childhood experienced higher rates of divorce as adults, and these associations were mediated by the cumulative educational, economic, and social consequences of childhood personality (Caspi, Elder, and Bem, 1987).

A more recent longitudinal study by these researchers confirmed these effects, demonstrating in a sample of over 900 children that undercontrolled temperament observed at age 3 predicts greater levels of conflict in romantic relationships at age 21 (Newman et al., 1997). Cross-sectional research on children self-identified as bullies suggests that such children experience deficits in their romantic relationships during adolescence specifically (Connolly et al., 2000). Research drawing upon the Minnesota Longitudinal Study refines this picture, exploiting the multiple assessments of this study to show how sociability and impulsivity assessed at less than 3 years of age predicts earlier initiation of romantic relationships in early adolescence, which in turn predicted greater alcohol use and a higher number of sexual partners by age 19 (Zimmer-Gembeck, Siebenbruner, and Collins, 2004).

Together, these studies suggest that an important way that personality affects adult relationship and marital outcomes may be through its direct effects on the timing of entry into dating and sexuality during adolescence.

A second individual characteristic that may also affect the initiation of romantic relationships is the timing of puberty and sexual maturation. Independent of personality or social context, some children enter puberty earlier or later than others. Most research on the effects of pubertal timing in adolescence has focused on its association with the initiation of sexual activity (Halpern, 2003). To date, the accumulated research on this effect indicates that earlier entry into puberty, however it is measured, predicts earlier sexual activity. For example, in the Add Health study, "early maturers" are more likely to have first sexual intercourse at a younger age compared with girls who mature later, particularly white early maturers (22 percent of white early maturers compared with 10 percent of white later maturers, $p < 0.01$) (Cavanagh, 2004). Girls who mature earlier also have fewer same-sex friendships and more boys in their friendship groups compared with other girls (Cavanagh, 2004). Although this finding has been consistent across several studies, Halpern (2003) points out that pubertal timing generally accounts for a relatively small amount (between 3 percent and 5 percent) of variance. Nevertheless, for girls, early physical maturation appears to bring about later negative outcomes like substance abuse and poor academic achievement through its direct association with sexual behavior (Caspi et al., 1993; Stattin and Magnusson, 1990).

For boys, in contrast, at least one longitudinal study finds evidence that pubertal timing may have positive long-term implications for life outcomes. Data from the Terman study, a longitudinal project begun in the 1920s that assessed gifted children repeatedly across their lives, revealed that boys who entered puberty earlier went on to experience higher levels of career and marital success (Taga, Markey, and Friedman, 2006). This is a provocative finding, suggesting biological influences on lifespan development, but its implications for understanding the impact of pubertal timing on less gifted youth in the present day are probably limited. For example, more recent analyses of data from the Add Health study finds early pubertal timing in boys to be associated with greater risk of being in physical fights, getting shot, or getting stabbed (Haynie and Piquero, 2006).

Research that directly examines associations between pubertal timing and dating behaviors, as opposed to sexual behaviors specifically, has found only modest effects. For example, analyses of data from adolescents 12–17 years old from the U.S. National Health Examination Survey examined whether levels of sexual maturation accounted for dating behaviors after controlling for the simple effects of age (Dornbusch et al., 1981). Whereas age was significantly associated with dating, so that older adolescents reported more dating, levels of sexual maturation accounted for little additional variance, suggesting that dating behaviors, more than sexual behaviors, may be shaped by social pressures rather than biological factors.

To the extent that temperament and pubertal timing may play a role in the development of adolescent romantic relationships, there may be genetic sources of influence on romantic relationships. To date, no research has examined genetic influence on relationship behaviors during adolescence, but behavioral genetic studies of identical and fraternal twins have demonstrated substantial heritabilities for divorce in adulthood (Jockin, McGue, and Lykken, 1996; McGue and Lykken, 1992). These genetic effects may be mediated by relationship behaviors during adolescence, but the intervening steps in this association have not been explored.

None of the research on individual characteristics in relationship development has addressed low-income populations specifically. In the absence of data, it is possible to speculate that the effects of individual characteristics on later romantic relationships are likely to be exacerbated by an impoverished environment. Exploring a similar idea, Caspi and his colleagues (Caspi et al., 1993) showed that the impact of early menarche on delinquency in adolescent girls is moderated by the sex composition of the schools they attend, such that early menarche predicts greater risk for girls at coeducational schools than at single-sex schools. It seems likely that similar interactions occur between individual characteristics and socioeconomic status, so that individual characteristics that place adolescents at risk in the general population have even greater effects in low-income contexts. Research confirming such a hypothesis could be used to target adolescents who are especially likely to be vulnerable and offer them specific or additional interventions.

Correlates of Adolescent Romantic Relationships

The distinction between antecedents and correlates of adolescent romantic relationships is more theoretical than empirical. In theory, the antecedent variables described in the previous section are in place long before the adolescent enters a romantic relationship for the first time. Because they precede the experience, antecedent variables are potential causes of relationship outcomes. The correlates described in this section, in contrast, are more proximal to the relationship experiences. They may precede relationship experiences, but they may also co-occur or change along with those experiences. In practice, because much of this research is cross-sectional, the causal relationships between adolescent relationship outcomes and the variables described in both sections remain an open question.

Peer Groups

Developmental models of adolescent relationships suggest that relationships with parents affect relationships with romantic partners in part through their direct effects on friendships with peers (e.g., Collins, 2003; Furman and Wehner, 1997). Perhaps as a result, peers are second only to the family of origin in the frequency with which they have been studied in research on adolescent romantic relationships. Stage models of the development of romantic relationships in adolescence propose an orderly sequence that begins with relationships with parents in infancy predicting the development and quality of relationships with same-sex friends in childhood. As the child enters adolescence and these early peer groups develop, they grow to include opposite-sex friendships, which in turn, for most adolescents, set the stage for the initiation of romantic relationships. Thus, peer networks form a proximal context for the initiation of romantic relationships in adolescence, and so should be associated with the timing and the quality of those relationships (Connolly and Goldberg, 1999; Furman, 1999).

Longitudinal research on relationships from childhood through late adolescence supports the general sequence of relationship experiences that stage models have proposed. In a three-year study of 180 high school students, having small groups of friends in childhood predicted having opposite-sex friends in early adolescence, which in turn predicted the initiation of romantic relationships in later adolescence (Connolly et al., 2000). A second study of an ethnically diverse sample of 1,284 adolescents observed the same progression (Connolly et al., 2004). To date, there have been no published attempts to determine whether this sequence replicates within low-income adolescents, or within specific racial or ethnic groups.

The majority of research on associations between peer and romantic relationships during adolescence has sought to move beyond the sequencing of these relationships toward an understanding of the aspects of peer relationships that contribute to more or less favorable romantic outcomes. To this end, a number of studies have examined how the size of an adolescent's peer network is associated with the timing and quality of his or her romantic relationships, with somewhat mixed results. For example, one longitudinal study of 92 white, middle class adolescents tracked the development of their relationships when they were 9, 13, and 18 years old. For both boys and girls, having a larger peer network in late childhood predicted having closer romantic relationships in middle adolescence, and in turn more enduring romantic relationships in later adolescence (Feiring, 1999b). The implication of these results is that having more friends in early adolescence is associated with qualities that promote healthier relationships. A separate study found that high school students rated as more popular by their peers also report dating more frequently (Franzoi, Davis, and Vasquez-Suson, 1994).

However, analyses of data from the Minnesota Longitudinal Study of Parents and Children paint a more complicated picture. Drawing upon the multiple assessments of that study, Zimmer-Gembeck, Siebenbruner, and Collins (2004) found that sociability and peer acceptance in early adolescence predicted both earlier entry into romantic relationships and greater use of alcohol. Together, these variables in turn predicted a greater number of sexual partners by the age of 19, not the result that would be expected based on the Feiring (1999b) study. The fact that the 2004 study explicitly measured alcohol use may help to account for the difference. Whereas having friends proves to be a necessary first step toward the development of sexual and romantic relationships in both studies, a large social network that includes alcohol might mean something very different from a social network of similar size that does not regularly use alcohol. Although these issues have yet to be examined in low-income populations specifically, these findings suggest that in populations where alcohol and other drugs are readily available, larger networks of friends may not benefit the development of healthy romantic relationships.

In addition to the size of the peer network, characteristics of peer and friendship groups have also been associated with age at which adolescents enter romantic and sexual relationships. In the NLSY study, children of the 1979 cohort who at ages 11–12 had primarily same-sex friendships and whose friendships tended to be with preteens in the same grade were significantly less likely to report weekly dating at ages 13–14 and 15–16 (Cooksey et al., 2002). Younger adolescents whose friends were primarily in higher grades were significantly more likely to become sexually experienced between ages 13–14 and 15–16. A study using Add Health data found a direct association between having friends who are sexually experienced and an adolescent becoming sexually experienced as well. As the authors noted, "for every 1 percent increase in sexually experienced friends at Wave 1, the odds that young people initiated sex by Wave 2 increased by 1%" (Sieving et al., 2006). In other words, in terms of shaping adolescents' entry into romantic relationships, what matters is not just the size of the peer network but also the composition of that network.

The associations between the quality of relationships with peers and with romantic partners are much clearer. Across several independent samples, adolescents' reports of the quality of their peer relationships are significantly correlated with their reports of the quality of their romantic relationships, such that adolescents who describe their friendships as close and supportive tend to describe their current and subsequent romantic relationships in similar terms (e.g., Collins et al., 1997; Connolly et al., 2000; Furman et al., 2002; Seiffge-Krenke, Shulman, and Kiessinger, 2001). Problems within peer groups may also have consequences for romantic relationships in adolescence. At least among white female adolescents, interpersonal problems in peer groups are associated with greater likelihood of initiating sexual intercourse (Cavanagh, 2004). Supporting the idea that peer relationships presage a new experience of intimacy for adolescents, two studies have explicitly shown that ratings of adolescent romantic relationships are more strongly correlated with ratings of peer relationships than with ratings of relationships with parents (Furman et al., 2002).

In addition to providing opportunities for developing romantic relationships, peers also seem likely to shape the standards that adolescents apply toward those relationships (Brown, 1999). Early research on peer relationships and sexual behavior found that adolescents tend to have friends whose levels of sexual experience match their own (Billy and Udry, 1985). Anticipated peer approval or disapproval is also a predictor of intercourse initiation among youth (Kirby, Lepore, and Ryan, 2005). Among gay and bisexual youth, the perception that certain factions in the gay community disapprove of romantic relationships may discourage participation in them (Myer, 1989). Such results are consistent with the idea that friends affect each other's decisions about when to enter romantic relationships and engage in sex, although they may also be evidence of a similarity bias in selecting friends.

Research on physical aggression in adolescent relationships offers additional evidence of a peer influence on standards within relationships. In an analysis of data from 391 adolescents, boys who believed that aggression was more common in the relationships of their peers engaged in more aggression in their own relationships (Kinsfogel and Grych, 2004). These data were collected at a single assessment, so it is not possible to infer a causal relationship from this association, but the result is consistent with the idea that peers teach each other the sorts of behaviors that are and are not appropriate within romantic relationships. It is also possible, however, that adolescents choose peers whose standards match their own, leaving the role of peers in setting standards for romantic relationships an open question for now.

Although it is common for peer relationships to be described as potential causes of subsequent romantic relationships, at least one study has described how the experience of romantic relationships may affect developing peer relationships during adolescence. Drawing upon retrospective data from 102 white female adolescents, Zimmer-Gembeck (1999) found that spending more time with a romantic partner was associated with spending less time with friends.

In general, research on the potential influence of peers on the development of romantic relationships in adolescence has been more suggestive than definitive. The idea that peer relationships form a crucial stepping stone from the intimacy of the family of origin to the intimacy of romantic relationships has received consistent support, but exclusively from studies of a relatively narrow range of adolescents. More precise questions about the paths through which relationships with peers may shape subsequent relationships with romantic partners have only been touched upon, and again never in research on low-income youth specifically. Although evidence from cross-sectional and longitudinal research is consistent with current theories about how peers may affect the development of romantic relationships, the causal role of peers in affecting the standards that adolescents apply to their relationships and the quality of those relationships has yet to be determined.

Qualities of the Relationship

Within adult relationships and marriages, a number of studies have explored which specific elements of the relationship are most strongly associated with partners' satisfaction. In adolescent relationships, several researchers have taken up this issue, but to date these studies have relied almost exclusively on cross-sectional self-report data from convenience samples, and so may be of limited value. For example, one study that examined self-report data from 304 adolescents found correlates of relationship satisfaction that generally echoed the correlates of satisfaction in adult relationships, e.g., commitment, being appreciated, good communication, feeling attracted to the partner (Levesque, 1993).

Another set of studies on this issue draws on assessments of 61 adolescent couples to examine correlates of relationship satisfaction and individual well-being (e.g., Galliher et al., 1999). Cross-sectionally, male and female partners who were more satisfied with their relationships tended also to be more satisfied with their communication (Galliher et al., 2004) and their relationships were less likely to end during the subsequent year (Rostosky et al., 2000). In a separate analysis of these data, these researchers also examined associations between feelings of commitment and sexual behavior, finding, perhaps counterintuitively, that physical expressions of affection (e.g., holding hands, kissing) were more strongly correlated with feelings of commitment than was engaging in sexual intercourse (Rostosky et al., 1999). Were this finding to be replicated in a larger and more representative sample, it would suggest that, at least for some adolescents, expressing physical affection reflects deeper commitment to a relationship than does engaging in sex.

A number of other qualities of adolescent romantic relationships may be associated with the concurrent and longitudinal implications of those relationships. For example, the Add Health study has used an innovative card sorting technique to assess the sequencing of specific behaviors within adolescent relationships (i.e., whether couples say "I love you" prior to or after having sex, when partners meet each other's parents, when partners appear in public as a couple). The timing of these behaviors may help to determine the impact of a specific relationship on the developing adolescent; to date, however, data from this part of the Add Health study have not been examined in published research. Other potential relationship qualities of interest might include the amount of time that adolescent partners spend together, how couples spend that time, and the specific age within adolescence when these relationships occur. None of these issues has yet been addressed in this area. Moreover, although it seems likely that the correlates of relationship satisfaction may vary significantly across low-income and upper-income populations, this question has yet to be addressed empirically.

Partner Characteristics

As noted earlier, virtually nothing is known about the ways that characteristics of adolescents' romantic partners affect the implications of adolescent romantic experiences (Collins and Van Dulmen, 2006). This seems a serious oversight, especially given Rutter's early research showing that characteristics of a partner can make a significant difference to the adult outcomes even of children who come from severely disadvantaged backgrounds (Rutter and Quinton, 1984).

Two studies that have addressed this issue examined the implications of a partner's age. For example, a study of 2,829 students recruited from sixth-grade classes in 19 urban schools assessed the presence of a partner, partner age, and sexual behaviors (VanOss Marín et al., 2000). Compared with those without steady partners, students with partners more than two years older than themselves were more likely to be Hispanic, less likely to be acculturated, and over 30 times more likely to have had sex.

In research on a middle school intervention to reduce sexual risk behaviors, the association between relationship status and sexual behavior was examined in detail for 2,829 seventh-, eighth-, and ninth-grade students in 19 predominantly Hispanic schools in urban Northern California (VanOss Marín et al., 2006). Having had a boyfriend or girlfriend in seventh grade increased the chances that the student had been sexually active by ninth grade. Having had a relationship with someone their own age doubled their odds of being sexually active in ninth grade, and girls who had a relationship with a boy in a higher grade by seventh grade were also more likely to be sexually experienced by ninth grade.

A smaller study of 146 girls recruited from ninth-grade classes found similar results, showing that girls whose partners were more than three years older than themselves were more likely to be engaging in all forms of sexual activity, more likely to be having sex while using drugs or alcohol, and more likely to report having been coerced into having sex, compared with girls whose partners were closer to their own age (Gowen et al., 2004). In terms of their attitudes and beliefs, girls with older boyfriends were more likely to endorse the belief that engaging in sex is associated with maturity. The authors of this study viewed these differences as evidence of power imbalances in the relationships of girls with older boyfriends, although power was not assessed directly.

To the extent that power imbalance is a salient issue in adolescent romantic relationships, it is possible to imagine numerous other partner characteristics that may lead to such imbalances, including physical attractiveness, physical strength, wealth, race and ethnicity, and social status. The associations among these partner characteristics and experiences in adolescent romantic relationships have not been studied.

Beliefs and Attitudes

Considering the number of studies that have described the beliefs and attitudes of adolescents with regard to romantic relationships and marriage (reviewed in Chapter Two), it is perhaps surprising that so few studies have examined whether adolescents' beliefs and attitudes are in fact associated with their experiences and behaviors in romantic relationships. Most studies that have examined links between cognitive variables and adolescent behaviors have focused narrowly on sexuality rather than romantic relationships.

For example, attitudes toward sexuality and exposure to sexuality in the media have been associated with sexual intentions and behaviors in several studies of adolescents (e.g., Collins et al., 2004; Pardun, L'Engle, and Brown, 2005). Analyses of the 1995 NSFG indicate that religious affiliation and frequency of attendance at religious services, variables that may be proxies for more conservative attitudes toward sexuality, account for the timing of first intercourse among adolescents, such that stronger affiliation and more frequent attendance are associated with delays, even after controlling for demographic variables (Jones, Darroch, and Singh, 2005). Intelligence, as measured by scores on the Peabody Picture Vocabulary Test (PPVT), is also associated with delays in initiating sex, according to analyses of data from Add Health (Halpern et al., 2000).

Yet aside from sexual behaviors, little is known about how other behaviors and choices relevant to romantic relationships are associated with adolescents' beliefs and attitudes. One exception is a cross-sectional study of 254 secondary school students that examined attitudes toward aggressive behavior in romantic relationships (Feiring et al., 2002). Although aggressive behaviors were rare in this sample, males and females who reported having engaged in aggressive behavior toward a romantic partner also endorsed statements indicating that aggressive behavior toward a romantic partner could be justified.

Links between other sorts of attitudes (e.g., beliefs about the importance of fidelity, the role of sexuality in intimacy, appropriate demonstrations of affection, the importance of relationships compared with other activities) and corresponding behaviors are unknown. In addition, no research linking attitudes to behaviors has been conducted among low-income adolescents. Given the prominent role that beliefs and attitudes play in the interventions currently being targeted toward adolescents in this population, such a lack of data must be considered a serious oversight. Filling this gap should be an immediate priority for research in this area.

Immediate Consequences of Adolescent Romantic Relationships for Adolescents

Accumulating evidence suggests that adolescents' experiences in romantic relationships have immediate and significant consequences for their well-being during adolescence. What is not currently clear is the extent to which experiences in romantic relationships may be said to cause those consequences. The studies reviewed in this section frequently demonstrate associations between specific experiences in relationships and specific outcomes during adolescence. Supporting a causal link between the experience and the outcome requires ruling out potential third variables that may in fact cause both the experience and the outcome. In cross-sectional studies, the problems are compounded by uncertainty about whether variables treated as outcomes in fact preceded the relationship experiences. The existing research in this area has rarely ruled out these alternative hypotheses. Thus, the studies described here can be said to have identified experiences associated with certain outcomes, but whether the experiences cause the outcomes (and so might appropriate targets of interventions designed to improve outcomes) remains an open question.

Psychological Well-Being

In a frequently cited paper drawing on data from the Add Health study, Joyner and Udry (2000) found that, relative to adolescents not involved in romantic relationships, adolescents in romantic relationships experienced greater increases in depressive symptoms over the period of one year, and this increase was greater for females than for males. An earlier review made a similar point, suggesting that early entry into dating is associated with lower self-esteem (Simmons et al., 1979). Girls who are involved in romantic relationships are also at higher risk for eating disorders (Cauffman and Steinberg, 1996; Smolak, Levine, and Gralen, 1993).

What may account for these associations? To determine whether the initiation of dating places youth at risk, researchers working with the Add Health data identified 2,344 participants in the initial assessment who had never had sex and never dated and examined their experiences and symptoms over the subsequent year (Grello et al., 2003). Adolescents who began dating, and those who had their first sexual experience in the context of a romantic relationship, did not experience significant changes in their depressive symptoms or delinquent behaviors. However, engaging in casual sex was associated with higher levels of depressive symptoms and problem behaviors.

Studies that have looked beyond relationship status to address qualities and processes in adolescent relationships offer a more refined picture. For example, research that assessed the degree of closeness in the relationships of 72 girls in late adolescence found that a lack of closeness in romantic relationships, but not a lack in other kinds of relationships, was associated with stronger tendency to experience negative moods (Williams, Connolly, and Segal, 2001). In a sample of 421 adolescents, those who described negative qualities in their romantic relationships also reported higher levels of depressive symptoms (La Greca and Harrison, 2005). Both these studies suggest that it is the quality of the romantic relationship, rather than the relationship status per se, that is associated with depressive symptoms during adolescence.

Consistent with this view, data from an epidemiological sample of 1,470 adolescents reveal that experiencing the breakup of a romantic relationship is a significant predictor of the first onset of major depression (Monroe et al., 1999). In contrast, a study of 480 Israeli adolescents found that those in steady dating relationships reported higher self-esteem and were rated more positively by their peers as well (Samet and Kelly, 1987).

Such findings place the Joyner and Udry (2000) research in perspective: Romantic relationships during adolescence provide an opportunity for emotional pain that puts young people at risk for experiencing depression, but this risk may be linked to unhealthy or unsuccessful relationships (Welsh, Grello and Harper, 2003). Thus, the converse may also be true: Healthy relationships may offer opportunities for growth and fulfillment that improve well-being and increase resilience. In other words, the quality of the romantic relationships that adolescents experience may moderate the implications of those experiences for their psychological well-being, just as is true in adult marriages (e.g., Beach, 2001). To date, there has been no research on these issues in low-income populations, but there is no reason to believe that the role of relationship quality is any less important in that population than in more affluent populations.

Sexual Behavior and Contraception

Experiencing a romantic relationship within the past 18 months is one of the most powerful predictors of sexual activity among adolescents (Blum, Beuhring, and Rinehart, 2000; Halpern et al., 2000; Miller et al., 1997), especially among girls (Marin et al., 2006). Because a romantic relationship provides a context that makes sex possible and rewarding, those who enter relationships earlier also tend to engage in sexual activities earlier (Thornton, 1990). In a sample of virgins ages 15–21 drawn from Add Health, the number of romantic relationships in the prior 18 months was strongly associated with likelihood of first intercourse in the subsequent year (Rostosky, Regenerus, and Wright, 2003). Analyses of data from the NLSY suggest that the romantic relationship per se, rather than mere dating, predicts sexual behavior: Having a steady partner accounts for first experiences of sex, but frequency of dating does not (Cooksey, Mott, and Neubauer, 2002). Research on a small sample of Australian young people ages 16 to 25 similarly found that, as dating relationships became more serious and committed, the desire for sexual intimacy and actual sexual behavior both increase (McCabe and Collins, 1984). Indeed, the modal reported reason for first intercourse among teens is to have the partner love them more (Rodgers, 1996). It is unknown whether these associations are replicated among low-income populations specifically.

Given the strong associations between romantic relationships and sexual behavior, an important question for policymakers is whether romantic relationships make safe sex and the use of contraception more or less likely among adolescents who are sexually active. Unfortunately, the existing research on this issue has produced mixed results (Giordano, 2003). Some studies suggest that involvement in romantic relationships is associated with more consistent use of condoms. For example, data from a subsample of adolescent girls in the 1995 NSFG survey who had had sexual intercourse for the first time before age 18 showed that roughly half (52 percent) of the female adolescents who had just met their sexual partner prior to having sexual intercourse used no method of contraception, compared with 24 percent of girls who reported that they were "going steady" with their partner. This relationship remained statistically significant when other variables linked to the likelihood of contraceptive use were controlled (Manning, Longmore, and Giordano, 2000). Analyses of data from the Add Health study also indicate that female adolescents who were acquainted with their partners before they were involved in a romantic relationship were more likely to use birth control consistently, compared with females who did not know their partners at all prior to entering the relationship (Kaestle et al., 2005) and that couples who are more similar to each other report more consistent condom use than couples who are less similar (Ford, Sohn, and Lepkowski, 2001). A smaller study of 625 inner-city black females, approximately one-third of whom were between ages 17 and 20, similarly observed that those who felt emotionally closer to their partners expressed stronger intentions to use condoms (Santelli et al., 1996). Together, these studies support the view that being in a romantic relationship—in particular, being in an emotionally close romantic relationship—is associated with higher levels of safe sex behavior among adolescents.

Yet several other studies have found no association between being in a relationship and condom use, or they have even found associations in the opposite direction. For example, a recently published study of 1,316 adolescents recruited from clinical settings found no difference in rates of self-reported condom use between those with a single partner and those who were sexually active with multiple partners (Lescano et al., 2006). Analyses of data from the NSAM indicate that, among sexually active adolescent males in exclusive romantic relationships, condom use declines as the length of the relationship increases (Ku, Sonenstein, and Pleck, 1994). Research on a smaller sample of 172 adolescent women paints a similar picture, showing that those in established relationships are quicker to have unprotected sex than those in new relationships (Fortenberry et al., 2002). By themselves, the results of these studies would suggest that adolescents in the strongest romantic relationships may be the least vigilant about contraception and safe sex.

How can we reconcile these two apparently contradictory sets of results? Clearly, more research is sorely needed to address this question. Still, in the absence of that research, we speculate that the explanation for these competing results may lie in the fact that, over the course of a single romantic relationship, adolescents' use of condoms changes over time. For example, a recent longitudinal study interviewed 176 adolescent women every three months for two years, asking about relationship status and use of condoms in each interview (Sayegh et al., 2006). Among those in ongoing relationships, condom use declined significantly over time. Yet condom use started out at the highest level among those who were in the most satisfying relationships at the initial interview. Together these results suggest that the predictors of condom use early in a relationship may differ from the predictors later in the same relationship. Early in a relationship, when adolescents are initiating sexual activity for the first time, they may be more comfortable discussing and enacting safe sex behaviors with partners that they feel closer to and trust. Over time, however, deepening trust in a partner may, ironically, encourage adolescent partners in lasting relationships to be less vigilant about condom use than partners in newer relationships.

Ethnographic data from low-income populations offers some support for this sort of process. For example, interviews with adolescent black females reveal their concerns that the use of contraception indicates a lack of intimacy and trust for a partner (Dash, 2003). To the extent that such sentiments generalize to low-income adolescents more broadly, those in more serious romantic relationships would be expected to use condoms less frequently than those in less established relationships, even if those in more serious relationships were more likely to use condoms initially. Evaluating this possibility requires longitudinal research that assesses trajectories of trust and condom use over time in adolescent romantic relationships, but to date we are aware of no studies that have collected this sort of data.

Intimate Partner Violence

As noted in Chapter Two, physical aggression between intimate partners is an all-too-frequent occurrence within adolescent romantic relationships. Data from Wave I of the Add Health study, for example, reveals that 12 percent of respondents had been the victim of physical violence from a dating partner in the previous 18 months, and rates are similar for males and females (Halpern et al., 2001). Because this is an outcome of particular concern to researchers and policymakers, research on the causes and correlates of violence between partners in adolescent relationships is somewhat more extensive than research on other outcomes has been. In recent years, two excellent reviews of research in this area have been published (Capaldi and Gorman-Smith, 2003; Wekerle and Avgoustis, 2003), so the current review will only briefly touch on that work here.

The dominant theory of relationship violence among adolescents focuses on the idea of intergenerational transmission, i.e., the idea that antisocial behaviors in parents, including violence toward the child, leads to children who view aggression between intimates as acceptable, and in turn makes aggressive behavior toward romantic partners more likely (Capaldi and Gorman-Smith, 2003). A number of longitudinal studies have found support for this general progression for males and females (e.g., Andrews et al., 2000; Capaldi and Clark, 1998; Magdol et al., 1998; Simons, Lin, and Gordon, 1998). Analyses of data from Add Health further suggest that violence is more likely to occur between adolescent romantic partners who have had sex than between partners who have not had sex (Kaestle and Halpern, 2005b). Additional analyses of the Add Health data reveal that, for both genders, engaging in intimate partner violence is significantly associated with increasing age and having a higher number of intimate partners (Roberts, Auinger, and Klein, 2005). Across a number of domains (e.g., socioeconomic resources, family relations, educational achievements, and problem behaviors), variables assessed during adolescence predict partner abuse at 21 more effectively than variables assessed prior to adolescence, suggesting that adolescence may be a crucial period during which the antecedents of partner violence take shape (Magdol et al., 1998).

Two longitudinal data sets have been particularly useful in examining the antecedents and correlates of partner violence in adolescence. One, the Oregon Youth Study, comprises primarily white males who were first assessed in fourth grade and have been followed yearly thereafter (Capaldi and Patterson, 1987). A second, the Chicago Youth Development Study, solicited fifth- and seventh-grade males from ethnically diverse communities with relatively high rates of poverty. Thus, the Chicago Youth Development Study provides specific insight into low-income youth, in marked contrast to most of the research reviewed in this report. It is especially noteworthy that the results of tests of the intergenerational model obtained from the Oregon Youth Study have generally replicated in the Chicago Youth Development Study, suggesting that the antecedents of partner violence may be similar across low-income and more affluent populations (Capaldi and Gorman-Smith, 2003). Both studies provide results supporting the idea of intergenerational transmission, showing that antisocial behaviors among parents predicts aggressive behaviors in their adolescent children (e.g., Capaldi and Clark, 1998).

One reason that understanding partner violence is particularly important for the current report is that the experience of partner violence during adolescence seems likely to have long-term implications for an individual's orientation toward future romantic relationships. The existing research in this area has yet to address these implications directly. There has been some research showing continuity among perpetrators of relationship violence, such that adolescents who are more accepting of violence against a partner are more likely to engage in violence within relationships as young adults (e.g., Capaldi et al., 2001). In addition, among female adolescents in the Add Health study, abuse by an intimate partner predicted significant increases in illicit substance use, antisocial behavior, and suicidal behavior one year later (Roberts, Klein, and Fisher, 2003). Studies of victims of partner violence during adolescence have not yet examined their consequences for outcomes assessed in adulthood.

Substance Abuse and Academic Achievement

Although substance abuse and academic achievement are quite different outcomes, they have often been examined in the same studies, perhaps because they tend to be negatively correlated (i.e., engaging in substance abuse is strongly associated with lower levels of academic achievement). Much of the research on the implications of romantic relationships for these outcomes has focused on the effects of early or later entry into romantic relationships on substance abuse and academic achievement in girls. The results of this research have been consistent across multiple studies: The earlier that girls become involved in romantic relationships, the higher their risks of later substance abuse and the lower their academic achievement (e.g., Aro and Taipale, 1987; Grinder, 1966; Pawlby, Mills, and Quinton, 1997). In later adolescence, the negative implications of romantic relationships appears to subside (Neemann, Hubbard, and Masten, 1995), but early entry into marriage continues to be associated with increased risk of substance abuse (e.g., Bachman et al., 1997; Schulenberg et al., 2005).

Throughout these studies, researchers have occasionally succumbed to the temptation to infer causal links from correlational data, suggesting that early involvement in romantic relationships causes later problems for girls. In fact, the nature of the causal influence in these studies is far from clear, because behavior problems that may predict later substance abuse and academic deficits have also been shown to predict early entry into romantic relationships (e.g., Aro and Taipale, 1987; Connolly et al., 2000). Nor is it clear that the same patterns of association would hold true for males. Indeed, Giordano (2003) speculates that early entry into romantic relationships may be positive for adolescent boys, although no data have addressed this possibility.

To the extent that early entry into romantic relationships is associated with a higher risk of substance abuse and lower academic achievement, at least for girls, late entry into romantic relationships may be associated with positive outcomes. For example, data from the Add Health study have been used to show that adolescents who postpone sexual activities score higher on measures of intelligence (Halpern et al., 2000). Other analyses of Add Health find that, compared with adolescents in dating relationships, those who do not date have the highest grades and the lowest levels of delinquent behavior (Giordano, Manning, and Longmore, 2006). Again, given the current state of the research on these issues, these associations are as likely to be the result of simple selection effects (i.e., students with greater academic prospects do not choose to devote time to romantic pursuits) as they are to reflect any causal effects of romantic relationships on academic outcomes.

The true relationship between romantic relationships and such outcomes as substance abuse and academic achievement is likely to be more complex than a simple focus on relationship status would suggest. For example, analyses of data from the Toledo Adolescent Relationships Study reveal that respondents' grades were significantly predicted by the grades of their romantic partners, controlling for parental monitoring (Giordano, Manning, and Longmore, 2006). It seems plausible that partners similarly affect substance abuse and delinquency. To the extent that partners do influence each other's behaviors in this regard, the closeness of the relationship may moderate this influence, such that close partners influence each other more than partners who are less close. In other words, it may be that the characteristics of the relationship interacting with the characteristics of the partner, rather than the mere presence of a romantic relationship, account for associations between romantic experiences, substance abuse, and academic achievement in adolescents. In the absence of data, these hypotheses must remain speculative.

Consequences of Adolescent Romantic Relationships for Outcomes in Adulthood

Current policies that target adolescents for relationship education are motivated less by the desire to promote favorable outcomes during adolescence (although that is clearly one goal) than by the desire to promote healthy marriages in adulthood. Thus, the guiding assumptions of current policies are (1) that experiences with romantic relationships in adolescence are associated with subsequent marital outcomes in adulthood, and (2) that the nature of these associations is causal, such that intervening during adolescence is likely to lead to improved outcomes during adulthood. Evaluating these assumptions requires, at minimum, long-term longitudinal research that follows adolescents into adulthood, assessing the nature of their romantic relationships at each stage of development. As many scholars in this area have noted (e.g., Collins and Van Dulmen, 2006; Furman and Shaffer, 2003; Giordano, 2003; Kan and Cares, 2006), almost no research of this type has been published to date. Data capable of addressing these issues have been collected in the Add Health and NLSY studies, but published research has tended to draw upon samples that have not yet extended far into adulthood.

The research that has attempted to link adolescent relationships to adult marital outcomes has so far been extremely limited in scope. For example, research focused specifically on the consequences of teen pregnancy has identified the economic and educational deficits that teen mothers experience relative to their peers who do not become pregnant (Furstenberg, Brooks-Gunn, and Chase-Lansdale, 1989), perhaps explaining the positive associations between premarital pregnancy and subsequent risk of divorce (Furstenberg, 1976). But research in this vein does not account for the relational context in which those pregnancies occurred.

To the extent that adolescents' experiences in romantic relationships have the immediate consequences reviewed in the previous section, it is reasonable to expect that evidence of long-term consequences may be found, because those immediate consequences have often been linked to adult marital outcomes. For example, depression in adolescence, which is predicted by the breakup of adolescent romantic relationships (Monroe et al., 1999), predicts earlier entry into marriage and higher risk of divorce in early adulthood (Gotlib, Lewinsohn, and Seeley, 1998). Intimate partner violence among young adults, which is predicted by violent behavior in adolescent relationships (Capaldi et al., 2001), is one of the strongest predictors of divorce in the early years of marriage (Rogge and Bradbury, 1999). The fact that these sorts of variables have been associated with adult marital outcomes in correlational and longitudinal research is consistent with models that view adolescent relationships as central to the foundation of healthy adult marriages.

Yet without direct evidence that rules out alternative explanations of the obtained associations, conclusions about the role of adolescent relationships in adult marriages must remain tentative. Research on the long-term implications of peer relationships provides a cautionary tale. In 1982, Giordano and colleagues conducted interviews with 942 adolescents regarding their relationships with their friends. Ten years later, the researchers recontacted 620 of their original respondents to examine whether aspects of peer relationships accounted for variance in a range of adult outcomes, controlling for economic and demographic variables and relationships with parents (Giordano et al., 1998). Analyses revealed that the quality of adolescent's relationships with peers did not account for significant variability in adult outcomes after sociodemographic and parental variables were controlled. However, sociodemographic and parental variables did account for adult outcomes, including marital satisfaction, after controlling for the quality of adolescent peer relationships.

Similar analyses of the long-term implications of adolescent romantic relationships are crucial to determine (1) whether associations between adolescent romantic experiences and adult marital outcomes exist, and (2) whether those associations are more than simply the by-product of the common effects of sociodemographic variables and the family of origin.

Summary and Conclusions

As Collins and Madsen (2006) recently observed,

> The agenda for filling gaps in research on relationships during early adulthood is a lengthy one. . . . The most compelling accounts would come from longitudinal data sets in which repeated accounts are sought from the same individuals across three age periods, using standard reporting devices and using standard metrics (p. 24).

Research fitting this description is being conducted, but the results of this work are not yet available. This leaves the available data to inform efforts to intervene in adolescent romantic relationships incomplete in several important ways.

First, as noted at the outset, the methods employed in much of the existing research have been quite limited. This report has emphasized the best of the available research, studies that have incorporated multiple assessments of individuals over time, multiple reporters (including the individual, parents, and peers), and a broad range of variables. However, the majority of this research has collected data at only a single occasion, relied exclusively on individuals' self-reports, and assessed only a few variables at a time. Importantly, even the strongest studies in this area have sampled almost exclusively from populations that are predominately middle-class and white and have not followed these samples beyond the earliest years of young adulthood.

Recognizing the limitations of the sampling in most research on adolescents has led some to question whether the results of the existing literature can be applied to nonwhite or low-income populations (McLoyd and Steinberg, 1998). Until more research is conducted on ethnically diverse and low-income samples, or until results from nationally representative studies are broken down by income, this remains an open question. Recognizing the limitations of the study interval has led others to question whether the existing research demonstrates a clear link between adolescent relationships and adult marital outcomes. The absence of data directly linking adolescents' experiences in romantic relationships to the outcomes of their marriages in adulthood leaves ongoing efforts to intervene in adolescent romantic relationships resting on an uncertain empirical foundation.

Second, despite the range of variables that have been addressed by this literature, broad classes of variables have nevertheless been overlooked. For example, whereas there have been several studies examining the timing of adolescents' entry into romantic relationships, the quality of those relationships, and processes within those relationships, have received far less attention (Collins and Van Dulmen, 2006). As a result, the ways that adolescents maintain their relationships, and the determinants of relationship satisfaction at different ages, remain unknown. Although most adolescents have multiple romantic relationships before they become young adults, the development of an individual across relationships, and the degree of consistency between relationships, has also not been studied (Bouchey and Furman, 2003). Research in this area has focused on the implications of being in relationships, rather than the implications that a specific relationship may have for an individual. Finally, given the emphasis on beliefs and values about marriage in current interventions targeting adolescent romantic relationships, it is noteworthy how seldom researchers studying these relationships have directly examined the implications of adolescents' beliefs and values about marriage. These variables have been described as dependent variables but not as independent variables that may account for subsequent adolescent outcomes. Each of these gaps in the existing literature represents a potentially fruitful direction for future research in this area.

Third, researchers in this area have tested specific hypotheses infrequently, and they have pitted alternative hypotheses or models against each other even less frequently. As a result, research has not accumulated to inform, refine, or elaborate upon theoretical frameworks, and competing frameworks have not emerged to guide research. The significant consequence of this limitation is a general failure to examine threats to causal inferences throughout the literature.

Too often, cross-sectional or longitudinal associations among variables of interest have been interpreted as support for models that consider only those variables (e.g., associations between relationships with parents and with romantic partners during adolescence have been taken as support for attachment perspectives). Yet these same analyses often overlook variables (such as socioeconomic status) that do not feature in those models but that might nevertheless influence both variables. Without such analyses, well-supported causal statements remain elusive.

Yet despite these significant limitations, the existing research on the antecedents and consequences of adolescent romantic relationships offers some justification for current efforts to target these relationships for intervention. Although no single study has yet addressed the entire framework, the results of correlational and longitudinal studies are generally consistent with specific paths of the integrative framework described in Chapter Three. Characteristics of children's family of origin and early environment are associated with their peer relationships. Peers do appear to influence timing of entry into romantic relationships. The immediate consequences of these relationships are the very ones that would be expected to influence adult marital outcomes. Moreover, studies that have followed individuals from early childhood through young adulthood do point to adolescence as a critical period during which significant antecedents of young adult outcomes take shape (e.g., Zimmer-Gembeck, Siebenbruner, and Collins, 2004). Thus, the existing data are consistent with a model that views adolescent romantic relationships as a key period during which the foundations of healthy adult marriages may be strengthened. To the extent that further research confirms this emerging picture of adolescent relationships as a link in a causal chain leading from the early environment to adult marriages, it would be warranted to intervene during adolescence, especially as a means of preventing the continuation of negative patterns in vulnerable youth. How are currently available interventions attempting to accomplish this? We turn to that question in the next chapter.

CHAPTER FIVE

Review of Relationship Education Programs for Adolescents

Thus far, the chapters of this report have reviewed theory and empirical research relevant to understanding the role of adolescent romantic relationships in the development of healthy adult marriages, with the explicit goal of informing programs and curricula targeting adolescents. To what extent are existing programs that address adolescents' romantic relationships informed by this literature? How well do the programs currently being administered to adolescents map onto the issues and topics that research indicates should be important?

To address these questions, this chapter surveys the current landscape of relationship education programs for adolescents, with a particular emphasis on materials likely to be directed toward low-income adolescents. These programs have typically been delivered in one of five formats. The first, Relationship and Marriage Education (RME), explicitly and more or less exclusively addresses interpersonal and romantic relationships and their implications. The other four programs include RME as a component of a broader curriculum. These broader formats include Family and Consumer Sciences (FACS) classes, character education (CE) programs, abstinence education (AE) programs, and community-based initiatives. Although the focus of this chapter is relationship education within community-based settings serving low-income adolescents (as opposed to schools), FACS classes are included in this discussion because they may be the program that routinely covers RME-related topics to which the largest number of low-income and other adolescents are exposed.

After reviewing the content and delivery of programs falling into each of these categories, we summarize the sparse evidence on the effectiveness of RME. Because the limited evidence is promising but still inconclusive, the analyses presented here, organized according to the integrative framework derived in Chapter Three, go one step further by comparing the content of examples of each type of curriculum with the content that the literature suggests might produce a potentially modifiable precursor to successful relationships. The results of this comparison can be used by policymakers and program implementers to identify, adapt, or develop new curricula targeting precursors to healthy relationships.

Reflecting the interest of the federal government and other policymakers in improving adult marital outcomes through interventions targeting adolescents, the chapter concludes with a review of the community-based organizations that provide relationship education to adolescents, using either an established curriculum described in this chapter, another of the available curricula, or a home-grown curriculum. The discussion highlights ways that community efforts to implement these curricula can be best supported.

In preparing this chapter, we relied heavily on conversations with decisionmakers, curriculum developers and distributors, and practitioners who are delivering relationship curricula to low-income adolescents. We spoke with a combination of FACS representatives and directors of organizations that currently or in the past were ACF grantees and are currently or have expressed an interest in offering relationship education to low-income or minority adolescents or young adults. Most of the practitioners are directors or executive directors of programs that are currently being funded by DHHS to implement relationship or marriage education curricula for low-income or minority youth (e.g., as part of the African-American Healthy Marriage Initiative). To ensure that these informants and others who receive funding in part from federal resources were comfortable discussing the issues and concerns they face in their practice, we promised to maintain confidentiality concerning their names and affiliations. However, all practitioners we spoke with represented a single program or coalition of programs targeting low-income or minority adolescents in community settings, including faith-based institutions and small and large community-based organizations serving different groups, including Hispanics, blacks, and fathers. Together, these organizations represented the four regions of the country, but they should not be considered representative of a larger universe of organizations.

In selecting particular relationship education curricula to review, our intent was to identify those that were most widely known and respected in their particular genre. Thus, the specific curricula and programs reviewed here cover the leading materials but do not represent a comprehensive list.

The Goals of Relationship Education for Adolescents and Youth

Marriage education programs designed for and mostly serving middle-class couples have been around for several decades. The broad objectives of these programs are to influence attitudes and beliefs and to teach skills and behaviors that are believed to contribute to positive relationships (Ooms, 2005). Relationship and marriage education programs for adolescents are generally similar. As with marriage education programs for couples, the objectives of RME curricula are to impart some combination of knowledge, values, and skills believed necessary to establish healthy romantic relationships. Drawing from each curriculum's Web site, Table 5.1 summarizes the objectives of the subset of curricula examined in this chapter that are entirely or largely focused on relationship education. Although each curriculum touches on the importance of a healthy marriage, only the two abstinence programs explicitly note healthy marriage as an objective. For the other curricula, no tangible short- or long-term measures of relationship outcomes are immediately apparent in the stated objectives. Others (e.g., *Connections*) aim to impart skills necessary to maintain a healthy marriage or relationship more generally but do not describe marriage itself as an objective.

As described below, the few efforts to evaluate the effectiveness of these programs have focused on different attitudinal and some behavioral outcomes, but choice of outcome is idiosyncratic to the specific program or preferences of the evaluation team. The field could benefit from a discussion about whether these programs should be targeting adolescent outcomes

Table 5.1
Objectives of RME Curricula Reviewed in This Chapter

Relationship and Marriage Education Curriculum	Objective
Connections (Kamper, 2004)	Teaches teens the skills that are essential for success in their dating relationships and in preparing for marriage. For younger teens, Connections includes a variety of exercises to teach teens how relationships develop, how to communicate effectively, how to recognize destructive patterns, how to deal with emotions, and other essential skills. For older teens, it teaches self-awareness, relationships, communication, conflict, and a Marriage Game.
The Art of Loving Well (Boston University School of Education, 1993)	Designed to help teenagers learn responsible sexual and social values through good literature, which reveals the complexity of life and love relationships. Additional goals include promoting literacy, critical thinking, and habits of reflection; resisting peer pressure; and reducing premature sexual activity, adolescent pregnancy, AIDS, other sexually transmitted diseases, and substance abuse; as well as countering school and family violence by providing positive models of conflict resolution.
Choosing the Best Soul Mate: A Relationship and Abstinence Curriculum (Cook, 2004)	Intended to inspire students to develop the communication skills and personal qualities essential for successful relationships of all kinds—with parents, peers, coworkers, teachers—and ultimately, for a lasting marriage.
A.C. Green's Game Plan Abstinence Program (Gray and Phelps, 2001)	The curriculum as a whole is intended to promote abstinence. Two secondary objectives are (1) to help students understand the importance of choosing friends wisely and to assist students in establishing guidelines for healthy dating relationships, and (2) to give students information on the positive benefits of marriage and to help them to consider this information for themselves and for their future.

only (based on a model, perhaps, that says that establishing solid relationships in adolescence naturally paves the way for establishment of solid relationships later) or if these programs need to try to affect longer-term relationship decisions directly. The field is at the point that stakeholders and program developers need to consider, prioritize, and select among a number of potential program goals, including promoting positive attitudes toward marriage; promoting greater rates of abstinence; promoting lower rates of date rape and abuse; promoting greater satisfaction with romantic relationships; increasing the chances of later healthy, stable marriage; lowering eventual divorce rates; lowering rates of conflict; and enhancing the ability to communicate to romantic partners and other people. An important direction for future development of these programs is to carefully think through the desired goals of these programs and try to link these goals to clear behavioral or attitudinal adolescent and/or adult outcomes. Greater clarity about program goals will help policymakers and others interested in investing in services for adolescents as a means to promoting later healthy marriage.

The Formats of Relationship Education

Based on our conversations with decisionmakers and program developers and distributors, we identified five formats in which relationship education is typically delivered. Although some may have been developed for a single setting, such as a school, these curricula, with the exception of the two textbooks reviewed here, are usually offered in a wide range of settings, including schools, the juvenile justice system, foster care programs, independent living facilities, programs for pregnant and parenting teens, camps, retreats, group homes, and after-school programs. For each of the five formats, Table 5.2 briefly describes the content of at least one curriculum nominated by our informants for inclusion in this report. Another commonality among most of the curricula reviewed (with the exception of abstinence education) is that the emphasis is on healthy relationships generally, which may include heterosexual or same-sex relationships. It is worth noting, however, that none of the curricula reviewed here explicitly mention same-sex relationships in the written materials. Rather, program developers mention that they discuss same-sex relationships when implementing the curricula.

Relationship and Marital Education (RME) Curricula

RME curricula are typically implemented in schools, faith-based settings, youth-serving organizations, and community-based organizations. In recent years, however, as part of welfare reform efforts, there has been an emphasis on supporting marriage and healthy relationships among welfare recipients, and most recently, as part of the African-American Healthy Marriage Initiative, on enhancing short- and long-term romantic and marriage outcomes for adolescents (Ooms, 2005). Typically, RME curricula contain some mix of intervention orientation and educational orientation. *Love U2,* for example, developed by Marline Pearson, contains content and structure that is similar to those used in marital education programs guided by behavioral or social learning theory, such as the Prevention and Relationship Enhancement Program (PREP; see, for example, Markman, Stanley, and Blumberg, 1994). This curriculum introduces a lot of background information for the instructor, and many activities for role-playing and practice skills. Other curricula, such as *Connections* (developed by Charlene Kamper), provide a mix of interactive activities and lessons, with less background information for instructors. There are now several registries of RME for adolescents, including Smart Marriages (Coalition for Marriage, Family and Couples Education, undated), and the National Healthy Marriage Resource Center (NHMRC, 2007).

Two RME curricula are described in Table 5.2. One of these, *Love U2*, is currently being revised. At the time this report was drafted, the lesson plan for only one of what will eventually be four revised modules was available, *Relationship Smarts*. The three other *Love U2* modules are *Baby Smarts*, which seeks to link marriage/relationships and childbearing by encouraging adolescents to assume a child's perspective; *Communication Smarts,* a version of PREP for adolescents aimed at preventing dating violence; and *Becoming Sex Smart*, a curriculum designed for sex education classes. Current versions of all *Love U2* modules are available from the Dibble Fund (Dibble Fund, 2007).

Family and Consumer Sciences (FACS) Textbooks

In most states, middle schools and/or high schools can offer family and consumer sciences classes, although these courses are not a graduation requirement. Florida, for example, currently requires most graduating seniors to complete a one-semester life skills management course (generally during ninth or tenth grade), but this requirement has been eliminated for

Table 5.2
Description of Exemplar Curricula, by Format

Curriculum Developer/Distributor	Content	Target Population/ Number of Sessions
	Relationship and Marital Education	
Connections. Charlene R. Kamper/ The Dibble Fund	*Dating and Emotions:* Self-awareness and readiness to date, how relationships develop, difficulties in relationships, ending a relationship, and moving past an ended relationship. *Relationships and Marriage:* Self-awareness, development of healthy friendships and dating relationships, good communication skills, and components of a healthy marriage.	*Connections: Dating and Emotions.* Grades 8–12 / 17 one-hour sessions. *Connections: Relationships and Marriage.* Grades 11–14 / 18 one-hour sessions. The materials indicate that curricula are appropriate for family life education, social studies, family consumer sciences, and health education.
Love U2. Marline Pearson/ The Dibble Fund	*Relationship Smarts* focuses on self-identity, peer pressure, maturity and mature love, communication, dating, models of healthy relationships, recognizing abuse, impact of healthy marriage on children, attitudes and beliefs about marriage. (At the time this report was written, only *Relationship Smarts* revised lessons were available.)	Curriculum was being revised at the time of this report to include *Relationship Smarts* (13 lessons + 1 interactive Internet booster lesson), designed for school and community settings; *Baby Smarts* (number of lessons to be determined), designed for school (especially FACS classes) and community settings; *Becoming Sex Smart* (administered over 3–4 weeks), designed specifically for health/sex education teachers; *Communication Smarts,* based on the communications parts of PREP, will be adapted for adolescents in schools and community settings.
	Family and Consumer Sciences Textbooks	
Families Today. Connie R. Sasse/ McGraw Hill/Glencoe	Text includes 13 (of 34) chapters that address romantic and sexual relationships including marriage. Topics include roles and relationships, interpersonal communication, conflict resolution, work and family life balance, divorce and remarriage, mature love, sexual identity and behavior, selecting a partner, marriage, and parenting.	Secondary students enrolled in FACS courses.
Contemporary Living. Verdene Ryder and Marjorie B. Harter/The Goodheart-Wilcox Company, Inc.	The text has seven parts, five of which cover much of the same material as RME, including self-concept and maturity, decisionmaking, communication, marriage relationship, parenting, and child development.	Secondary students enrolled in FACS courses.
	Character Education	
The Art of Loving Well. Developed by College of Communication and School of Education, Boston University/The Loving Well Project, Boston University	A compendium of short stories and activities intended to promote student conversation and reflection about love and sexuality. Ethnically diverse stories address three broad themes: early loves and losses, romance, and commitment and marriage.	Originally field-tested with eighth and ninth graders, the curriculum is designed for grades 7–12, depending on which stories are selected by individual teachers. Contains 40 stories plus a broad spectrum of activities.

Table 5.2—continued

	Abstinence Education	
Choosing the Best Soul Mate: A Relationship and Abstinence Curriculum. Bruce Cook/Choosing the Best Publishing	The curriculum uses a "teaching approach that moves students from a cognitive understanding of the facts to a personal awareness that leads to a changed behavior." Each lesson incorporates some aspect of RME; e.g., for upper high school grades, lessons include tips on finding a good partner, self-confidence and self-awareness, developing relational skills, understanding dating, marriage and commitment.	There are four age-appropriate versions (grades 6 and 7; 7 and 8; 9 and 10; and 11 and 12). Each version has 5–8 50-minute lessons. Lessons include short videos or case studies, discussion, group activities (e.g., role playing), and demonstrations. Can be used in school or community settings.
A.C. Green's Game Plan Abstinence Program. Libby Gray and Scott Phelps/Project Reality	The developers describe this curriculum as a "sports-themed, positive approach to abstinence education." Topics related to RME include making future plans, boundaries within relationships, the consequences of premarital sex, choosing friends, and looking at marriage as a goal.	Grades 7–9. Game Plan is designed primarily as a public school health curriculum with each of 8 lessons intended for one class period.
	National Organization Initiatives	
Project Alpha. March of Dimes Birth Defects Foundation and the Alpha Phi Alpha Fraternity, Inc.	Program designed to provide education, motivation and skill-building on the issues of responsibility, relationships, teen pregnancy and sexually transmitted diseases to black males.	Black males ages 12–15. Designed to be delivered in half-day workshops, weekend long retreats, or shorter informational sessions.

students entering high school in 2007–2008. The national standards for FACS education include Interpersonal Relationships ("understanding personal needs and characteristics and their impact on interpersonal relationships" and "effective conflict prevention and management techniques") (National Association of State Administrators for Family and Consumer Sciences, 1998). States are free to adopt or adapt national standards according to state-specific perspectives underpinning FACS education (most states that we contacted have a standard that is very similar to Interpersonal Relationships).

Because FACS classes are almost always optional, it is difficult without specific information on student enrollment to know how many and which students may be exposed to relationship education curricula within FACS courses. Limited information indicates that these classes reach females and students who are not college-bound (Jennifer Kerpelman, personal communication, April 21, 2006)—which represents at least some of the target population.

Character Education (CE) Curricula

CE is the most nebulous type of curriculum identified by informants. While it is sometimes defined as "teaching and learning for personal development" and may include "moral reasoning/cognitive development," "social and emotional learning," and "moral education/virtue" (Otten, 2000), informants noted that they themselves were not clear about the definition of character education and expressed discomfort with the concept (or term) for two reasons. First, there is the well-known question: "Whose 'values' are to be taught?" (Otten, 2000). A second closely related concern raised by an educator we spoke with is that there is a lack of clear standards against which youth are expected to be held. As one state education representative we spoke with noted,

> Character education is soft and done in pieces. . . . [I]t doesn't really hold kids accountable from one district to the next. It says "This is how we are nice to each other" rather than setting a standard of behavior that affects your relationship and this is the way you need to act.

By extension, a lack of standards or clear expectations of outcomes makes it difficult for curriculum developers to design an intervention that can effectively change attitudinal or behavioral relationship outcomes.

One of the earliest developed relationship-focused curricula, *The Art of Loving Well*, is described as a literature-based CE curriculum, although one of its key developers, Nancy McLaren, emphasizes that originators of the curriculum define character education as essentially synonymous with the development of social-emotional intelligence (Nancy McLaren, personal communication, August 7, 2006). *The Art of Loving Well* is an anthology of short stories intended to help adolescents learn about responsible sexual and social values through literature. The goals of the curriculum include convincing adolescents that good relationships require hard work but contribute to quality of life; reducing sexual activity, adolescent pregnancy, and AIDS; and countering family and school violence by providing models of conflict resolution. The curriculum is also designed to promote conversations between adolescents and parents, and many of the stories provide positive models of healthy relationships and marriages. Stories and activities from *Loving Well* are sometimes integrated into lessons in other multicomponent curricula (e.g., *Love U2*).

Abstinence Education (AE) Curricula

Increasingly, policymakers have criticized AE and comprehensive sex education for too often ignoring relationships and romance, suggesting that abstinence and sex education should be taught within the context of relationship education (Whitehead and Pearson, 2006). This is reflected in a recent ACF program announcement that emphasized a preference for AE applicants to address healthy relationships during adolescence and healthy marriages in adulthood (Department of Health and Human Services, 2006). On a practical level, incorporating RME curricula into abstinence education curricula may be an effective strategy for moving RME curricula into schools. At least one distributor of AE and RME curricula we spoke with noted that he was having difficulty selling the latter to schools, even those schools with whom they have an established relationship selling AE curricula. This distributor believed that incorporating RME into AE curricula would be the most effective way of getting RME curricula into the schools he works with and would have the added benefit of strengthening the RME curricula at the same time.

National Organization Initiatives

The fifth category of programs includes efforts or initiatives by national organizations that seek to improve relationship outcomes as a primary or secondary objective of programs targeting at-risk youth. The one example of such an initiative that we reviewed for this project is Project Alpha, collaboratively developed and implemented by Alpha Phi Alpha Fraternity, Inc., and the March of Dimes Birth Defects Foundation. Project Alpha is designed to provide "education, motivation, and skill-building on issues including responsibility, relationships, teen pregnancy, and sexually transmitted diseases" for young black male students ages 12–15. The program is cosponsored by local college and alumni fraternity chapters and local March of Dimes units and is delivered in anything ranging from half-day workshops to weekend retreats.

Are Relationship Education Curricula Effective?

How can policymakers evaluate whether any relationship education curriculum is effective? As we have already noted, one obstacle faced by efforts to assess the effectiveness of these programs is the fact that program objectives are often vague. To the extent that it is not clear whether programs are designed to promote healthy marriages in adulthood or healthy relationships in adolescence, the criteria for measuring the effectiveness of these programs are not obvious. A second obstacle is that conducting rigorous evaluation research is difficult and costly. The "gold standard" for evaluating interventions requires random assignment, or, failing that, quasi-experimental designs involving careful matching of treatment and comparison groups. If students who participate in a relationship education program have better relationship outcomes during adolescence (however those are defined) or better marital outcomes as adults, then the program is deemed effective. Because relationship education curricula for adolescents are relatively new (Gardner, 2001), no experimental evaluations have yet been completed.

Three of the curricula described in Table 5.2—*The Art of Loving Well, Connections,* and *Love U2*—have been evaluated with quasi-experimental studies (Gardner, 2001, 2005; Kreitzer, 1998; Jennifer Kerpelman, personal communication, April 21, 2006). Combined, the results of these evaluations are at most suggestive that relationship education curricula may improve relationship outcomes during adolescence. Each of these evaluations measured some combination of short-term (i.e., adolescent) attitude and/or behavioral outcomes (which may or may not be related to later adult marital outcomes).

Based on the promising findings from the quasi-experimental evaluation of *Relationship Smarts,* Jennifer Kerpelman and colleagues were recently funded by ACF to conduct a more rigorous evaluation of the intervention, with Alabama teachers working in schools having a high percentage of minority and low-income students. One problem with the earlier evaluation of *Relationship Smarts* and *Connections* is that they were delivered in FACS classes. A strength of the new evaluation is that it will test whether the intervention is effective in health courses (which are required of all high school students prior to graduation) as well as FACS, to assess the portability of the intervention to different courses and to evaluate whether the program is effective for a more representative group of students (such as males, who are underrepresented in FACS classes).

The study investigators are working closely with *Relationship Smarts* curriculum developer Marline Pearson to produce a streamlined version of *Love U2 (Relationship Smarts* module) for use in this larger evaluation and to replace the current version being distributed. We review this streamlined version later in this chapter. The evaluation will examine short- and long-term knowledge (up to three years post-intervention), attitudes, identity styles, behaviors, and skills, both pre- and post-intervention, for control and intervention students. Because the investigators of this study carefully examined extant curricula at the time that they were formulating the study design and chose the one that they thought most appropriate developmentally, the results of this study will contribute substantially to assessing if and how the current generation of relationship curricula is effective, and should highlight areas of the curriculum that can be improved.

The fact that quasi-experimental evaluations have yielded suggestive results does not necessarily portend that the results from the experimental evaluation will be positive. In particular, when quasi-experimental evaluations have relatively weak comparison groups, such as in the case of the three completed evaluations described above, the results from experimental designs can often differ substantially, and just as likely in a negative direction as a positive one (see Lipsey and Corday, 2000, for discussion of this literature).

Nevertheless, even if the results of the ongoing study are disappointing, the field stands to gain from this rigorous evaluation. First, based on the opinion of several informants we spoke with, *Love U2* is the curriculum that many believe is the strongest. If the results of this evaluation are disappointing, it is likely that other curricula would not have fared better if they had been examined. Yet, as seen in the next section, *Love U2* covers many of the same concepts as other curricula. Thus, lessons learned from the implementation analysis of this evaluation are likely to apply to other curricula.

Second, disappointing results can also provide the impetus necessary to generate a second or third generation of programs that are more effective than earlier generations, as happened in the drug prevention field. About two decades ago, vast quantities of money were being funneled into subsequently disproved program strategies or into programs like D.A.R.E. (Drug Abuse Resistance Education) that had not been carefully evaluated. Later evaluations showed that D.A.R.E. had very little or no effect and that the costs were not justified. As a result, the federal government has pushed for adopting better-designed programs, like Project ALERT, that have rigorous evaluations and yield credible and positive results. Such evaluations have shown that drug prevention can work and, perhaps even more important, have helped to confirm the value of these programs to policymakers who fund them. Moreover, such evaluations have shown which drug intervention programs work and which do not, critical information for schools selecting a program to implement. In the event that the ongoing evaluation by Kerpelman and colleagues is disappointing, the relationship education field could still benefit greatly if it used these results as an impetus to push the curricula to be more effective in producing better relationships (however such outcomes are eventually defined).

A third reason to push for more rigorous evaluations of relationship education is that, given the nature of the research in this field, and the impracticality and the ethical issues involved in random assignment in terms of romantic and marital behaviors, studying the effect of interventions on immediate and long-term consequences of adolescent romantic relationships may be one of very few feasible ways to evaluate models of romantic relationships rigorously. For the most part, researchers can only measure correlations among relationship precursors, including attitudes and behaviors, and make educated guesses about underlying processes. If they include random assignment and a valid control group, careful evaluations of interventions that modify specific precursors can help to demonstrate whether changes in those precursors affect other precursors or subsequent relationships and marital outcomes.

Are Major Relationship Education Curricula Aligned with the Research Base?

When results from rigorous evaluations are lacking, an alternative way of evaluating the likely effectiveness of curricula is to assess how well the content of the curricula aligns with what the basic research literature suggests is likely to be important. There is solid research demonstrating that interventions targeting general and at-risk youth positively affect many of the precursors of healthy adolescent relationships identified in Chapters Three and Four of this report (and summarized in Figure 3.1), including relationships with parents, stress, and prevalence of substance abuse (Johnson et al., 1990; Johnson et al., 1996; Weiss and Nicholson, 1998); timing of entry into sexual relationships; sexual behavior; and incidence of sexually transmitted diseases and pregnancy (Philliber et al., 2002); and longer-term outcomes, such as educational attainment (Myers and Schirm, 1999). Some effective interventions are multicomponent interventions; others seek to impart knowledge or teach skills to affect attitudinal and behavioral changes. Unfortunately, as with almost all evaluations, it is not possible to isolate what intervention component or knowledge or skills produced the desired outcome. We can only conclude that research demonstrates that specific precursors can be positively affected by an intervention.

For each curriculum reviewed for this chapter, we indicate in Table 5.3 whether the content seeks to modify (not just discuss or address) each adolescent health relationship precursor listed in the first column. In the case of *Art of Loving Well,* which is a compendium of short stories, we only coded efforts to affect precursors based on the stated objectives of the developers on their Web site because otherwise it was difficult to ascertain from the text exactly what behavioral or attitudinal changes are sought. Unlike the other curricula, the intended impact on attitudes or behaviors is not typically obvious with each story.[1]

In the remainder of this section, we illustrate the variety of ways that each precursor is addressed in these curricula. In some cases, a curriculum seeks to impart some knowledge as a way to effect behavior. In other cases, the curriculum clearly tries to help students build skills necessary to modify the precursor. There are few consistent approaches to addressing the precursors across the curricula.

Immediate Context

Four of the five precursors that our integrative framework identifies as relevant elements of the immediate context of the adolescent are addressed by at least one of the curricula reviewed here. The one (possible) exception is family structure, where we allocate partial credit to three curricula for addressing future (rather than current) family structure. For example, the two textbooks emphasize the difficulties resulting from parental divorce. None of the curricula tries

[1] As of May 6, 2007:
http://www.bu.edu/education/lovingwell/LovingWell_Goals.html

Table 5.3
Precursors of Relationship Outcomes Addressed by Exemplar Relationship and Marriage Education Curricula

	RME		CE	FACS		AE		National Organization
Precursors of Relationship Outcomes	Connections	Relationship Smarts	Art of Loving Well	Families Today	Contemporary Living	Choosing the Best	The Game Plan	Project Alpha
Immediate Context								
Peer group	√	√		√	√		√	√
School environment			√					
Family structure		*		*	*			*
Relations with parents			√	√	√			√
Stress	√	√		√	√			√
Individual Differences								
Self-esteem	√	√	√	√	√	√	√	√
Substance use			√	√	√			
Academic delinquency			√					
Personality								
Attitudes and Beliefs								
Models of intimacy and relationships	√	√	√	√	√	√	√	√
Attitudes toward dating and marriage	√	√	√	√	√	√	√	√
Beliefs about sex and childbearing	√	√	√	√	√	√	√	√
Relationship Behaviors								
Timing of (relationship) entry	√	√	√	√		√	√	√
Relationship commitment	√	√	√	√	√	√	√	√
Duration and number	√	√					√	√
Sexual behavior	√	√	√	√	√	√	√	√
Partner choice	√	√	√	√	√	√	√	√
Violence	√	√	√	√				√
STDs and pregnancy	√	√	√	√	√	√	√	√

* The precursor is partially addressed in the curricula.
√ The precursor is addressed in the curricula.

to modify the structure of the current family of the youth. The only curriculum that seeks to affect school environment is *The Art of Loving Well*—the stated objectives of this curriculum (as of many character education efforts), as described on its Web site, is to "counter school violence by providing positive models of conflict resolution" as well as to "enhance mutual respect among adolescents, parents, and teachers." The most commonly addressed of the immediate context precursors are peer groups, followed by stress. Peer groups are discussed in two ways: (1) emphasizing the importance of selecting friends who share the same attitudes (e.g., *Game Plan);* and (2) describing peer pressure and providing resistance strategies (e.g., *Families Today, Connections: Dating and Emotions, Art of Loving Well*).

Individual Differences

All eight curricula address self-esteem or a related concept in relation to interpersonal relationships. The two RME curricula (*Connections: Relationships and Dating* and *Love U2)* devote a lesson to self-awareness and developing a vision of how students would like to be in the future. Both textbooks define self-esteem and provide exercises for strengthening it, and one textbook (*Contemporary Living*) links self-esteem to marital quality. The CE and FACS texts are each intended to address substance abuse—CE through literature and the FACS texts by describing the adverse consequences of substance abuse. Although most of the curricula address personality and ways that it can interact with romantic and marital relationships, none seems to seek to modify personality.

Attitudes and Beliefs

All the curricula we reviewed touch on each of the attitude and belief precursors. Each curriculum introduces one or more models of relationships and intimacy—in most cases, these include positive models, although one, *Choosing the Best Soul Mate*, emphasizes negative examples of relationships and intimacy to highlight problems that can plague relationships. The curricula seek to shape attitudes and beliefs about dating and marriage, emphasizing the value of postponing dating and suggesting that the purpose of dating is to get to know someone and assess compatibility. All the curricula emphasize the importance of abstinence.

Relationship Behavior

Relationship behavior is the second most comprehensively covered domain in the curricula we reviewed. All the curricula address commitment, sexual behavior, partner choice, and STDs and pregnancy as factors that influence the quality of romantic and/or marital relationships. Six of the eight curricula encourage youth to postpone entry into serious relationships. Four of the curricula address duration and/or number of relationships and five address violence. With respect to violence, the emphasis is on helping youth define or identify abusive or violent relationships and providing recommendations for how to end such relationships.

Practical Concerns in Delivering Relationship Education Curricula to Low-Income Youth

One of the goals of the ACF Healthy Marriage Initiative is to increase the percentage of youth and young adults with the skills and knowledge necessary to form healthy relationships and marriages (Department of Health and Human Services, 2006). To explore this issue, we spoke with several ACF staff who are overseeing efforts to extend HMI efforts to include programs targeting adolescents, as well as with ACF grantees that have some experience providing relationship education programming to adolescents in community settings (or sometimes AE with a relationship education emphasis) or that are preparing to do so. Among the organizations we spoke with that have some experience encouraging healthy relationships among adolescents, there is uniform agreement that this programming is vital and that the additional funds will help them better address the needs of the adolescents they work with. Moreover, there is also consensus that youth who participate in these efforts are highly receptive to them. For these two reasons, these organizations said that they would, if possible, continue to refine and provide this programming. The remainder of this section discusses the practical and resource issues that emerged in our discussion with ACF decisionmakers and grantees.

Most organizations we spoke with said that the major curricula they selected from were those featured at Smart Marriages conferences. It is important to note that the organizations we spoke with were not necessarily using the specific curricula reviewed in this chapter. We asked informants from these organizations to describe for us, in generic terms, the types of issues and concerns they perceived in implementing relationship education curricula, but we did not attempt to map whether these issues and concerns apply to one or more of the curricula reviewed here.

The Need for More Culturally Appropriate Curricula

Perhaps the most commonly cited difficulty that organizations expressed is a shortage of relationship education curricula that appear suitable for their specific target population. This ranged from a concern that the curricula are too explicit for the youth that are served (and their parents) to a concern that the curricula do not accurately reflect youth culture (e.g., hip-hop). Grantees in the latter group acknowledged that curricula (particularly abstinence-only curricula) are increasingly incorporating media (especially commercials and hip-hop) and that these efforts are well received by youth. AE programs were most frequently mentioned as doing a good job at incorporating culture (sometimes defined as hip-hop music or explicit commercials)—but we did not hear this comment applied to RME curricula. Given the limitations of this review, we were not able to ascertain whether organizations perceived that lack of culturally appropriate curricula reflects a failure to adequately incorporate media into the curriculum. Because we did not speak with youth directly, we were unable to assess whether these perceptions are those of the informants we spoke with, those of the youth they work with, or of the parents of the youth. We also could not assess the validity of these perceptions. The RME field, in particular, may benefit from exploring the potential reasons for these perceptions and whether the extent of their cultural adaptation is insufficient, on average, or whether they need to address perceptual barriers.

Problem with Curricula Overlooking Young Parents

Grantees mentioned two key segments of the youth population that they believe existing curricula largely ignore: young mothers and fathers and pregnant women. At best, grantees said that they believed that certain sessions are simply awkward for these young adults to attend (and one grantee said that they recommend young mothers and pregnant women be pulled out of certain sessions) and in other cases they thought the entire curriculum was inappropriate for these population segments. Because teen fathers are not always recognized as such, there was a particular concern that teen fathers were most at risk of not benefiting from the programming. We are aware of some efforts to develop programming tailored for at-risk teens. For example, Marline Pearson (personal communication) reports that she may produce tailored editions of *Love U2* for teen parents, foster teens, and possibly Hispanic teens. Pearson has also developed, in collaboration with Scott Stanley and Galena Kline, *Within My Reach: Low Income PREP*, a decisionmaking and relationship skill-building and marriage promotion program designed specifically for low-income single mothers, who may be older adolescents or young adults. As another example, *Connections* is now available in Spanish. Another grantee we spoke with that provides technical assistance is likewise exploring ways to adapt other curricula so that they are appropriate for Hispanics and other groups. Finally, we note that other marriage education curricula not reviewed in this report are actively working to adapt curricula specific for different subgroups.

Insufficient Implementation Tools

Several organizations said that they could benefit from greater assistance in delivering curricula. In particular, they expressed the need for assistance or guidelines for adapting curricula. One organization we spoke with said that it picks and chooses components it thinks are best. Another grantee said that it does not have the necessary time to implement its selected curriculum with fidelity, so it removed some components. Grantees said they would appreciate some guidance for which curriculum components are believed to be essential to achieving a desired outcome versus which are likely to be duplicative and considered optional. Currently, grantees that must shorten the number or length of sessions combine two approaches to modifying the curricula: (1) pre-tests for youth to assess what components are core, and (2) asking staff to assess which curricula components are core. Several grantees said that they would prefer some guidance from the program developers on the issue of which components are core and which are optional. We also heard confusion expressed about whether organizations could modify curriculum without violating the terms of the agreement with the distributor.

Many argue that policymakers and funders should recognize the need to produce guidelines that communities can use to think about when and how science-based program components can be adapted to fit their setting. Among other definitions, adaptation has been defined as the deliberate or accidental modification of a program (Center for Substance Abuse Prevention, 2002). Adaptation can include deletions or additions of program components, changes in the manner or intensity of components, or cultural modifications (Center for Substance Abuse Prevention, 2002).

Although the impact of adaptation on participant outcomes is largely unknown, most believe that low fidelity is associated with worse outcomes (Blakely et al., 1987). If this is true, reports that organizations are commonly adapting curricula mean that target populations are not enjoying maximum benefits. It is also possible that, in the absence of easy-to-follow and effective adaptation guidelines, organizations may not bother with proven curricula to avoid the burden of adaptation, although we have not seen empirical evidence on this point. At this time there are no "proven" marriage education curricula, but assuming such curricula are developed, adolescent public health as a whole may benefit as much from making effective adaptation guidelines available to organizations as from commercially available curricula.

Although tools to guide adaptation are currently missing within the marriage education movement, this may be changing. One grantee we spoke with is developing a toolkit that organizations can use to design RME programs. This toolkit is intended to be a step-by-step guide in workbook form. It begins by walking the organization through such steps as developing the vision; building a foundation; creating a mission statement, goals, and activities (worksheets); determining participants; identifying barriers; and reviewing all aspects of marriage curricula (e.g., the pros and cons of different curricula, when and where to meet, how often, and how to perform an evaluation). Aspects of this tool overlap with similar efforts being undertaken in other fields, such as youth development and community health. Organizations can use all these tool to help them with needs assessment, setting of priorities, planning and delivering programs, monitoring, and evaluation (e.g., Chinman, Imm, and Wandersman, 2003). Such a toolkit would be useful to organizations that want to provide RME to youth, and it could be extended to incorporate adaptation guidelines.

Questions About the Age-Appropriateness of Some Curricula Components

Some informants we spoke with questioned the age-appropriateness of some of the RME curricula and their components. In particular, they expressed concern about whether PREP (or PREP-like components), a tool developed to improve communication of (primarily white, middle-class) adult married and premarital couples, is appropriate for adolescents and, if so, whether sufficient work has been done to tailor it to the developmental stage of youth. We heard that many in the marriage education field believe that PREP (or an adaptation of it) should be distributed for youth, and many of the curricula we reviewed incorporate PREP-like components. But we heard from some informants with a background in adolescence (rather than in marriage education) a concern that insufficient research has been conducted to confirm that the widespread use of such components is warranted at this time.

We note that this same criticism is applicable to all RME curricula and their components. A danger in not rigorously evaluating a curriculum or component that is primed to be widely distributed, such as PREP in adolescent programming, is that it may be enormously successful but subsequently found to not be as effective in accomplishing the desired outcome as an alternative. Yet, once programs accept and buy into a given curricula, it can be very difficult to disabuse them of the effectiveness of the intervention. For example, D.A.R.E., the drug abuse prevention program shown to be ineffective nearly 15 years ago, is still the most widely used drug prevention program in the United States and internationally, even though more effective alternatives are available.

Need for Training in the Logistics of Serving At-Risk Youth

Given the goal of the programming, some youth who could most benefit have logistical challenges. For example, one grantee said that there is need for training on how to incorporate child-care logistics to deal with the children of young parents. Given the nature of some of the discussion, there is also need for guidance on when male and female participants in these programs should be separated. For example, should separations be based on topic, age, or some combination of the two? And if so, how should the genders be separated? For the full course? For specific sessions? During breakout sessions? Some logistical issues are relevant for all curricula (e.g., child care), whereas other issues may be especially pertinent to a specific curriculum. Other logistical issues organizations recommend guidance on include if and when to offer incentives to potential participants (such as food or prizes) and where and when to deliver the curriculum. Many of these issues are relevant to all populations. However, because these grantees in many cases were considering expanding the scope of programming they provide to include RME—or expanding their target populations to include youth—grantees are revisiting logistical questions they faced before.

Marketing Relationship Education to Adult Decisionmakers

We heard concerns from grantees that while relationship education efforts were well-received by youth, parents and other adult decisionmakers were sometimes less enthusiastic. One grantee opined that part of this may be due to unfortunate terms—many parents interpret "relationship education" to mean a dating or "hook-up" service and protest that such service is not what their children need. If the issue is only one of terminology, then the recommendation for overcoming this limitation is to conduct a series of focus groups with parents to assess the appropriateness of other terms.

However, another grantee indicated that there may be a larger problem of the way adults and parents perceive the need for RME targeting youth. This organization delivers RME and AE services to service providers in the geographic area for a modest fee. It found that while most organizations were open to RME programming if the programming were cross-subsidized by other programming (such as abstinence education), these same organizations, when faced with restricted resources, would pay for AE programming but not for relationship education. They viewed relationship education as less important for youth than abstinence education. Ultimately, the board of directors decided that, financially, the grantee organization could no longer afford to cross-subsidize relationship education programming and would cease offering it.

This may reflect a larger need to assess whether parents and community decisionmakers believe that relationship education is important for their youth and are willing to back it. At the same time that ACF is reaching out to youth to understand how it can craft messages for youth, there may be a need to reach out to community leaders and parents who are not involved in the relationship and marriage education movement to assess where they stand on these matters. There may be a need to reach and educate adults about the need and potential benefits from RME efforts that coincides with or supersedes efforts to deliver this programming to youth.

Summary and Conclusions

The field of relationship education is relatively new and, consequently, the effects of the curricula on improving relationship outcomes in adolescence and subsequent adulthood have not been established. On the positive side, these curricula are evidence-based in that they draw on cutting-edge research on adolescent relationships. This cannot be said of first- and second-generation interventions in other fields (such as drug prevention). However, most of the evidence in the relationship education field is correlational, so it is unclear whether the precursors of healthy relationships identified in Chapters Three and Four are caused by third factors that have not been identified or if a change in these precursors really affects relationship outcomes. If the latter, then the existing curricula that all tend to touch on at least one precursor within each of the domains are likely to be at least somewhat effective. If the former, future research evaluating the effect of these interventions on relationship outcomes will be invaluable. If carefully done, it will provide a unique opportunity to rigorously test aspects of the model that are not otherwise available because of practical and ethical considerations. One such evaluation is currently under way, although the results will not be available for a few years. A key challenge facing the field will be to arrive at a consensus about what the clear and measurable short- and long-term goals of these programs ought to be.

In this chapter, we reviewed exemplar RME, CE, FACS, and AE curricula nominated by experts in the field. In terms of addressing the domains in the integrative framework developed in Chapter Three, the key strengths of these curricula are that they cover most of the attitudes and beliefs and most of the relationship behaviors that current research and theory suggest are relevant for the development of healthy relationships and marriages. The curricula are less consistent in how they address immediate context and individual difference precursors. An open question is whether RME programs should address these other factors at all, given that for some of these precursors, such as substance use prevention, there are already proven curricula.

We spoke with decisionmakers and community-based organizations that are offering or considering relationship education curricula about the issues they encounter. From these conversations, we derived a number of observations. First, there is a perceived need for more culturally appropriate curricula, which the field appears to be addressing. Second, some key subpopulations (e.g., teen fathers, pregnant teens) are not adequately addressed by existing curricula. At least one curriculum developer we spoke with said there were plans to address one or more of these subpopulations. More such efforts may be necessary.

Third, organizations almost unanimously indicated that they adapt existing curricula because of limited time or physical resources and that these adaptations are occurring with no guidance from the program developer. Some organizations are concerned that their adaptations are compromising the effectiveness of the curricula and would appreciate guidance. We recommend that there be more emphasis on adaptation guidelines and other implementation tools to use when delivering a new curriculum.

A fourth concern expressed by some organizations is that relationship education curricula are not always age-appropriate. These concerns ranged from questioning the appropriateness of the explicit sexual content of some of the materials (especially media examples) to whether the content of core materials (such as PREP) that were originally developed for adult couples is developmentally appropriate for teens.

Fifth, some organizations said that the relationship education programming often attracts some youth with special logistical needs (e.g., babysitting) that the organization is unequipped to handle. These organizations say they could benefit from technical assistance in how to deal with such logistics.

Finally, we saw evidence that adults, such as parents and leaders of community organizations, may not understand the purpose or need for relationship education programming. Since these adults are often in a position to influence whether relationship education programming is made available to youth, more attention to marketing to these influential adults may be required.

We conclude with an observation on the RME field. As in any field, the program developers, distributors, implementers, and some funders generally believe deeply in the importance and value of the curricula for improving the lives of adolescents. As a result, these individuals and organizations devote an enormous amount of energy and talent to developing and disseminating these programs. Among these parties, there appears to be a certain level of frustration with the failure to make sufficient inroads in schools and community settings. There is some disagreement as to which setting is ideal or realistic. On the one hand, schools are highly desirable because most adolescents attend them. On the other hand, schools are under enormous pressure to meet performance standards set by state and federal departments of education and are reluctant to add any curricula that would distract from time devoted to meeting these standards. Unfortunately, in the current environment, RME curricula are most likely to be incorporated in schools if they meet one of two criteria. One route would be to integrate this material into required courses (e.g., health education), as some distributors recommend. The concern with the health education route is that many of these classes are taught by coaches or others who may be less effective educators than standard teachers. The challenge here would be to modify the curricula so that anyone, particularly those who are likely to teach health classes, can effectively teach the curricula. A second route to gain entry into schools would be to convincingly demonstrate that RME curricula produce other outcomes by which schools are evaluated (e.g., attendance, standardized test scores). The results from the Auburn, Alabama, study described previously should provide evidence on whether such evidence is likely to be forthcoming (at least based on the current generation of RME curricula).

Alternatively, RME curricula may be pitched to other settings that desire curricula to address specific issues they care about. In this case, the field may be more successful with some mix of evidence and marketing. Increasingly, some nonschool practitioners are sophisticated about the evidence base. For example, after-school programs are very aware of the lack of evidence showing that participation in their programs leads to improved outcomes (such as higher standardized test scores or reduced behavioral problems). Nonetheless, these programs meet an important need (for childcare), so their viability, particularly in elementary schools, is assured. The issue they are facing is how to engage kids in their programs (particularly students in fifth grade and higher). Those in the RME field may find themselves welcomed by these programs if the RME field can rigorously demonstrate their that curricula have low resource demands (e.g., do not require staff to have much education or training); that students like the curriculum;

and, most importantly, that it improves program attendance, behavioral problems, or staff-student relationships (Bodilly and Beckett, 2005). Similarly, other out-of-school-time settings may have unique needs that RME may be well qualified to help address.

CHAPTER SIX

Future Directions for Research and Intervention

Public health educators distinguish among three forms of disease prevention (Butler, 1997). *Primary prevention* involves activities designed to ward off threats to health before they occur (e.g., public service announcements, vaccinations). *Secondary prevention* involves activities designed to screen for early signs of disease and limit the consequences (e.g., mammograms). Finally, *tertiary prevention* involves activities designed to treat disease directly and avoid recurrence (e.g., antibiotics, chemotherapy).

Over the past several decades, the history of efforts to promote marriages and families may be understood as moving gradually backward through these three stages. Initially, the sharp rise in divorce rates during the 1970s and early 1980s inspired efforts at tertiary prevention, i.e., efforts to provide therapy to distressed couples and manage the consequences of divorce (Jacobson and Margolin, 1979; Weiss, 1980). As studies began to question the effectiveness of these treatments (Jacobson and Addis, 1993), the emphasis in research and policy shifted toward secondary prevention, i.e., efforts to identify vulnerable newlyweds and provide them with relationship education before their relationships decline (e.g., Bradbury and Fincham, 1990b; Markman et al., 1994). In turning toward adolescence, researchers and policymakers appear to have arrived at last at primary prevention, i.e., developing programs and policies designed to sow the seeds of healthy adult marriages prior to adulthood and reduce subsequent risk of divorce and marital distress (e.g., Barber and Eccles, 2003).

The success of programs that attempt to promote healthy adult marriages by targeting adolescents will depend on (1) whether these programs are addressing behaviors, beliefs, and attitudes that are in fact causally linked to subsequent adult marriages, (2) whether these programs are effective at changing the behaviors and attitudes being addressed, and (3) whether these programs, even if effective in the general population, are equally effective in the specific population of interest, i.e., low-income groups (Greene and Simons-Morton, 1984).

The broad goal of the current report has been to evaluate each of these questions by reviewing existing research and theory on the role of adolescent romantic relationships in adult development and by reviewing relationship education curricula currently being offered to adolescents. The results of this review indicate that none of these issues has yet been settled. Although the available research is consistent with theories that view experiences with romantic relationships in adolescence as central to the development of healthy marriages in adulthood, direct support for causal links between adolescent experiences and adult outcomes does not yet exist. Third-variable explanations (for example, the possibility that genetic or contextual variables shape relationships in adolescence and adulthood without additional causal effects of adolescent experiences on adulthood) have not been ruled out. Although the available relationship education curricula address many of the variables that existing theories suggest are important to adolescent and adult romantic relationships, the effectiveness of these curricula at altering these variables and promoting desired outcomes has yet to be evaluated in controlled studies that employ random assignment to conditions. Although adolescent romantic relationships have begun to receive attention from researchers and curricula developers, data specific to low-income adolescents remain rare.

Recognizing the limitations of the existing empirical base for understanding and intervening in adolescent romantic relationships, this final chapter offers an agenda for building upon existing research and advancing programs to promote the development of healthy adult marriages. The rest of this chapter describes this agenda in three parts. The first section recommends specific priorities for further research to clarify the role of adolescent romantic relationships in adult development. The second section draws upon the research and theory reviewed in this report to offer guidelines and new strategies for current efforts to strengthen the foundation of healthy marriages during adolescence. The final section identifies future directions for interventions addressing adolescent romantic relationships.

Immediate Priorities for Research on Adolescent Romantic Relationships

If programs and curricula targeting adolescent romantic relationships are to be effective, they must be grounded in an accurate understanding of how these relationships function and the role that they play in the development of healthy adult marriages. As Bouchey and Furman (2003) have pointed out, most of what is known about these questions is based on data from white, middle-class adolescents, and even that literature is quite limited. Research that addresses the following immediate priorities would strengthen the empirical base of current programs and substantially advance efforts to promote healthy adult marriages.

Exploit existing data sets. No one studying or intervening in low-income populations denies that the data describing romantic relationships in low-income populations are thin and that what data there are often come from small, ethnographic studies rather than nationally representative data sets. Yet nationally representative data sets (e.g., the Add Health study, the NLSY79, the NLSY97) include data from substantial numbers of well-sampled low-income adolescents. To date, analyses of these data sets have not included many comparisons across levels of income, but comparisons across racial and ethnic groups are common. As noted in Chapter Two, race and ethnicity are poor proxies for level of income, because most members of racial or ethnic minority groups are not low-income (Bachrach, 1998).

Analyses of these and other data sets that address the role of income directly would have relatively low costs and potentially high yield for informing policies that target low-income youth. Such studies would be limited by the assessments already included in these studies, but across the data sets there are enough variables relevant to understanding adolescents and their relationships to offer a much clearer picture of low-income youth than currently exists—in particular, the ways that low-income youth may resemble or differ from more affluent youth.

Analyses of existing data sets would provide valuable descriptive data on prevalence of specific relationship behaviors and experiences, as well as providing opportunities to determine if models of relationships among variables generalize across different income groups and different racial and ethnic groups within low-income populations.

It is worth noting that level of income is not the only dimension of relevance that has been overlooked in existing national data sets. It may also be possible to examine the effects of schools and neighborhoods in shaping and constraining adolescents' access to partners and opportunities (Furstenberg, 2000).

Address diversity directly. Although all low-income adolescents may have common needs that distinguish them from more affluent adolescents, subgroups of low-income adolescents may also have unique needs for which programs and interventions might be tailored. For example, research has rarely addressed ethnically diverse populations of adolescents, and so there has not been much systematic attention to the ways that racial and ethnic diversity combine with level of income to affect adolescent romantic relationships. Yet culture and ethnicity are likely to be important sources of the beliefs and values that all existing programs and interventions are targeting. A priority for new research in this area is to directly examine how adolescents from different cultures may approach their first experiences of romantic relationships differently, and especially how culture and income may interact to shape the impact that experiences during adolescence have on subsequent adult outcomes.

A second source of overlooked diversity in existing research and intervention efforts is diversity in sexual orientation (Diamond et al., 1999; Savin-Williams, 2001). As noted in Chapter Four, there has been little research on the development of healthy relationships for this population, in either adolescence or adulthood. As noted in Chapter Five, existing interventions attempt to be inclusive, but none addresses issues related to sexual orientation directly. As a first step toward promoting healthy relationships for all adolescents, this research gap should be addressed.

Examine the consequences of adolescent romantic relationships for adult outcomes. The fundamental assumption of current efforts to target adolescent romantic relationships—that these experiences can contribute to the success or failure of adult marriages—has never been addressed empirically. Justifying the allocation of marriage promotion resources toward adolescence requires addressing this gap in the literature. There are several ways to do this.

First, as has been noted throughout this report, the Add Health study and a number of high-quality smaller studies (e.g., the Toledo Adolescent Relationships Study, the Minnesota Longitudinal Study of Parents and Children) have followed infants or children throughout adolescence and into the earliest years of adulthood, but these studies have not yet progressed far enough to provide much insight into marriage. These studies deserve continued support because their considerable investments may pay the greatest dividends when the participants in these studies progress through adulthood and the long-term implications of their early experiences begin to emerge.

Second, because most existing studies have sampled narrowly from middle-class populations (the Add Health study being the exception), additional data are needed that describe low-income populations specifically. Samples of convenience, even if drawn from low-income populations, are unlikely to be sufficient. Rather, to inform current efforts, research on adolescent romantic relationships in low-income populations must pay careful attention to obtaining samples representative of low-income groups in general, yet capable of allowing comparisons between subgroups of particular interest (e.g., groups that vary by race and ethnicity or by urban versus rural context). New studies of low-income adolescents must be descriptive, inclusive of a broad range of assessments, and longitudinal (Eccles and Gootman, 2002), in order to capture the course of adolescent romantic relationships during adolescence, examine the long-term implications of these experiences, and identify the specific elements that account for those implications.

Rule out alternative explanations. Establishing direct associations between experiences in romantic relationships during adolescence and marital outcomes during adulthood would be a major advance for research in this area. By itself, however, establishing these associations would not be sufficient to justify intervening in adolescent romantic relationships to promote healthy marriages among adults. Even if they are effective at improving adolescent relationships, programs that target adolescents are only likely to improve adult marriages to the extent that adolescent experiences account for adult outcomes even after controlling for third variables that may give rise to both adolescent experiences and adult outcomes. For example, if socioeconomic status directly shapes adolescent romantic relationships and adult marriages, then adolescent relationships will be associated with adult marriages even if adolescent relationships have no causal influence on adult marriages after the effects of socioeconomic status are controlled.

Future research in this area must acknowledge this threat to causal inference and address it directly when possible. This is not an easy task. Even well-considered longitudinal research can never account for all potential third variables. Lacking the ability to randomly assign adolescents to different kinds of romantic experiences, the best that researchers can do is design studies that allow the largest number of confounding variables to be controlled. The Add Health study, for example, contains data from siblings within the same families. Comparing the relationship experiences of siblings goes a long way toward controlling for family of origin effects. The Add Health study also contains a subset of data from monozygotic and dizygotic twins. Analyses of these data have already examined genetic contributions to adolescent behaviors as diverse as alcohol and tobacco use, aggression, and sex-typed behaviors (Cleveland, 2003; Cleveland, Udry, and Chantala, 2001; Cleveland, Wiebe, and Rowe, 2005). There is every reason to expect genetic contributions to adolescent relationship outcomes as well; analyses of twin data would allow this contribution to be identified and the remaining effects of adolescent relationships on adult outcomes to be evaluated.

Describe how adolescent relationships function. Once evidence has accumulated to support causal links between adolescent experiences in romantic relationships and adult marital outcomes, designing effective interventions requires a clear understanding of the elements of adolescent relationships that account for their long-term impact. Available data on adolescent relationships tend to focus on the external features of those relationships, e.g., timing, duration, number of partners. Far less attention has been directed toward understanding processes within those relationships, e.g., relationship maintenance, conflict resolution, social support (Shulman, 2003). Particularly notable by their absence are data that capture adolescents' perspectives on what make their relationships worth maintaining, how they go about maintaining them, and how they decide whether to remain in them or leave them.

A deeper understanding of the day-to-day process of adolescent relationships would go far in informing interventions and curricula that connect directly to these processes. Addressing these issues may require methods that have yet to be employed in research on adolescent relationships, such as daily diary assessments or experience sampling approaches. Detailed assessments such as these, which have shown great value in research on adult marriage (e.g., Thompson and Bolger, 1999), may begin to describe how adolescents spend time with their partners, and how time spent with partners affects time spent on other activities, such as school, work, and family life (Furstenberg, 2000). These data in turn may point out how romantic relationships in adolescence affect marital and other outcomes in adulthood.

Strategies for Programs and Curricula Aimed at Adolescent Relationships

Regardless of the fact that the empirical foundation linking adolescent experiences to adult outcomes remains incomplete, it is reasonable to consider adolescents as targets of interventions designed to improve adult outcomes, as adolescence is characterized by transitions that pave the way for adulthood (Magdol et al., 1998). Indeed, the programs reviewed in Chapter Five are currently administering relationship education to adolescents as a means of promoting healthy marriage in adulthood. Although collectively these programs address a wide range of content, Chapter Five notes that existing curricula devote most of their attention to behavior in relationships and thoughts and feelings about relationships.

Expanding the focus of relationship education beyond romantic relationships themselves is warranted for several reasons. First, given the limited research on adolescent romantic relationships, many of these programs are forced to draw upon research conducted on married couples. It is not clear to what extent this research will generalize to adolescents, let alone the low-income adolescents that are the primary focus of current efforts. For example, relationship education programs developed for married couples emphasize skill-building within the marital relationship. Because adolescents may not be in relationships while participating in an education program and are likely to experience multiple relationships before they marry, programs targeting adolescents must aim to develop skills that generalize across relationships. Research on married couples does not offer much guidance about how well skills developed within a particular relationship are maintained in subsequent relationships.

Second, it is not even clear that participating in romantic relationships during adolescence is the best route to healthy adult marriages. For example, as has been noted in this report, early experience with romantic relationships is associated with substance abuse and behavioral problems (e.g., Aro and Taipale, 1987). Other research described in this report observes that students who have the highest levels of academic achievement are also those with the least experience with romantic relationships during adolescence (Halpern et al., 2000). As yet unpublished research by Madsen and Collins (as described in Shellenbarger, 2005) similarly observes that teens with fewer dating relationships during adolescence have a higher likelihood of experiencing healthy relationships in adulthood, compared to those with more dating relationships. Studies such as these serve as reminders that the associations between adolescent experiences in romantic relationships and adult experiences in marriage have not yet been fully described and may be complex.

Acknowledging this evolving empirical base offers two ways to strengthen existing programs targeting adolescent romantic relationships. First, the integrative framework proposed in Chapter Three, by mapping the range of possible content that relationship education curricula may contain, suggests dividing that content into three broad topics, illustrated by different sorts of questions:

1. *Antecedent conditions of relationships.* Where do our ideas about romantic relationships come from? Why are we attracted to the partners we are attracted to? Why do different people have different sorts of experiences in their relationships? How do family members, peers, and the media affect the way we approach relationships?
2. *Relationships in adolescence.* What is a romantic relationship, and what do we want from it? What makes a relationship satisfying and worthwhile? When is the right time for romantic relationships? What role should sex play in romantic relationships during adolescence? How are romantic relationships affected by the contexts in which they occur?
3. *Consequences of relationships for adult outcomes.* How do choices during adolescence affect development? What behaviors during adolescence predict healthy marriages in adulthood?

By drawing explicit links among all three topics, the integrative framework suggests that understanding each topic requires understanding the other topics also. Thus, programs and curricula targeting adolescents' relationships may be most effective to the extent that they are wide-ranging and comprehensive, taking each of these topics into account and acknowledging the ways that antecedents, correlates, and consequences of adolescent relationships may fit together. As the analyses in Chapter Five revealed, to date existing programs targeting adolescents have not been comprehensive or systematic in covering the full range of potentially relevant content. The checklist provided in Table 5.3 may prove a useful tool for evaluating the coverage of current and future programs in this area.

Second, beyond suggesting the range of potential content for relationship education curricula, the theories and research reviewed in this report also suggest specific strategies to address each of the three broad topics. Several of those strategies have been described throughout this report. In the rest of this section, to assist program developers, we repeat, add to, and elaborate upon these strategies, noting ways that interventions and programs might design curricula to address the full range of relevant content. The primary contribution here is not the strategies themselves because several existing curricula have described innovative ways of addressing some of these same topics. Rather, the primary contributions are the identification of crucial themes, i.e., the suggestion that a complete program will include content addressing each of these topics, and the fact that the specific strategies described here are explicitly connected to empirical research on adolescents.

Strategies Addressing Antecedent Conditions

Research and theory on the antecedents of adolescent romantic relationships indicate that beliefs, values, and habits developed in relationships with family members and friends are often continued and reinforced within romantic relationships (e.g., Collins and Sroufe, 1999). Relationship education curricula may seek to directly affect some of the sources of adolescents' thoughts and behaviors in romantic relationships, or, to the extent that some antecedent conditions are impossible for individuals to change (e.g., family history), these curricula might help adolescents recognize the impact that their backgrounds and personal histories have on their current relationships. Specific strategies include the following:

- *Relationships education should help adolescents identify and express their models and beliefs about romantic relationships.* The data summarized in Chapter Two indicate that, before they enter their first relationships, adolescents have well-developed models of what relationships are like and what they can expect from them. Because these models are likely to shape their choices and behaviors in their relationships, adolescents may benefit from the opportunity to examine their models explicitly. Many adolescents may take for granted that their own expectations for romantic relationships are the same as those of their peers, and they may be surprised to find that this is not always the case. Through free writing or group discussions, adolescents might be encouraged to articulate their assumptions about relationships and compare their assumptions with each other. A benefit of this strategy is that it is appropriate for adolescents at any age, regardless of whether or not they have experienced romantic relationships themselves. Some existing curricula already include activities of this sort, but the current framework suggests that they may be an essential first step in any relationship education program.
- *Adolescents might be directly encouraged to explore the sources of their models of relationships.* Although the studies summarized in Chapter Four reveal substantial continuity between adolescents' romantic relationships and their relationships with family members and friends, adolescents may not be aware of this continuity themselves. When asked to consider where their ideas about relationships come from, many adolescents may spontaneously look to their families of origin, relationships with peers, their cultural identity, or the media. Those who have already had experiences in romantic relationships may look to those. A facilitator might help adolescents to explore sources of continuity and discontinuity in their own ideas about relationships, and to identify patterns that they wish to continue and relationship habits they may wish to break.
- *Relationship education should include training in interacting effectively with parents, siblings, and friends.* Relationships with family members and peers are more than sources of values and habits. The studies reviewed in Chapter Four indicate that the nature of adolescents' social network is also associated with the timing of their entry into romantic relationships, as well as risk of substance abuse and behavioral problems (e.g., Pawlby , Mills, and Quinton, 1997). Targeting family and peer relationships directly may be a way of directing adolescents toward more optimal life paths, especially if programs could be targeted to adolescents whose family circumstances are already troubled. Several existing curricula already address communication skills that can be applied across a variety of interpersonal

situations. To the extent that skills training in adolescence is effective, and to the extent that those skills could be applied to existing relationships with family members and peers, the potential impact of such programs is great, especially because adolescents are likely to have the same family members in adulthood as they do in adolescence (something that cannot be said about adolescents' romantic relationship partners).

Strategies Addressing Relationships in Adolescence

As noted above, relationship education curricula devote most of their attention to topics directly related to the conduct of romantic relationships during adolescence, i.e., attitudes, beliefs, and behaviors. As noted in Chapter Five, adolescents are likely to benefit from a greater understanding of these topics and from gaining relevant skills. Yet the current framework also suggests that relationship education should acknowledge how the context external to a romantic relationship (e.g., the stresses that each partner faces, the resources and opportunities available to the couple, the physical environment) may affect how partners behave within the relationship. Examples of both types of strategies include the following:

- *Program facilitators can help adolescents understand how their models of relationships affect their behavior in their current and future relationships.* The research reported in Chapter Four suggests that ideas and beliefs about relationships may affect the way adolescents interact with their relationship partners. By making these effects explicit, adolescents may have opportunities to change or improve their own behaviors. This need not be tied directly into dry presentations of research findings, nor must it necessarily involve self-disclosure. For example, a facilitator might use a series of vignettes that describe individuals with different styles of attachment (e.g., "Tasha has never felt she could trust her partners completely," "Sanjay feels he can do pretty well on his own without romantic relationships") and then ask participants to discuss how those different individuals might respond to common interpersonal scenarios (e.g., "A friend made a date to have lunch with you at noon, but was 30 minutes late"). By examining how general ideas about relationships might affect specific behaviors in these scenarios, adolescents may come to see how their own behavior in specific relationships, and possible continuities between their experiences of relationships in different contexts, might be affected by their own assumptions and beliefs.
- *Adolescents can be encouraged to explore how their own behaviors affect how other people respond to them, reinforcing their modes of interacting with others (e.g., interactional continuity).* The lifespan developmental perspective summarized in Chapter Three highlights interactions with others as an important way that an individual's personality gets reinforced throughout the lifespan. Adolescents may benefit from the opportunity to attend to these processes and consider whether or not they value the traits and habits that their interactions with others reinforce. This need not involve personal disclosure. For example, adolescents might be encouraged to adopt a persona and then role-play an interaction with someone who does not know the persona that they have adopted. How does the naïve participant interact with someone who has adopted a shy persona? How are the same person's behaviors different when interacting with an aggressive persona? How

do the reactions of the naïve participant reinforce the personas that adolescents have adopted? By examining these questions in a neutral environment, adolescents may gain a clearer understanding of the sources of interactional continuity in their own lives.

- *Adolescents should be encouraged to appreciate how their own or a partner's behavior might be changed or constrained in different environments.* As discussed in Chapter Four, a common tendency in adolescents and adults is to view other people's behavior as a reflection of their personalities, overlooking the external forces that can affect what people say and do (Gilbert and Malone, 1995). Indeed, one of the most reliable findings in marital research is that spouses who appreciate the role that situations play in their interactions experience happier, more stable marriages (Bradbury and Fincham, 1990a; Karney and Bradbury, 2000). Adolescence is an appropriate time to begin learning this lesson. For example, adolescents might be asked to consider a couple trying to resolve a disagreement about money. Would it change the nature of their discussion if they were relatively affluent and discussing whether to remodel a room in the house, compared to if they were low-income and discussing how to pay the bills? Would it matter if the conversation took place on a weekday or a weekend? Whether or not young children are around? How would these scenarios play out differently in the context of a marriage versus other relationships? By drawing out the links between what happens inside relationships and what is going on outside of relationships, adolescents may better appreciate, and account for, the external forces that impact their experiences within their own relationships.
- *To address the environment of adolescent romantic relationships directly, relationship education should be offered in conjunction with or alongside programs aimed at improving adolescents' lives in other ways.* As noted in Chapter Four, negative experiences in romantic relationships are, for some adolescents, part of a constellation of problematic behaviors and circumstances that includes substance abuse and delinquency (e.g., Aro and Taipale, 1987). It therefore may not be possible or warranted to address relationship experiences separately from the broader contexts in which they occur. On the contrary, to the extent that problems with substance abuse or delinquency precede difficulties in romantic relationships, then interventions that directly target the problematic behaviors may improve adolescents' relationship experiences indirectly, and may provide environments conducive to expressing relationship skills. Any efforts to provide adolescents with greater opportunities for healthy development (e.g., job training or substance abuse prevention programs) may therefore provide a suitable arena for promoting healthy relationships as well.
- *Curricula that address safe sex and contraception must emphasize that using condoms does not indicate a lack of trust in a partner.* One of the troubling findings in Chapter Four is that, at least in some cases, adolescents become less vigilant about using condoms as their romantic relationships grow longer and more committed. To account for this association, some research finds that adolescents believe using condoms expresses a lack of faith in or commitment to their partners. The potential consequences of this belief (i.e., unwanted pregnancy and STDs) are so severe that it deserves to be addressed directly and refuted in relationship education curricula.
- *Relationship education must address beliefs about intimate partner violence directly.* The data reviewed in Chapter Four suggest that violence between dating partners is preva-

lent among adolescents, especially among adolescents who view aggressive behavior as appropriate. Both the behaviors and the beliefs warrant direct attention. Program leaders should create a neutral environment in which adolescents can express their attitudes and beliefs about violence between intimate partners, but they should also be exposed to data regarding the consequences of violence, in particular the fact that violence between spouses is one of the most powerful predictors of divorce (Rogge and Bradbury, 1999; Rogge et al., 2006).

Strategies Addressing the Consequences of Relationships for Adult Outcomes

Programs aimed at adolescents obviously cannot target adult outcomes directly. However, they can address the consequences of adolescent romantic relationships that are likely to have the greatest effect on adult outcomes, either by encouraging adolescents to consider the possible consequences of their choices and behaviors more carefully or by teaching skills that help adolescents to manage possible negative consequences of their relationships more effectively. Examples of both strategies include the following:

- *Relationship education can help adolescents to understand the ways that their behaviors and decisions in adolescence can affect their options in later life* (i.e., the implications of cumulative continuity). The lifespan developmental perspective summarized in Chapter Three suggests that experiences in adolescence may have consequences that accumulate over time to shape the options available to individuals during adulthood. To encourage consideration of these processes, adolescents might be guided in thinking about the potential outcomes of their decisions regarding romantic relationships, and about the sequence of consequences that might follow from those outcomes on into adulthood. For example, a group of participants might consider the possible immediate consequences of deciding not to enter into a relationship at all, and then the consequences of different sorts of decisions within relationships. It would be important to include the broadest possible range of potential outcomes in this sort of discussion and to include both positive and negative outcomes, so that all participants might identify with the possible paths being outlined. By drawing out these sequences, adolescents may come to appreciate the range of effects that their decisions about romantic relationships can have on their lives.
- *Relationship education should emphasize that successful marriages are an achievable goal for adults.* The data summarized in Chapter Two suggest that, although almost all adolescents value marriage in the abstract, many believe that successful marriages are out of reach for them personally, and this belief may be especially prevalent among low-income populations. To the extent that lack of hope for a successful marriage affects decision-making among low-income adolescents, they may benefit from exposure to the idea that successful marriages are achievable for everyone. The developers of the PREP program have recently developed a new program addressing these issues aimed at low-income adult women. To the extent that this program is shown to have an effect on the choices and outcomes of its target population, it is worth considering what a translation of this program for low-income adolescents might look like.

- *Especially for adolescents known to be at risk, relationship education programs should offer assistance in preventing or managing negative consequences of adolescent relationships.* In Chapter Two, the review of research describing adolescents' experiences in romantic relationships indicated that most adolescents experience a small number of romantic relationships that are relatively intense and relatively long-lasting. With respect to predicting the outcome of adult marriages, adolescent relationships may be most consequential for the minority of adolescents who have severely negative experiences in their relationships, such as pregnancy, sexual or physical violence, or harassment. Such experiences may be disruptive to educational and developmental trajectories, giving rise to adult circumstances that impede the formation and maintenance of healthy marriages. An alternative to offering relationship education for all adolescents would be to identify those who are vulnerable to negative experiences or those who have had negative experiences, and offer support directly to these youths to prevent or minimize the adverse cumulative consequences of negative events in their lives. Programs that combine relationship education with efforts to prevent teen pregnancy, substance abuse, or truancy, for example, should have the cumulative effect of promoting more favorable trajectories into adulthood and thus more favorable circumstances for eventual healthy marriages. To the extent that adolescents who have experienced teen pregnancy, problems with criminal behavior, or substance abuse can be assisted in gaining access to opportunities for recovery and advancement, these adolescents may have a better chance of maintaining healthy marriages in adulthood than they otherwise would have had.

Future Directions for Interventions Targeting Adolescent Relationships

The specific strategies described above are intended as guidelines for program developers seeking to design comprehensive relationship education curricula for adolescents. This final section of the report offers three more general recommendations for improving the focus and effectiveness of relationship education aimed at promoting healthy marriages by targeting adolescents.

Discuss Goals and Objectives of These Programs Explicitly

Although all current programs geared toward adolescents are generally designed to improve their lives, their specific goals and objectives are often left vague. As a result, it is not always clear what these programs are trying to accomplish. Some may prioritize improving romantic relationships during adolescence, others may focus on providing skills that lead to improved romantic relationships during adulthood (even if that means delaying or forgoing romantic relationships in adolescence). Some programs may seek to enhance all romantic relationships that adolescence may experience (including cohabitation and same-sex relationships), whereas others are aimed at promoting and supporting marriage in particular. Policymakers and others interested in services for adolescents as a means of promoting later healthy marriage should consider programs' stated goals as well as the implicit goals reflected in the programs' content. Program designers can strengthen their own programs and better inform policy decisions by making their programs' goals more clear.

Evaluate the Effectiveness of Existing Programs

In an atmosphere of limited resources, those resources should be directed toward programs that have demonstrated their ability to bring about desired changes. As noted in Chapter Five, the gold standard for demonstrating program effectiveness involves randomly assigning participants to receive either the program or a control treatment and then observing the outcomes. An even stronger design would include multiple groups, allowing comparisons among treatments that adopt different approaches. Massive experimental studies are currently under way to evaluate the effectiveness of programs to promote the formation of marriages among new unmarried parents (the Building Strong Families study) and programs to support married parents (the Supporting Healthy Marriages study). Rigorous evaluations of abstinence education programs are also under way. If policymakers remain committed to primary prevention of divorce during adolescence, especially within low-income populations, then a similar effort to evaluate programs targeting adolescent romantic relationships may be warranted.

Coordinate with Other Services Offered to Adolescents

Adolescents are the targets of many and varied programs designed to improve their lives, each of which tends to be developed, distributed, and administered by independent entities. A recurring theme in this chapter is that efforts to provide relationship education may be more effective to the extent that they are coordinated with programs that provide other services and programs to adolescents. By presenting relationship skills as a subset of the broad range of life skills that further adolescents' development into healthy adults, an integrated approach would offer benefits to program developers and to adolescents. From the perspective of program developers, coordinating with programs offering other skills and services would reduce the risk of duplicating efforts and would allow relationship education programs to capitalize on lessons learned in connecting with adolescents in other domains that have longer histories (e.g., drug abuse and pregnancy prevention). From the perspective of adolescents, presenting relationship education in the context of other programs would recognize and reinforce the idea that their experiences in romantic relationships are embedded in the broader trajectories of their lives. Acknowledging the other challenges that adolescents face may make relationship education itself more effective.

Conclusion

None of the alternative intervention strategies described here are mutually exclusive or incompatible with current relationship education programs and curricula. On the contrary, it seems likely that the programs most effective at promoting healthy adult marriages will be multifaceted, acknowledging that adolescents' experiences in romantic relationships, and the long-term consequences of those experiences, are woven into the broader fabric of their lives. Relationship education is likely to be one element in a repertoire of approaches. Reviewing the theory and evidence on the links between adolescence and later healthy marriage yields a number of ways that approaches to serving adolescents could be strengthened.

References

Abma, J. C., Martinez, G. M., Mosher, W. D., and Dawson, B. S. (2004). Teenagers in the United States: Sexual activity, contraceptive use and childbearing, 2002. *Vital Health Statistics, 23,* 58.

Adam, E. K., and Chase-Lansdale, P. L. (2002). Home sweet home(s): Parental separations, residential moves, and adjustment problems in low-income adolescent girls. *Developmental Psychology, 38,* 792–805.

Administration for Children and Families. (2005). *The Healthy Marriage Initiative (HMI).* Web site. As of May 6, 2007:
http://www.acf.hhs.gov/healthymarriage/about/program_planning.html#Connections

Ainsworth, M. D. S., Blehar, M. C., Waters, E., and Wall, S. (1978). *Patterns of Attachment: A Psychological Study of the Strange Situation.* Hillsdale, N.J.: Lawrence Erlbaum Associates.

Ainsworth, M. S. (1989). Attachments beyond infancy. *American Psychologist, 44,* 709–716.

Albert, B. (2004). *With One Voice 2004: America's Adults and Teens Sound Out About Teen Pregnancy. An Annual Survey.* Washington, D.C.: The National Campaign to Prevent Teen Pregnancy.

Amato, P. R. (1996). Explaining the intergenerational transmission of divorce. *Journal of Marriage and the Family, 58,* 628–640.

Amato, P. R. (2001). Children of divorce in the 1990s: An update of the Amato and Keith (1991) meta-analysis. *Journal of Family Psychology, 15,* 355–370.

Amato, P. R., and Booth, A. (2001). The legacy of parents' marital discord: Consequences for children's marital quality. *Journal of Personality and Social Psychology, 81,* 627–638.

Amato, P. R., and DeBoer, D. D. (2001). The transmission of marital instability across generations: Relationship skills or commitment to marriage? *Journal of Marriage and the Family, 63,* 1038–1051.

Amato, P. R., Johnson, D. R., Booth, A., and Rogers, S. J. (2003). Continuity and change in marital quality between 1980 and 2000. *Journal of Marriage and the Family, 65,* 1–22.

Anderson, D. A. (1993). Lesbian and gay adolescents: Social and developmental considerations. *High School Journal, 77,* 13–19.

Andrews, J. A., Foster, S. L., Capaldi, D., and Hops, H. (2000). Adolescent and family predictors of physical aggression, communication, and satisfaction in young adult couples: A prospective analysis. *Journal of Consulting and Clinical Psychology, 68,* 195–208.

Aro, H., and Taipale, V. (1987). The impact of timing of puberty on psychosomatic symptoms among fourteen- to sixteen-year-old Finnish girls. *Child Development, 58,* 261–268.

Bachman, J. G., Wadsworth, K. N., O'Malley, P. M., Schulenberg, J., et al. (1997). Marriage, divorce, and parenthood during the transition to young adulthood: Impacts on drug use and abuse. In J. Schulenberg, J. L. Maggs, and K. Hurrelmann (eds.), *Health Risks and Developmental Transitions During Adolescence* (pp. 246–279). New York: Cambridge University Press.

Bachrach, C. A. (1998). The changing circumstances of marriage and fertility in the United States. In R. Moffitt (ed.), *Welfare, the Family, and Reproductive Behavior: Research Perspectives* (pp. 9–32). Washington, D.C.: National Academy Press.

Baltes, P. B. (1987). Theoretical propositions of life-span developmental psychology: On the dynamics between growth and decline. *Developmental Psychology, 23,* 611–626.

Bandura, A. (1994). Social cognitive theory of mass communication. In J. Bryant and D. Zillman (eds.), *Media Effects: Advances in Theory and Research.* Hillsdale, N.J.: Lawrence Erlbaum Associates.

Barber, B. L. (2006). To have loved and lost . . . Adolescent romantic relationships and rejection. In A. C. Crouter and A. Booth (eds.), *Romance and Sex in Adolescence and Emerging Adulthood: Risks and Opportunities* (pp. 29–40). Mahwah, N.J.: Lawrence Erlbaum Associates.

Barber, B. L., and Eccles, J. S. (2003). The joy of romance: Healthy adolescent relationships as an educational agenda. In P. Florsheim (ed.), *Adolescent Romantic Relations and Sexual Behavior: Theory, Research, and Practical Implications* (pp. 355–370). Mahwah, N.J.: Lawrence Erlbaum Associates.

Beach, S. R. H. (2001). *Marital and Family Processes in Depression: A Scientific Foundation for Practice.* Washington, D.C.: American Psychological Association.

Bearman, P. S., Moody, J., and Stovel, K. (2004). Chains of affection: The structure of adolescent romantic and sexual networks. *American Journal of Sociology, 110,* 44–91.

Bell, L. G., and Bell, D. C. (2005). Family dynamics in adolescence affect midlife well-being. *Journal of Family Psychology, 19,* 198–207.

Benson, M. J., Larson, J., Wilson, S. M., and Demo, D. H. (1993). Family of origin influences on late adolescent romantic relationships. *Journal of Marriage and the Family,* 55, 663–672.

Billy, J. O., and Udry, J. R. (1985). Patterns of adolescent friendship and effects on sexual behavior. *Social Psychology Quarterly, 48,* 27–41.

Bissell, M. (2000). Socio-economic outcomes of teen pregnancy and parenthood: A review of the literature. *Canadian Journal of Human Sexuality, 9,* 191–204.

Black, M., Noonan, R., Legg, M., Eaton, D., and Breiding, M. (2006). Physical dating violence among high school students—United States, 2003. *MMWR Weekly, 55,* 532–535.

Blakely, C., Mayer, J., Gottschalk, R., Schmitt, N., Davidson, W., Roitman, D., et al. (1987). The fidelity-adaptation debate: Implications for the implementation of public sector social programs. *American Journal of Community Psychology, 15,* 253–268.

Blum, R. W., Beuhring, T., and Rinehart, P. M. (2000). *Protecting Teens: Beyond Race, Income, and Family Structure.* Minneapolis, Minn.: Center for Adolescent Health, University of Minnesota.

Bodilly, S. J., and Beckett, M. (2005). *Making Out-of-School-Time Matter: Evidence for an Action Agenda.* Santa Monica, Calif.: RAND Corporation. As of May 5, 2007: http://www.rand.org/pubs/monographs/MG242/

Bonell, C. (2004). Why is teenage pregnancy conceptualized as a social problem? A review of quantitative research from the USA and UK. *Culture, Health and Sexuality, 6,* 255–272.

Boston University School of Education. (1993). *The Art of Loving Well.* As of May 7, 2007: http://www.bu.edu/education/lovingwell/

Bouchey, H. A., and Furman, W. (2003). Dating and romantic experiences in adolescence. In G. R. Adams and M. D. Berzonsky (eds.), *Blackwell Handbook of Adolescence* (pp. 313–329). Malden, Mass.: Blackwell Publishing.

Bowlby, J. (1969). *Attachment and Loss.* Volume I. *Attachment.* New York: Basic Books.

Bowlby, J. (1973). *Attachment and Loss.* Volume II. *Separation: Anxiety and Anger.* New York: Basic Books.

Bowlby, J. (1980). *Attachment and Loss.* Volume III. *Loss: Sadness and Depression.* New York: Basic Books.

Bradbury, T. N., and Fincham, F. D. (1990a). Attributions in marriage: Review and critique. *Psychological Bulletin, 107,* 3–33.

Bradbury, T. N., and Fincham, F. D. (1990b). Preventing marital dysfunction: Review and analysis. In F. D. Fincham and T. N. Bradbury (eds.), *The Psychology of Marriage* (pp. 375–401). New York: Guilford.

Bramlett, M. D., and Mosher, W. D. (2002). *Cohabitation, Marriage, Divorce, and Remarriage in the United States* (Vital and Health Statistics, Series 23, Number 22). Hyattsville, Md.: National Center for Health Statistics.

Brehm, S. S. (1985). *Intimate Relationships.* New York: Random House.

Brewin, C. R., Andrews, B., and Gotlib, I. H. (1993). Psychopathology and early experience: A reappraisal of retrospective reports. *Psychological Bulletin, 113,* 82–98.

Brooks-Gunn, J., and Paikoff, R. (1997). Sexuality and developmental transitions during adolescence. In J. Schulenberg, J. L. Maggs, and K. Hurrelmann (eds.), *Health Risks and Developmental Transitions During Adolescence* (pp. 190–219). New York: Cambridge University Press.

Brooks-Gunn, J., Petersen, A. C., and Eichorn, D. (1985). The study of maturational timing effects in adolescence. *Journal of Youth and Adolescence, 14,* 149–161.

Brown, B. B. (1999). "You're going out with who?" Peer group influences on adolescent romantic relationships. In W. Furman, B. B. Brown, and C. Feiring (eds.), *The Development of Romantic Relationships in Adolescence* (pp. 291–329). New York: Cambridge University Press.

Brown, B. B. (2006). A few "course corrections" to Collins and Van Dulmen's "The course of true love." In A. C. Crouter and A. Booth (eds.), *Romance and Sex in Adolescence and Emerging Adulthood: Risks and Opportunities* (pp. 113–123). Mahwah, N.J.: Lawrence Erlbaum Associates.

Brown, B. B., Feiring, C., and Furman, W. (1999). Missing the love boat: Why researchers have shied away from adolescent romance. In W. Furman, B. B. Brown, and C. Feiring (eds.), *The Development of Romantic Relationships in Adolescence* (pp. 1–16). New York: Cambridge University Press.

Brown, J. D., L'Engle, K. L., Pardun, C. J., Guo, G., Kenneavy, K., and Jackson, C. (2006). Sexy media matter: exposure to sexual content in music, movies, television, and magazines predicts black and white adolescents' sexual behavior. *Pediatrics, 117,* 1018–1027.

Brown, S. L. (2000). Union transitions among cohabitors: The significance of relationship assessments and expectations. *Journal of Marriage and the Family, 62,* 833–846.

Bryant, C. M. (2006). Pathways linking early experiences and later relationship functioning. In A. C. Crouter and A. Booth (eds.), *Romance and Sex in Adolescence and Emerging Adulthood: Risks and Opportunities* (pp. 103–111). Mahwah, N.J.: Lawrence Erlbaum Associates.

Bryant, C. M., and Conger, R. D. (2002). An intergenerational model of romantic relationship development. In A. L. Vangelisti and H. T. Reis (eds.), *Stability and Change in Relationships* (pp. 57–82). New York: Cambridge University Press.

Bryant, J. (1985). *Frequency of Exposure, Age of Initial Exposure and Reactions to Initial Exposure to Pornography.* Hillsdale, N.J.: Lawrence Erlbaum Associates.

Bulcroft, R. A., and Bulcroft, K. A. (1993). Race differences in attitudinal and motivational factors in the decisions to marry. *Journal of Marriage and the Family, 55,* 338–355.

Bumpass, L., and Lu, H. H. (2000). Trends in cohabitation and implications for children's family contexts in the United States. *Population Studies, 54,* 29–41.

Bumpass, L. L., Sweet, J. A., and Cherlin, A. (1991). The role of cohabitation in declining rates of marriage. *Journal of Marriage and the Family, 53,* 913–927.

Burton, L. (1995). *Family Structure and Nonmarital Fertility: Perspectives from Ethnographic Research. Report to Congress on Out-of-Wedlock Childbearing.* Hyattsville, Md.: U.S. Department of Health and Human Services.

Butler, J. T. (1997). *Principles of Health Education and Health Promotion* (2nd ed.). Englewood, Colo.: Morton Publishing Company.

Cantor, M. G. (1990). Prime-time fathers: A study in continuity and change. *Critical Studies in Mass Communication, 7,* 275–285.

Capaldi, D. M., and Clark, S. (1998). Prospective family predictors of aggression toward female partners for at-risk young men. *Developmental Psychology, 34,* 1175–1188.

Capaldi, D. M., Dishion, T. J., Stoolmiller, M., and Yoerger, K. (2001). Aggression toward female partners by at-risk young men: The contribution of male adolescent friendships. *Developmental Psychology, 37,* 61–73.

Capaldi, D. M., and Gorman-Smith, D. (2003). The development of aggression in young male/female couples. In P. Florsheim (ed.), *Adolescent Romantic Relations and Sexual Behavior: Theory, Research, and Practical Implications* (pp. 243–278). Mahwah, N.J.: Lawrence Erlbaum Associates.

Capaldi, D. M., and Patterson, G. R. (1987). An approach to the problem of recruitment and retention rates for longitudinal research. *Behavioral Assessment, 9,* 169–177.

Card, J. J. (1999). Teen pregnancy prevention: Do any programs work? *Annual Review of Public Health, 20,* 257–285.

Carlson, E. A., Sroufe, L. A., and Egeland, B. (2004). The construction of experience: A longitudinal study of representation and behavior. *Child Development, 75,* 66–83.

Carroll, J. S., and Doherty, W. J. (2003). Evaluating the effectiveness of premarital prevention programs: A meta-analytic review of outcome research. *Family Relations, 52,* 105–118.

Carver, K. P., Joyner, K., and Udry, J. R. (2003). National estimates of adolescent romantic relationships. In P. Florsheim (ed.), *Adolescent Romantic Relations and Sexual Behavior: Theory, Research, and Practical Implications* (pp. 23–56). Mahwah, N.J.: Lawrence Erlbaum Associates.

Carver, K. P., and Udry, J. R. (1997, March). *Reciprocity in the Identification of Adolescent Romantic Partners.* Paper presented at the Population Association of America, Washington, D.C.

Caspi, A. (1987). Personality in the life course. *Journal of Personality and Social Psychology, 53,* 1203–1213.

Caspi, A., Bem, D. J., and Elder, G. H. (1989). Continuities and consequences of interactional styles across the life course. *Journal of Personality, 57,* 375–406.

Caspi, A., Elder, G. H., and Bem, D. J. (1987). Moving against the world: Life-course patterns of explosive children. *Developmental Psychology, 23,* 308–313.

Caspi, A., Elder, G. H., Jr., and Bem, D. J. (1988). Moving away from the world: Life-course patterns of shy children. *Developmental Psychology, 24,* 824–831.

Caspi, A., Lynam, D., Moffitt, T. E., and Silva, P. A. (1993). Unraveling girls' delinquency: Biological, dispositional, and contextual contributions to adolescent misbehavior. *Developmental Psychology, 29,* 19–30.

Cauffman, E., and Steinberg, L. (1996). Interactive effects of menarcheal status and dating on dieting and disordered eating among adolescent girls. *Developmental Psychology, 32,* 631–635.

Cavanagh, S. (2004). The sexual debut of girls in early adolescence: The intersection of race, pubertal timing, and friendship group characteristics. *Journal of Research on Adolescence, 14,* 285–312.

Ceci, S. J., and Hembrooke, H. A. (1995). A bioecological model of intellectual development. In P. Moen, G. H. Elder and K. Lüscher (eds.), *Examining Lives in Context: Perspectives on the Ecology of Human Development* (pp. 303–345): Washington, D.C.: APA Books.

Center for Substance Abuse Prevention. (2002). *Finding the Balance. Program Fidelity and Adaptation in Substance Abuse Prevention* (June 2001 Conference Edition). Rockville, Md.: Center for Substance Abuse Prevention.

Cherlin, A. J. (1988). *The Changing American Family and Public Policy.* Washington D.C.: Urban Institute Press.

Cherlin, A. J. (1992). *Marriage, Divorce, Remarriage* (2nd ed.). Cambridge, Mass.: Harvard University Press.

Cherlin, A. J. (2004). The deinstitutionalization of American marriage. *Journal of Marriage and the Family, 66,* 848–861.

Cherlin, A. J. (2005). American marriage in the early 21st century. *The Future of Children, 15,* 33–56.

Cherlin, A. J., Burton, L. M., Hurt, T. R., and Purvin, D. M. (2004). The influence of physical and sexual abuse on marriage and cohabitation. *American Sociological Review,* 69, 768–789.

Child Trends. (2006). Dating. As of June 1, 2006:
http://www.childtrendsdatabank.org/indicators/73Dating.cfm

Chinman, M., Imm, P., and Wandersman, A. (2003). *Getting to Outcomes 2004: Promoting Accountability Through Methods and Tools for Planning, Implementation, and Evaluation.* Santa Monica, Calif.: RAND Corporation, TR-101-CDC. As of May 6, 2007:
http://www.rand.org/pubs/technical_reports/TR101/

Cleveland, H. H. (2003). Disadvantaged neighborhoods and adolescent aggression: Behavioral genetic evidence of contextual effects. *Journal of Research on Adolescence, 13,* 211–238.

Cleveland, H. H., Udry, J. R., and Chantala, K. E. (2001). Environmental and genetic influences on sex-typed behaviors and attitudes of male and female adolescents. *Personality and Social Psychology Bulletin, 27,* 1587–1598.

Cleveland, H. H., Wiebe, R. P., and Rowe, D. C. (2005). Sources of exposure to smoking and drinking friends among adolescents: A behavioral-genetic evaluation. *Journal of Genetic Psychology, 166,* 153–169.

CNN. (February 27, 2002). Bush welfare plan promotes marriage, work. As of August 22, 2005:
http://archives.cnn.com/2002/ALLPOLITICS/02/26/welfare.reform/index.html

Coalition for Marriage, Family and Couples Education (undated). Smart Marriages Web site. As of May 6, 2007:
http://www.smartmarriages.com/

Coates, D. L. (1999). The cultured and culturing aspects of romantic experience in adolescence. In W. Furman, B. B. Brown, and C. Feiring (eds.), *The Development of Romantic Relationships in Adolescence* (pp. 330–363). New York: Cambridge University Press.

Coley, R. L., and Chase-Lansdale, P. L. (1998). Adolescent pregnancy and parenthood recent evidence and future directions. *American Psychologist, 53,* 152–166.

Collins, R. L., Elliott, M. N., Gerry, S. H., Kanouse, D. E., Kunkel, D., Hunter, S. B., et al. (2004). Watching sex on television predicts adolescent initiation of sexual behavior. *Pediatrics, 114,* e280–e289.

Collins, W. A. (1997). Relationships and development during adolescence: Interpersonal adaptation to individual change. *Personal Relationships, 4,* 1–14.

Collins, W. A. (2003). More than myth: The developmental significance of romantic relationships during adolescence. *Journal of Research on Adolescence, 13,* 1–24.

Collins, W. A., Hennighausen, K. C., Schmit, D. T., and Sroufe, L. A. (1997). Developmental precursors of romantic relationships: A longitudinal analysis. In S. Shulman and W. A. Collins (eds.), *Romantic Relationships in Adolescence: Developmental Perspectives* (pp. 69–84). San Francisco, Calif.: Jossey-Bass.

Collins, W. A., and Madsen, S. D. (2006). Close relationships in adolescence and early adulthood. In D. Perlman and A. Vangelisti (eds.), *Handbook of Personal Relationships* (pp. 191–209). New York: Cambridge University Press.

Collins, W. A., and Sroufe, L. A. (1999). Capacity for intimate relationships: A developmental construction. In W. Furman, B. B. Brown and C. Feiring (eds.), *The Development of Romantic Relationships in Adolescence* (pp. 125–147). New York: Cambridge University Press.

Collins, W. A., and Van Dulmen, M. (2006). "The course of True Love(s). . . .": Origins and pathways in the development of romantic relationships. In A. C. Crouter and A. Booth (eds.), *Romance and Sex in Adolescence and Emerging Adulthood: Risks and Opportunities* (pp. 63–86). Mahwah, N.J.: Lawrence Erlbaum Associates.

Comstock, J., and Strzyzewski, K. (1990). Interpersonal interaction on television: Family conflict and jealousy on primetime. *Journal of Broadcasting and Electronic Media, 34,* 263–282.

Conger, R. D., Cui, M., Bryant, C. M., and Elder, G. H. J. (2000). Competence in early adult romantic relationships: A developmental perspective on family influences. *Journal of Personality and Social Psychology, 79,* 224–237.

Connolly, J., Furman, W., and Konarski, R. (2000). The role of peers in the emergence of heterosexual romantic relationships in adolescence. *Child Development, 71,* 1395–1408.

Connolly, J. A., Craig, W., Goldberg, A., and Pepler, D. (1999). Conceptions of cross-sex friendships and romantic relationships in early adolescence. *Journal of Youth and Adolescence, 28,* 481–494.

Connolly, J. A., Craig, W., Goldberg, A., and Pepler, D. (2004). Mixed-gender groups, dating, and romantic relationships in early adolescence. *Journal of Research on Adolescence, 14,* 185–207.

Connolly, J. A., and Goldberg, A. (1999). Romantic relationships in adolescence: The role of friends and peers in their emergence and development. In W. Furman, B. B. Brown, and C. Feiring (eds.), *The Development of Romantic Relationships in Adolescence* (pp. 266–290). New York: Cambridge University Press.

Connolly, J. A., and Johnson, A. (1996). Adolescents' romantic relationships and the structure and quality of their close interpersonal ties. *Personal Relationships, 2,* 185–195.

Connolly, J. A., and Konarski, R. (1994). Peer self-concept in adolescence: Analysis of factor structure and of associations with peer experience. *Journal of Research on Adolescence, 4,* 385–403.

Connolly, J. A., Pepler, D., Craig, W., and Taradash, A. (2000). Dating experiences of bullies in early adolescence. *Child Maltreatment: Journal of the American Professional Society on the Abuse of Children, 5,* 299–310.

Cook, B. (2004). *Choosing the Best Soul Mate: A Relationship and Abstinence Curriculum.* Atlanta, Ga.: Choosing the Best Publishing. As of May 6, 2007:
http://www.choosingthebest.org/curriculum/abstinence_education_4.html

Cooksey, E. C., Mott, F. L., and Neubauer, S. A. (2002). Friendships and early relationships: Links to sexual initiation among American adolescents born to young mothers. *Perspectives on Sexual and Reproductive Health, 34,* 118–126.

Crouter, A. C., and Booth, A. (2006). *Romance and Sex in Adolescence and Emerging Adulthood: Risks and Opportunities.* Mahwah, N.J.: Lawrence Erlbaum Associates.

D'Augelli, A. (1988). The adolescent closet: Promoting the development of the lesbian or gay male teenager. *The School Psychologist, 42,* 2–3.

Darling, N., Dowdy, B. B., Van Horn, M. L., and Caldwell, L. L. (1999). Mixed-sex settings and the perception of competence. *Journal of Youth and Adolescence, 28,* 461–480.

Dash, L. (2003). *When Children Want Children: The Urban Crisis of Teenage Childbearing.* Urbana-Champaign, Ill.: University of Illinois Press.

Deficit Reduction Act of 2005, P.L. No. 109-171, Section 7103 (2006).

Department of Health and Human Services. (2006). Community Based Abstinence Education Program announcement. As of July 3, 2006: http://www.acf.hhs.gov/grants/open/HHS-2006-ACF-ACYF-AE-0099.html

Diamond, L. M. (2003). Love matters: Romantic relationships among sexual-minority adolescents. In P. Florsheim (ed.), *Adolescent Romantic Relations and Sexual Behavior: Theory, Research, and Practical Implications* (pp. 85–107). Mahwah, N.J.: Lawrence Erlbaum Associates.

Diamond, L. M., Savin-Williams, R. C., and Dubé, E. M. (1999). Sex, dating, passionate friendships, and romance: Intimate peer relations among lesbian, gay, and bisexual adolescents. In W. Furman, B. B. Brown, and C. Feiring (eds.), *The Development of Romantic Relationships in Adolescence* (pp. 175–210). New York: Cambridge University Press.

Dibble Fund (2007). Relationship Skills for Teens. Web site. As of May 6, 2007: http://www.dibblefund.org

DiIorio, C., Pluhar, E., and Belcher, L. (2003). Parent-child communication about sexuality: A review of the literature from 1980–2002. *Journal of HIV/AIDS Prevention and Education for Adolescents and Children, 5,* 7–32.

Doljanac, R. F., and Zimmerman, M. A. (1998). Psychosocial factors and high-risk sexual behavior: Race differences among urban adolescents. *Journal of Behavioral Medicine, 21,* 451–467.

Dornbusch, S. M., Carlsmith, J. M., Gross, R. T., Martin, J. A., Jennings, D., Rosenberg, A., and Duke, P. (1981). Sexual development, age, and dating: A comparison of biological and social influences upon one set of behaviors. *Child Development, 52,* 179–185.

Douvan, E., and Adelson, J. (1966). *The Adolescent Experience.* New York: Wiley.

East, P. L. (1998). Racial and ethnic differences in girls' sexual, marital and birth expectations. *Journal of Marriage and the Family, 6,* 150–162.

Eaton, D., Kann, L., Kinchen, S., Ross, J., Hawkins, J., Harris, W., Lowry, R., McManus, T., Chyen, D., Shanklin, S., Lim, C., Grunbaum, J., and Wechsler, H. (2006). Youth risk behavior surveillance—United States, 2005. *MMWR Surveillance Summaries, 55,* 1–108.

Eccles, J., and Gootman, J. A. (eds.). (2002). *Community Programs to Promote Youth Development.* Washington, D.C.: National Academy of Sciences.

Edin, K. (2000). What do low-income single mothers say about marriage? *Social Problems, 47,* 112–133.

Edin, K., and Reed, J. M. (2005). Why don't they just get married? Barriers to marriage among the disadvantaged. *The Future of Children, 15,* 117–138.

Elder, G. H., Pavalko, E. K., and Hastings, T. J. (1991). Talent, history, and the fulfillment of promise. *Psychiatry, 54,* 251–267.

Elwood, D. T., and Jencks, C. (2004). The uneven spread of single-parent families: What do we know? What do we need to know? Where do we look for answers? In K. M. Neckerman (ed.), *Social Inequality* (pp. 3–118). New York: Russell Sage Foundation.

Erikson, E. H. (1968). *Identity, Youth, and Crisis.* New York: Norton.

Eyre, S. L., Auerswald, C., Hoffman, V., and Millstein, S. G. (1998). Fidelity management: African-American adolescents' attempts to control the sexual behavior of their partners. *Journal of Health Psychology Qualitative Research, 3,* 393–406.

Feeney, J. A., Noller, P., and Patty, J. (1993). Adolescents' interactions with the opposite sex: Influence of attachment style and gender. *Journal of Adolescence, 16,* 169–186.

Fein, D. J. (2004). *Married and Poor: Basic Characteristics of Economically Disadvantaged Married Couples in the U.S. Supporting Healthy Marriage Evaluation,* Working Paper SHM-01. Cambridge, Mass.: Abt Associates.

Fein, D. J., Burstein, N. R., Fein, G. G., and Lindberg, L. D. (2003). *The Determinants of Marriage and Cohabitation Among Disadvantaged Americans: Research Findings and Needs.* Cambridge, Mass.: Abt Associates.

Feinstein, S. C., and Ardon, M. S. (1973). Trends in dating patterns and adolescent development. *Journal of Youth and Adolescence, 2,* 157–166.

Feiring, C. (1996). Learning the ways of romance. *Journal of Research on Adolescence, 6,* 181–200.

Feiring, C. (1999a). Gender identity and the development of romantic relationships in adolescence. In W. Furman, B. B. Brown, and C. Feiring (eds.), *The Development of Romantic Relationships in Adolescence* (pp. 211–232). New York: Cambridge University Press.

Feiring, C. (1999b). Other-sex friendship networks and the development of romantic relationships in adolescence. *Journal of Youth and Adolescence, 28,* 495–512.

Feiring, C., Deblinger, E., Hoch-Espada, A., and Haworth, T. (2002). Romantic relationship aggression and attitudes in high school students: The role of gender, grade, and attachment and emotional styles. *Journal of Youth and Adolescence, 31,* 373–385.

Feldman, S. S., and Gowen, L. K. (1998). Conflict negotiation tactics in romantic relationships in high school students. *Journal of Youth and Adolescence, 27,* 691–717.

Feldman, S. S., Gowen, L. K., and Fisher, L. (1998). Family relationships and gender as predictors of romantic intimacy in young adults: A longitudinal study. *Journal of Research on Adolescence, 8,* 263–286.

Feldman, S. S., Turner, R. A., and Araujo, K. (1999). Interpersonal context as an influence on sexual timetables of youths: Gender and ethnic effects. *Journal of Research on Adolescence, 9,* 25–52.

Fincham, F. D., and Bradbury, T. N. (1987). The assessment of marital quality: A reevaluation. *Journal of Marriage and the Family, 49,* 797–809.

Flanagan, A. S., and Furman, W. C. (2000). Sexual victimization and perceptions of close relationships in adolescence. *Child Maltreatment, 5,* 350–359.

Flanigan, C., Huffman, R., and Smith, J. (2005). Science says: Teens' attitudes toward marriage, cohabitation and divorce, 2002. *National Campaign to Prevent Teen Pregnancy, 16.*

Florsheim, P. (2003a). Adolescent romantic and sexual behavior: What we know and where we go from here. In P. Florsheim (ed.), *Adolescent Romantic Relations and Sexual Behavior: Theory, Research, and Practical Implications* (pp. 371–385). Mahwah, N.J.: Lawrence Erlbaum Associates.

Florsheim, P. (ed.). (2003b). *Adolescent Romantic Relations and Sexual Behavior: Theory, Research, and Practical Implications.* Mahwah, N.J.: Lawrence Erlbaum Associates.

Flouri, E., and Buchanan, A. (2002). What predicts good relationships with parents in adolescence and partners in adult life? Findings from the 1958 British birth cohort. *Journal of Family Psychology, 16,* 186–198.

Ford, K., Sohn, W., and Lepkowski, J. (2001). Characteristics of adolescents' sexual partners and their association with use of condoms and other contraceptive methods. *Family Planning Perspectives, 33,* 100–105, 132.

Fortenberry, J. D., Tu, W., Harezlak, J., Katz, B. P., and Orr, D. P. (2002). Condom use as a function of time in new and established adolescent sexual relationships. *American Journal of Public Health, 92,* 211–213.

Franzoi, S. L., Davis, M. H., and Vasquez-Suson, K. A. (1994). Two social worlds: Social correlates and stability of adolescent status groups. *Journal of Personality and Social Psychology, 67,* 462–473.

Furman, W. (1984). Some observations on the study of personal relationships. In J. C. Masters and K. Yarkin-Levin (eds.), *Boundary Areas in Social and Developmental Psychology* (pp. 15–42). Orlando, Fla.: Academic Press.

Furman, W. (1999). Friends and lovers: The role of peer relationships in adolescent romantic relationships. In W. A. Collins and B. Laursen (eds.), *Relationships as Developmental Contexts* (pp. 133–154). Mahwah, N.J.: Lawrence Erlbaum Associates.

Furman, W., Brown, B. B., and Feiring, C. (eds.). (1999). *The Development of Romantic Relationships in Adolescence.* New York: Cambridge University Press.

Furman, W., and Buhrmester, D. (1992). Age and sex differences in perceptions of networks of personal relationships. *Child Development, 63,* 103–115.

Furman, W., Feiring, C., and Brown, B. B. (1999). Love is a many-splendored thing: Next steps for theory and research. In W. Furman, B. B. Brown, and C. Feiring (eds.), *The Development of Romantic Relationships in Adolescence* (pp. 399–414). New York: Cambridge University Press.

Furman, W., and Flanagan, A. S. (1997). The influence of earlier relationships on marriage: An attachment perspective. In W. K. Halford and H. J. Markman (eds.), *Clinical Handbook of Marriage and Couples Interventions* (pp. 179–202). Hoboken, N.J.: John Wiley and Sons, Inc.

Furman, W., and Hand, L. S. (2006). The slippery nature of romantic relationships: Issues in definition and differentiation. In A. C. Crouter and A. Booth (eds.), *Romance and Sex in Adolescence and Emerging Adulthood: Risks and Opportunities* (pp. 171–178). Mahwah, N.J.: Lawrence Erlbaum Associates.

Furman, W., and Shaffer, L. (2003). The role of romantic relationships in adolescent development. In P. Florsheim (ed.), *Adolescent Romantic Relations and Sexual Behavior: Theory, Research, and Practical Implications* (pp. 3–22). Mahwah, N.J.: Lawrence Erlbaum Associates.

Furman, W., and Simon, V. A. (1999). Cognitive representations of adolescent romantic relationships. In W. Furman, B. B. Brown, and C. Feiring (eds.), *The Development of Romantic Relationships in Adolescence* (pp. 75–98). New York: Cambridge University Press.

Furman, W., Simon, V. A., Shaffer, L., and Bouchey, H. A. (2002). Adolescents' working models and styles for relationships with parents, friends, and romantic partners. *Child Development, 73,* 241–255.

Furman, W., and Wehner, E. A. (1994). Romantic views: Toward a theory of adolescent romantic relationships. In R. Montemayor, G. R. Adams, and T. P. Gullotta (eds.), *Personal Relationships During Adolescence* (pp. 168–195). Thousand Oaks, Calif.: Sage Publications, Inc.

Furman, W., and Wehner, E. A. (1997). Adolescent romantic relationships: A developmental perspective. In S. Shulman and W. A. Collins (eds.), *Romantic Relationships in Adolescence: Developmental Perspectives* (pp. 21–36). San Francisco, CA: Jossey-Bass.

Furstenberg, F. F. (1976). Premarital pregnancy and marital instability. *Journal of Social Issues, 32,* 67–86.

Furstenberg, F. F. (1979). Premarital pregnancy and marital instability. In G. Levinger and O. C. Moles (eds.), *Divorce and Separation: Context, Causes, and Consequences* (pp. 83–98). New York: Basic Books.

Furstenberg, F. F. (1980). Burdens and benefits: The impact of early childbearing on the family. *Journal of Social Issues, 36,* 64–87.

Furstenberg, F. F. (1995). Fathering in the inner city: Paternal participation and public policy. In W. Marsiglio (ed.), *Fatherhood: Contemporary Theory, Research, and Social Policy.* Thousand Oaks, Calif.: Sage Publications, Inc.

Furstenberg, F. F. (2000). The sociology of adolescence and youth in the 1990s: A critical commentary. *Journal of Marriage and the Family, 62,* 896–910.

Furstenberg, F. F., Brooks-Gunn, J., and Chase-Lansdale, L. (1989). Teenaged pregnancy and childbearing. *American Psychologist, 44,* 313–320.

Furstenberg, F. F., Jr., Brooks-Gunn, J., and Morgan, S. P. (1987). *Adolescent Mothers in Later Life.* New York: Cambridge University Press.

Galliher, R. V., Rostosky, S. S., Welsh, D. P., and Kawaguchi, M. C. (1999). Power and psychological well-being in late adolescent romantic relationships. *Sex Roles, 40,* 689–710.

Galliher, R. V., Welsh, D. P., Rostosky, S. S., and Kawaguchi, M. C. (2004). Interaction and relationship quality in late adolescent romantic couples. *Journal of Social and Personal Relationships, 21,* 203–216.

Galotti, K. M., Kozberg, S. F., and Appleman, D. (1990). Younger and older adolescents' thinking about commitments. *Journal of Experimental Child Psychology, 50,* 324–339.

Gardner, S. (2001). Evaluation of the Connections: Relationships and Marriage curriculum. *Journal of Family and Consumer Sciences Education, 19,* 1.

Gardner, S. (2005). Final Summary Report for the Evaluation of the Connections: Dating and Emotions Curriculum. As of August 7, 2006:
http://www.dibblefund.org/Documents/CDE-FER.pdf

Garofalo, R., Wolf, R. C., Kessel, S., Palfrey, S. J., and DuRant, R. H. (1998). The association between health risk behaviors and sexual orientation among a school-based sample of adolescents. *Pediatrics, 101,* 895–902.

Garofalo, R., Wolf, R. C., Wissow, L. S., Woods, E. R., and Goodman, E. (1999). Sexual orientation and risk of suicide attempts among a representative sample of youth. *Archives of Pediatric Adolescent Medicine, 153,* 487–493.

Gerbner, G., Gross, L., Morgan, M., and Signorielli, N. (1994). Growing up with television: The cultivation perspective. In J. Bryant and D. Zillman (eds.), *Media Effects: Advances in Theory and Research.* Hillsdale, N.J.: Lawrence Erlbaum Associates.

Gilbert, D. T., and Malone, P. S. (1995). The correspondence bias. *Psychological Bulletin, 117,* 21–38.

Giordano, P. C. (2003). Relationships in adolescence. *Annual Review of Sociology, 29,* 257–281.

Giordano, P. C., Cernkovich, S. A., Groat, H. T., Pugh, M. D., and Swinford, S. P. (1998). The quality of adolescent friendships: Long term effects? *Journal of Health and Social Behavior, 39,* 55–71.

Giordano, P. C., Longmore, M. A., and Manning, W. D. (2006). Gender and the meanings of adolescent romantic relationships: A focus on boys. *American Sociological Review, 71,* 260–287.

Giordano, P. C., Manning, W. D., and Longmore, M. A. (2005). The romantic relationships of African-American and white adolescents. *Sociological Quarterly, 46,* 545–568.

Giordano, P. C., Manning, W. D., and Longmore, M. A. (2006). Adolescent romantic relationships: An emerging portrait of their nature and developmental significance. In A. C. Crouter and A. Booth (eds.), *Romance and Sex in Adolescence and Emerging Adulthood: Risks and Opportunities* (pp. 127–150). Mahwah, N.J.: Lawrence Erlbaum Associates.

Goodburn, E. A., and Ross, D. A. (1995). *A Picture of Health: A Review and Annotated Bibliography of the Health of Young People in Developing Countries.* Geneva: World Health Organization and UNICEF.

Gotlib, I. H., Lewinsohn, P. M., and Seeley, J. R. (1998). Consequences of depression during adolescence: Marital status and marital functioning in early adulthood. *Journal of Abnormal Psychology, 107,* 686–690.

Gowen, L. K., Feldman, S. S., Diaz, R., and Yisrael, D. (2004). A comparison of the sexual behaviors and attitudes of adolescent girls with older vs. similar-aged boyfriends. *Journal of Youth and Adolescence, 33,* 167–175.

Gray, M. R., and Steinberg, L. (1999). Adolescent romance and the parent-child relationship: A contextual perspective. In W. Furman, B. B. Brown, and C. Feiring (eds.), *The Development of Romantic Relationships in Adolescence* (pp. 235–262). New York: Cambridge University Press.

Gray, S., and Phelps, S. (2001). *A.C. Green's Game Plan Abstinence Program.* Glencoe, Ill.: Project Reality. As of May 6, 2007:
http://www.projectreality.org/about/index.php?id=47

Greenberg, B. S. (1994). Content trends in media sex. In D. Zillman, J. Bryant, and A. C. Huston (eds.), *Media, Children and the Family.* Hillsdale, N.J.: Lawrence Erlbaum Associates.

Greenberg, B. S., and Busselle, R. W. (1996). Soap operas and sexual activity: A decade later. *Journal of Communication, 46,* 153–160.

Greene, W. H., and Simons-Morton, B. G. (1984). *Introduction to Health Education.* Prospect Heights, Ill.: Waveland Press.

Grello, C. M., Welsh, D. P., Harper, M. S., and Dickson, J. W. (2003). Dating and sexual relationship trajectories and adolescent functioning. *Adolescent and Family Health, 3,* 103–112.

Grinder, R. E. (1966). Relations of social dating attractions to academic orientation and peer relations. *Journal of Educational Psychology, 57,* 27–34.

Halford, W. K., Markman, H. J., Kline, G. H., and Stanley, S. M. (2003). Best practice in couple relationship education. *Journal of Marital and Family Therapy, 29,* 385–406.

Halpern, C. T. (2003). Biological influences on adolescent romantic and sexual behavior. In P. Florsheim (ed.), *Adolescent Romantic Relations and Sexual Behavior: Theory, Research, and Practical Implications* (pp. 57–84). Mahwah, N.J.: Lawrence Erlbaum Associates.

Halpern, C. T., Joyner, K., Udry, J. R., and Suchindran, C. (2000). Smart teens don't have sex (or kiss much either). *Journal of Adolescent Health, 26,* 213–225.

Halpern, C. T., Oslak, S. G., Young, M. L., Martin, S. L., and Kupper, L. L. (2001). Partner violence among adolescents in opposite-sex romantic relationships: Findings from the National Longitudinal Study of Adolescent Health. *American Journal of Public Health, 91,* 1679–1685.

Hamilton, B. E., Ventura, S. J., Martin, J. A., and Sutton, P. D. (2005). Preliminary births for 2004 [Electronic Version]. Health E-Stats, National Center for Health Statistics. As of October 28, 2005: http://www.cdc.gov/nchs/products/pubs/pubd/hestats/prelim_births/prelim_births04.htm

Harris, K. M., Florey, F., Tabor, J., Bearman, P.S., Jones, J., and Udry, J.R. (1997). *The National Longitudinal Study of Adolescent Health: Research Design.* As of May 18, 2007: http://www.cpc.unc.edu/projects/addhealth/design

Haynie, D. L., and Piquero, A. R. (2006). Pubertal Development and Physical Victimization in Adolescence. *Journal of Research in Crime and Delinquency, 43,* 3–35.

Hazan, C., and Shaver, P. R. (1987). Romantic love conceptualized as an attachment process. *Journal of Personality and Social Psychology, 52,* 511–524.

Heintz, K. E. (1992). Children's favorite television families: A descriptive analysis of role interactions. *Journal of Broadcasting and Electronic Media, 36,* 443–451.

Herdt, G., and Boxer, A. M. (1993). *Children of Horizons: How Gay and Lesbian Teens Are Leading a New Way Out of the Closet.* Boston, Mass.: Beacon Press.

Hernandez, D. J. (1997). Poverty trends. In G. J. Duncan and J. Brooks-Gunn (eds.), *Consequences of Growing Up Poor* (pp. 18–34). New York: Russell Sage Foundation.

Herold, E. S., and Marshall, S. K. (1996). Adolescent sexual development. In G. R. Adams, R. Montemayor, and T. P. Gullotta (eds.), *Psychosocial Development During Adolescence* (pp. 62–94). Thousand Oaks, Calif.: Sage Publications, Inc.

Hill, J. P., and Palmquist, W. J. (1978). Social cognition and social relations in early adolescence. *International Journal of Behavioral Development, 1,* 1–36.

Hogan, D. P., Astone, N. M., and Kitagawa, E. M. (1985). Social and environmental factors influencing contraceptive use among black adolescents. *Family Planning Perspectives, 17,* 165–169.

Hogan, D. P., and Kitagawa, E. M. (1985). The impact of social status, family structure, and neighborhood on the fertility of black adolescents. *American Journal of Sociology, 90,* 825–855.

Howard, D. E., and Wang, M. Q. (2003). Psychosocial factors associated with adolescent boys' reports of dating violence. *Adolescence, 38,* 519–533.

Jacobson, N. S., and Addis, M. E. (1993). Research on couples and couple therapy: What do we know? Where are we going? *Journal of Consulting and Clinical Psychology, 61,* 85–93.

Jacobson, N. S., and Margolin, G. (1979). *Marital Therapy: Strategies Based on Social Learning and Behavior Exchange Principles.* New York: Brunner/Mazel.

Jacobson, N. S., and Moore, D. (1981). Spouses as observers of the events in their relationship. *Journal of Consulting and Clinical Psychology, 49,* 269–277.

Jakubowski, S. F., Milne, E. P., Brunner, H., and Miller, R. B. (2004). A review of empirically supported marital enrichment programs. *Family Relations, 53,* 528–536.

Jockin, V., McGue, M., and Lykken, D. T. (1996). Personality and divorce: A genetic analysis. *Journal of Personality and Social Psychology, 71,* 288–299.

Johnson, C. A., Pentz, M. A., Weber, M. D., Dwyer, J. F., Baer, N., MacKinnon, D. P., et al. (1990). Relative effectiveness of comprehensive community programming for drug abuse prevention with high-risk and low-risk adolescents. *Journal of Consulting and Clinical Psychology, 58,* 447–456.

Johnson, J. D., Adams, M. S., Ashburn, L., and Reed, W. (1995). Differential gender effects of exposure to rap music on African American adolescents' acceptance of teen dating violence. *Sex Roles, 33,* 597–605.

Johnson, K., Bryant, D., Strader, T., Bucholtz, G., Berbaum, M., Collins, D., et al. (1996). Reducing alcohol and other drug use by strengthening community, family, and youth resiliency: An evaluation of the Creating Lasting Connections program. *Journal of Adolescent Research, 11,* 36–67.

Johnston, L. D., Bachman, J. G., and O'Malley, P. M. (1995). *Monitoring the Future. Questionnaire Responses from the Nation's High School Seniors, 1993.* Ann Arbor, Mich.: Institute for Social Research.

Jones, E. E., and Harris, V. A. (1967). The attribution of attitudes. *Journal of Experimental Social Psychology Quarterly, 3,* 1–24.

Jones, R. K., Darroch, J. E., and Singh, S. (2005). Religious differentials in the sexual and reproductive behaviors of young women in the United States. *Journal of Adolescent Health, 36,* 279–288.

Joyner, K., and Campa, M. (2006). How do adolescent relationships influence the quality of romantic and sexual relationships in young adulthood? In A. C. Crouter and A. Booth (eds.), *Romance and Sex in Adolescence and Emerging Adulthood: Risks and Opportunities* (pp. 93–101). Mahwah, N.J.: Lawrence Erlbaum Associates.

Joyner, K., and Udry, J. R. (2000). You don't bring me anything but down: Adolescent romance and depression. *Journal of Health and Social Behavior, 41,* 369–391.

Kaestle, C. E., and Halpern, C. T. (2005a). Sexual activity among adolescents in romantic relationships with friends, acquaintances, or strangers. *Archives of Pediatric Adolescent Medicine, 159,* 849–853.

Kaestle, C. E., and Halpern, C. T. (2005b). Sexual intercourse precedes partner violence in adolescent romantic relationships. *Journal of Adolescent Health, 36,* 386–392.

Kaestle, C. E., Halpern, C. T., Miller, W. C., and Ford, C. A. (2005). Young age at first sexual intercourse and sexually transmitted infections in adolescents and young adults. *American Journal of Epidemiology, 161,* 774–780.

Kamper, C. R. (2004). *Connections.* Berkeley, Calif.: The Dibble Fund. As of May 6, 2007: http://www.buildingrelationshipskills.org/catalog-con.htm

Kan, M. L., and Cares, A. C. (2006). From "friends with benefits" to "going steady": New directions in understanding romance and sex in adolescence and emerging adulthood. In A. C. Crouter and A. Booth (eds.), *Romance and Sex in Adolescence and Emerging Adulthood: Risks and Opportunities* (pp. 241–258). Mahwah, N.J.: Lawrence Erlbaum Associates.

Karney, B. R., and Bradbury, T. N. (1995). The longitudinal course of marital quality and stability: A review of theory, methods, and research. *Psychological Bulletin, 118,* 3–34.

Karney, B. R., and Bradbury, T. N. (2000). Attributions in marriage: State or trait? A growth curve analysis. *Journal of Personality and Social Psychology, 78,* 295–309.

Karney, B. R., Garvan, C. W., and Thomas, M. S. (2003). *Family Formation in Florida: 2003 Baseline Survey of Attitudes, Beliefs, and Demographics Relating to Marriage and Family Formation.* Gainesville, Fla.: University of Florida.

Kennedy, D. P. (2005). Young people and their companions: Reciprocation of adolescent romantic partner nominations. Arlington, Va.: Battelle Weekly Seminar.

Kim, K. J., Conger, R. D., Lorenz, F. O., and Elder, G. H. J. (2001). Parent-adolescent reciprocity in negative affect and its relation to early adult social development. *Developmental Psychology, 37,* 775–790.

Kinsfogel, K. M., and Grych, J. H. (2004). Interparental conflict and adolescent dating relationships: Integrating cognitive, emotional, and peer influences. *Journal of Family Psychology, 18,* 505–515.

Kirby, D., Lepore, G., and Ryan, J. (2005). *Sexual Risk and Protective Factors. Factors Affecting Teen Sexual Behavior, Pregnancy, Childbearing and Sexually Transmitted Disease: Which Are Important? Which Can You Change?* Washington, D.C.: National Campaign to Prevent Teenage Pregnancy.

Kreider, R. M., and Fields, J. M. (2001). Number, timing, and duration of marriages and divorces: Fall 1996. In *Current Population Reports* (pp. 70–80). Washington, D.C.: U.S. Census Bureau.

Kreitzer, A. (1998). Summary: Evaluation of the "Loving Well" curriculum. As of July 3, 2006: http://www.bu.edu/education/lovingwell/Formal_Evaluation.html

Ku, L., Sonenstein, F. L., and Pleck, J. H. (1994). The dynamics of young men's condom use during and across relationships. *Family Planning Perspectives, 26,* 246–251.

Kubey, R., and Donovan, B. W. (2001). Media and the family. In D. G. Singer and J. L. Singer (eds.), *Handbook of Children and the Media* (pp. 323–340). Thousand Oaks, Calif.: Sage Publications, Inc.

Kunkel, D., Eyal, K., Finnerty, K., Biely, E., and Donnerstein, E. (2005). Sex on TV4: A Kaiser Family Foundation Report. Menlo Park, Calif.: Kaiser Family Foundation.

La Greca, A. M., and Harrison, H. M. (2005). Adolescent peer relations, friendships, and romantic relationships: Do they predict social anxiety and depression? *Journal of Clinical Child and Adolescent Psychology, 34,* 49–61.

La Guardia, J. G., Ryan, R. M., Couchman, C. E., and Deci, E. L. (2000). Within-person variation in security of attachment: A self-determination theory perspective on attachment, need fulfillment, and well-being. *Journal of Personality and Social Psychology, 79,* 367–384.

Laursen, B., and Collins, W. A. (1994). Interpersonal conflict during adolescence. *Psychological Bulletin, 115,* 197–209.

Lempers, J. D., and Clark-Lempers, D. S. (1993). A functional comparison of same-sex and opposite sex friendships during adolescence. *Journal of Adolescent Research, 81,* 89–108.

Lescano, C. M., Vazquez, E. A., Brown, L. K., Litvin, E. B., and Pugatch, D. (2006). Condom use with "casual" and "main" partners: What's in a name? *Journal of Adolescent Health, 39,* e1–e7.

Levesque, R. J. (1993). The romantic experience of adolescents in satisfying love relationships. *Journal of Youth and Adolescence, 22,* 219–251.

Lichter, D. T., Graefe, D. R., and Brown, J. B. (2003). Is marriage a panacea? Union formation among economically disadvantaged unwed mothers. *Social Problems, 50,* 60–86.

Linder, J. R., and Collins, W. A. (2005). Parent and peer predictors of physical aggression and conflict management in romantic relationships in early adulthood. *Journal of Family Psychology, 19,* 252–262.

Lipsey, M. W., and Corday, D. S. (2000). Evaluation methods of social intervention. *Annual Review of Psychology, 51,* 345–375.

Longmore, M. A., Manning, W. D., and Giordano, P. C. (2001). Preadolescent parenting strategies and teens' dating and sexual initiation: A longitudinal analysis. *Journal of Marriage and the Family, 63,* 322–335.

Magdol, L., Moffitt, T. E., Caspi, A., and Silva, P. A. (1998). Developmental antecedents of partner abuse: A prospective-longitudinal study. *Journal of Abnormal Psychology, 107,* 375–389.

Malamuth, N. M., and Impett, E. A. (2001). Research on sex in the media. What do we know about effects on children and adolescents? In D. G. Singer and J. L. Singer (eds.), *Handbook of Children and the Media* (pp. 269–287). Thousand Oaks, Calif.: Sage Publications, Inc.

Manlove, J., Franzetta, K., Ryan, S., and Moore, K. (2006). Adolescent sexual relationships, contraceptive consistency, and pregnancy prevention approaches. In A. C. Crouter and A. Booth (eds.), *Romance and Sex in Adolescence and Emerging Adulthood: Risks and Opportunities* (pp. 181–212). Mahwah, N.J.: Lawrence Erlbaum Associates.

Manning, W., Longmore, M., and Giordano, P. (2000). The relationship context of contraceptive use at first intercourse. *Family Planning Perspectives, 32,* 104–110.

Marin, B. V., Kirby, D. B., Hudes, E. S., Coyle, K. K., and Gomez, C. (2006). Boyfriends, girlfriends and teenagers' risk of sexual involvement. *Perspectives on Sexual and Reproductive Health, 38,* 76–83.

Markman, H. J., Stanley, S. M., and Blumberg, S. L. (1994). *Fighting for Your Marriage: Positive Steps for Preventing Divorce and Preserving a Lasting Love.* San Francisco: Jossey-Bass.

Martin, J. A., Hamilton, B. E., Ventura, S. J., Menacker, F., and Park, M. M. (2002). Births: final data for 2000. *National Vital Statistics Reports,* Vol. 50, No. 5. Hyattsville, Md.: Centers for Disease Control and Prevention, National Center for Health Statistics.

Martin, S. P. (2004). Growing Evidence for a "Divorce Divide"? Education and Marital Dissolution Rates in the U.S. Since the 1970s. New York: Russell Sage Foundation. As of June 1, 2007: http://www.russellsage.org/publications/workingpapers/divorcedivide/document

Martinez, G., Chandra, A., Abma, J., Jones, J., and Mosher, W. (2006). Fertility, contraception, and fatherhood: Data from the 2002 National Survey of Family Growth. *Vital Health Statistics, 23,* 246.

Martino, S. C., Collins, R. L., Elliott, M. N., Strachman, A., Kanouse, D. E., and Berry, S. H. (2006). Exposure to degrading versus non-degrading music lyrics and sexual behavior among youth. *Pediatrics, 118,* e430–e441.

Masten, A. S., Coatsworth, J. D., Neemann, J., Gest, S. D., Tellegen, A., and Garmezy, N. (1995). The structure and coherence of competence from childhood through adolescence. *Child Development, 66,* 1635–1659.

Maynard, R. (1995). Teenage childbearing and welfare reform: Lessons from a decade of demonstration and evaluation research. *Children and Youth Services Review, 17,* 309–332.

McCabe, M. P., and Collins, J. K. (1984). Measurement of depth of desired and experienced sexual involvement at different stages of dating. *Journal of Sex Research, 20,* 377–390.

McGue, M., and Lykken, D. T. (1992). Genetic influence on risk of divorce. *Psychological Science, 3,* 368–373.

McLanahan, S. (2004). Diverging destinies: How children are faring under the second demographic transition. *Demography, 41,* 607–627.

McLanahan, S., and Sandefur, G. (1994). *Growing Up with a Single Parent: What Hurts, What Helps?* Cambridge, Mass.: Harvard University Press.

McLoyd, V. C., and Steinberg, L. (eds.). (1998). *Studying Minority Adolescents: Conceptual, Methodological, and Theoretical Issues.* Mahwah, N.J.: Lawrence Erlbaum.

Miller, B. C., and Benson, B. (1999). Romantic and sexual relationship development during adolescence. In W. Furman, B. B. Brown, and C. Feiring (eds.), *The Development of Romantic Relationships in Adolescence* (pp. 99–121). New York: Cambridge University Press.

Miller, B. C., Norton, M. C., Curtis, T., Hill, E. J., Schvaneveldt, P., and Young, M. H. (1997). The timing of sexual intercourse during adolescence: Family peer, and other antecedents. *Youth and Society, 29,* 54–83.

Miller, K. S., Forehand, R., and Kotchick, B. A. (2000). Adolescent sexual behavior in two ethnic minority groups: A multisystem perspective. *Adolescence, 35,* 313–333.

Monroe, S. M., Rohde, P., Seeley, J. R., and Lewinsohn, P. M. (1999). Life events and depression in adolescence: Relationship loss as a prospective risk factor for first onset of major depressive disorder. *Journal of Abnormal Psychology, 108,* 606–614.

Montgomery, M. J. (2005). Psychosocial intimacy and identity: From early adolescence to emerging adulthood. *Journal of Adolescent Research, 20,* 346–374.

Murry, V. M., Hurt, T. R., Kogan, S. M., and Luo, Z. (2006). Contextual processes of romantic relationships: Plausible explanations for gender and race effects. In A. C. Crouter and A. Booth (eds.), *Romance and Sex in Adolescence and Emerging Adulthood: Risks and Opportunities* (pp. 151–160). Mahwah, N.J.: Lawrence Erlbaum Associates.

Myer, J. (1989). Guess who's coming to dinner this time? A study of gay intimate relationships and the support for those relationships. *Marriage and Family Review, 14,* 59–82.

Myers, D., and Schirm, A. (1999). *The Impacts of Upward Bound: Final Report for Phase I of the National Evaluation.* Washington, D.C.: U.S. Department of Education, Planning and Evaluation Service.

National Association of State Administrators for Family and Consumer Sciences. (1998). National Standards for Family and Consumer Sciences Education. Decatur, Ga.: V-TECS Southern Association of Colleges and Schools.

National Healthy Marriage Resource Center (NHMRC). 2007. Fairfax, Va.: National Healthy Marriage Clearing House. As of May 17, 2007:
http://www.healthymarriageinfo.org/

Neemann, J., Hubbard, J., and Masten, A. S. (1995). The changing importance of romantic relationship involvement to competence from late childhood to late adolescence. *Development and Psychopathology, 7,* 727–750.

Newman, D. L., Caspi, A., Moffitt, T. E., and Silva, P. A. (1997). Antecedents of adult interpersonal functioning: Effects of individual differences in age 3 temperament. *Developmental Psychology, 33,* 206–217.

O'Donnell, B. L., O'Donnell, C. R., and Stueve, A. (2001). Early sexual initiation and subsequent sex-related risks among urban minority youth: The reach for health study. *Family Planning Perspectives, 33,* 268–275.

O'Donnell, W. J. (1979). Affectional patterns of adolescents. *Adolescence, 14,* 681–686.

Ooms, T. (2005). *The New Kid on the Block: What Is Marriage Education and Does It Work?* (Couples and Marriage Series Brief No. 7). Washington, D.C.: Center for Law and Social Policy.

Otten, E. H. (2000). *Character Education.* Bloomington, Ind.: ERIC Clearinghouse for Social Studies/Social Science Education, Indiana University.

Pardun, C. J., L'Engle, K. L., and Brown, J. D. (2005). Linking exposure to outcomes: Early adolescents' consumption of sexual content in six media. *Mass Communication and Society, 8,* 75–91.

Parke, R. D. (1998). A developmentalist's perspective on marital change. In T. N. Bradbury (ed.), *The Developmental Course of Marital Dysfunction* (pp. 393–409). New York: Cambridge University Press.

Pawlby, S. J., Mills, A., and Quinton, D. (1997). Vulnerable adolescent girls: Opposite-sex relationships. *Journal of Child Psychology and Psychiatry, 38,* 909–920.

Pearson, M. (2007). *Love U2.* Berkeley, Calif.: The Dibble Fund.

Personal Responsibility and Work Opportunity Reconciliation Act, P.L. 104-193 (1996).

Philliber, S., Williams, K. J., Herrling, S., and West, E. (2002). Preventing pregnancy and improving health care access among teenagers: An evaluation of the Children's Aid Society-Carrera Program. *Perspectives on Sexual and Reproductive Health, 34,* 244–251.

Project Alpha (2007). Web site. As of June 12, 2007:
http://www.alphaphialpha.net/Page.php?id=165

Raffaelli, M. (2005). Adolescent dating experiences described by Latino college students. *Journal of Adolescence, 28,* 559–572.

Raley, K., and Bumpass, L. (2003). The topography of the divorce plateau: Levels and trends in union stability in the United States after 1980. *Demographic Research, 8,* 245–259.

Reese-Weber, M., and Marchand, J. F. (2002). Family and individual predictors of late adolescents' romantic relationships. *Journal of Youth and Adolescence, 31,* 197–206.

Roberts, D. F., Foehr, U. G., and Rideout, V. (2005). *Generation M: Media in the Lives of 8–18 Year-Olds. A Kaiser Family Foundation Study.* Menlo Park, Calif.: Kaiser Family Foundation.

Roberts, T. A., Auinger, P., and Klein, J. D. (2005). Intimate partner abuse and the reproductive health of sexually active female adolescents. *Journal of Adolescent Health, 36,* 380–385.

Roberts, T. A., Klein, J. D., and Fisher, S. (2003). Longitudinal effect of intimate partner abuse on high-risk behavior among adolescents. *Archives of Pediatric Adolescent Medicine, 157,* 875–881.

Rodgers, J. (1996). Sexual transitions in adolescence. In J. Graber, J. Brooks-Gunn, and A. Peterson (eds.), *Transitions Through Adolescence: Interpersonal Domains and Context* (pp. 85–110). Mahwah, N.J.: Lawrence Erlbaum Associates.

Rogge, R., and Bradbury, T. N. (1999). Till violence does us part: The differing roles of communication and aggression in predicting adverse marital outcomes. *Journal of Consulting and Clinical Psychology, 67,* 340–351.

Rogge, R. D., Bradbury, T. N., Hahlweg, K., Engl, J., and Thurmaier, F. (2006). Predicting marital distress and dissolution: Refining the two-factor hypothesis. *Journal of Family Psychology, 20,* 156–159.

Roisman, G. I., Collins, W. A., Sroufe, L. A., and Egeland, B. (2005). Predictors of young adults' representations of and behavior in their current romantic relationship: Prospective tests of the prototype hypothesis. *Attachment and Human Development, 7,* 105–121.

Roisman, G. I., Madsen, S. D., Hennighausen, K. H., Sroufe, L. A., and Collins, W. A. (2001). The coherence of dyadic behavior across parent-child and romantic relationships as mediated by the internalized representation of experience. *Attachment and Human Development, 3,* 156–172.

Roscoe, B., Diana, M. S., and Brooks, R. H. (1987). Early, middle, and late adolescents' views on dating and factors influencing partner selection. *Adolescence, 22,* 59–68.

Rose, S., and Frieze, I. H. (1989). Young singles' scripts for a first date. *Gender and Society, 3,* 258–268.

Rostosky, S. S., Galliher, R. V., Welsh, D. P., and Kawaguchi, M. C. (2000). Sexual behaviors and relationship qualities in late adolescent couples. *Journal of Adolescence, 23,* 583–597.

Rostosky, S. S., Regenerus, M. D., and Wright, M. L. C. (2003). Coital debut: The role of religiosity and sex attitudes in the Add Health survey. *Journal of Sex Research,* 40, 358–367.

Rostosky, S. S., Welsh, D. P., Kawaguchi, M. C., and Galliher, R. V. (1999). Commitment and sexual behaviors in adolescent dating relationships. In J. M. Adams and W. H. Jones (eds.), *Handbook of Interpersonal Commitment and Relationship Stability* (pp. 323–338). Dordrecht, Netherlands: Kluwer Academic Publishers.

Rutter, M., and Quinton, D. (1984). Long-term follow-up of women institutionalized in childhood: Factors promoting good functioning in adult life. *British Journal of Developmental Psychology, 2,* 191–204.

Ryder, V., and Harter, M. B. (1995). *Contemporary Living.* Tinley Park, Ill.: The Goodheart-Wilcox Company, Inc.

Salts, C. J., Seismore, M. D., Lindholm, B. W., and Smith, T. A. (1994). Attitudes toward marriage and premarital sexual activity of college freshmen. *Adolescence, 29,* 775–779.

Samet, N. R., and Kelly, E. W. (1987). The relationship of steady dating to self-esteem and sex role identity among adolescents. *Adolescence, 22,* 231–245.

Santelli, J., Ott, M. A., Lyon, M., Rogers, J., Summers, D., and Schleifer, R. (2006). Abstinence and abstinence-only education: A review of U.S. policies and programs. *Journal of Adolescent Health, 38,* 72–81.

Santelli, J. S., Kouzis, A. C., Hoover, D. R., Polacsek, M., Burwell, L. G., and Celentano, D. D. (1996). Stage of behavior change for condom use: The influence of partner type, relationship and pregnancy factors. *Family Planning Perspectives, 28,* 101–107.

Sasse, C. R. (2004). *Families Today.* Blacklick, Ohio: McGraw Hill/Glencoe.

Savin-Williams, R. C. (1994). Verbal and physical abuse as stressors in the lives of lesbian, gay male, and bisexual youths: Associations with school problems, running away, substance abuse, prostitution, and suicide. *Journal of Consulting and Clinical Psychology, 62,* 261–269.

Savin-Williams, R. C. (2001). A critique of research on sexual-minority youths. *Journal of Adolescence, 24,* 5–13.

Sayegh, M. A., Fortenberry, J. D., Shew, M., and Orr, D. P. (2006). The developmental association of relationship quality, hormonal contraceptive choice and condom non-use among adolescent women. *Journal of Adolescent Health, 39,* 388–395.

Sayers, S. L., Kohn, C. S., and Heavey, C. (1998). Prevention of marital dysfunction: Behavioral approaches and beyond. *Clinical Psychology Review, 18,* 713–744.

Schoen, R., and Standish, N. (2001). The retrenchment of marriage: Results from Marital Life Tables for the United States, 1995. *Population and Development Review, 27,* 553–563.

Schulenberg, J., Bachman, J. G., Johnston, L. D., and O'Malley, P. M. (1995). American adolescents' views on family and work: Historical trends from 1976–1992. In P. Noack, M. Hofer, and J. Youniss (eds.), *Psychological Responses to Social Change.* New York: Walter de Gruyter.

Schulenberg, J., O'Malley, P. M., Bachman, J. G., and Johnston, L. D. (2005). Early adult transitions and their relation to well-being and substance use. In R. A. Settersten, F. F. Furstenberg, and R. G. Rumbaut (eds.), *On the Frontier of Adulthood: Theory, Research, and Public Policy* (pp. 417–453). Chicago, Ill.: University of Chicago Press.

Schwarz, N. (1999). Self-reports: How the questions shape the answers. *American Psychologist, 54,* 93–105.

Seefeldt, K. S., and Smock, P. J. (2004). *Marriage on the Public Policy Agenda: What Do Policy Makers Need to Know from Research?* (PSC Research Report No. 04-554). Ann Arbor, Mich.: Population Studies Center, University of Michigan.

Seiffge-Krenke, I. J., Shulman, S., and Kiessinger, N. (2001). Adolescent precursors of romantic relationships in young adulthood. *Journal of Social and Personal Relationships, 18,* 327–346.

Seltzer, J. A. (2004). Cohabitation in the United States and Britain: Demography, kinship, and the future. *Journal of Marriage and the Family, 66,* 921–928.

Shadish, W. R., Cook, T. D., and Campbell, D. T. (2002). *Experimental and Quasi-Experimental Designs for Generalized Causal Inference.* Boston, Mass.: Houghton Mifflin Co.

Shellenbarger, S. (2005). The case for going steady: Studies say teen dating habits affect marriage skills. *Wall Street Journal,* p. D.1, September 8.

Shulman, S. (2003). Conflict and negotiation in adolescent romantic relationships. In P. Florsheim (ed.), *Adolescent Romantic Relations and Sexual Behavior: Theory, Research, and Practical Implications* (pp. 109–135). Mahwah, N.J.: Lawrence Erlbaum Associates.

Sieving, R. E., Eisenberg, M. E., Pettingell, S., and Skay, C. (2006). Friends' influence on adolescents' first sexual intercourse. *Perspectives on Sexual and Reproductive Health, 38,* 13–19.

Signorielli, N. (1982). Marital status in television drama: A case of reduced options. *Journal of Broadcasting and Electronic Media, 26,* 585–597.

Silver, E., and Bauman, L. (2006). The association of sexual experience with attitudes, beliefs, and risk behaviors of inner-city adolescents. *Journal of Research on Adolescence, 16,* 29–45.

Silverman, J. G., Raj, A., Mucci, L. A., and Hathaway, J. E. (2001). Dating violence against adolescent girls and associated substance use, unhealthy weight control, sexual risk behavior, pregnancy, and suicidality. *JAMA: Journal of the American Medical Association, 286,* 572–579.

Simmons, R. G., Blyth, D. A., Vancleave, E. F., and Bush, D. M. (1979). Entry into early adolescence—impact of school structure, puberty, and early dating on self-esteem. *American Sociological Review, 44,* 948–967.

Simon, R. W., Elder, D., and Evans, C. (1992). The development of feeling norms underlying romantic love among adolescent females. *Social Psychology Quarterly, 55,* 29–46.

Simons, R. L., Lin, K.-H., and Gordon, L. C. (1998). Socialization in the family of origin and male dating violence: A prospective study. *Journal of Marriage and the Family, 60,* 467–478.

Singer, E., and Presser, S. (1989). *Survey Research Methods: A Reader.* Chicago: University of Chicago Press.

Singh, G. K., Matthews, T. J., Clarke, S. C., Yannicos, T., and Smith, B. L. (1995). Annual summary of births, marriages, divorces, and deaths: United States, 1994. *Monthly Vital Statistics Reports,* Vol. 43, No. 13. Atlanta, Ga.: National Center for Health Statistics.

Smolak, L., Levine, M. P., and Gralen, S. (1993). The impact of puberty and dating on eating problems among middle school girls. *Journal of Youth and Adolescence, 22,* 355–368.

Sprague, H. E., and Kinney, J. M. (1997). The effects of interparental divorce and conflict on college students' romantic relationships. *Journal of Divorce and Remarriage,* 27, 85–104.

Sprecher, S., Barbee, A., and Schwartz, P. (1995). "Was it good for you too?" Gender differences in first sexual intercourse experience. *Journal of Sex Research, 32,* 3–15.

Sroufe, L. A., Egeland, B., Carlson, E., and Collins, W. A. (2005). Placing early attachment experiences in developmental context: The Minnesota Longitudinal Study. In K. E. Grossmann, K. Grossmann, and E. Waters (eds.), *Attachment from Infancy to Adulthood: The Major Longitudinal Studies* (pp. 48–70). New York: Guilford Publications, Inc.

Stattin, H., and Magnusson, D. (1990). *Pubertal Maturation in Female Development.* Hillsdale, N.J.: Lawrence Erlbaum Associates.

Steinberg, S. J., Davila, J., and Fincham, F. D. (2006). Adolescent marital expectations and romantic experiences: Associations with perceptions about parental conflict and adolescent attachment security. *Journal of Youth and Adolescence, 35,* 314–329.

Story, L. B., Karney, B. R., Lawrence, E., and Bradbury, T. N. (2004). Interpersonal mediators in the intergenerational transmission of marital dysfunction. *Journal of Family Psychology, 18,* 519–529.

Story, L. B., Rothman, A. D., and Bradbury, T. N. (2002). Risk factors, risk processes, and the longitudinal course of newlywed marriage. In P. Noller and J. A. Feeney (eds.), *Understanding Marriage: Developments in the Study of Couple Interaction* (pp. 468–492). New York: Cambridge University Press.

Sullivan, H. S. (1953). *The Interpersonal Theory of Psychiatry.* New York: W. W. Norton.

Summers, P., Forehand, R., Armistead, L., and Tannenbaum, L. (1998). Parental divorce during early adolescence in Caucasian families: The role of family process variables in predicting the long-term consequences for early adult psychosocial adjustment. *Journal of Consulting and Clinical Psychology, 66,* 327–336.

Taga, K. A., Markey, C. N., and Friedman, H. S. (2006). A longitudinal investigation of associations between boys' pubertal timing and adult behavioral health and well-being. *Journal of Youth and Adolescence, 35,* 380–390.

Tallman, I., Burke, P. J., and Gecas, V. (1998). Socialization into marital roles: Testing a contextual, developmental model of marital functioning. In T. N. Bradbury (ed.), *The Developmental Course of Marital Dysfunction* (pp. 312–342). New York: Cambridge University Press.

Tasker, F. L., and Richards, M. P. M. (1994). Adolescents' attitudes toward marriage and marital prospects after parental divorce: A review. *Journal of Adolescent Research, 9,* 340–362.

Thompson, A., and Bolger, N. (1999). Emotional transmission in couples under stress. *Journal of Marriage and the Family, 61,* 38–48.

Thorbecke, W., and Grotevant, H. D. (1982). Gender differences in adolescent interpersonal identity formation. *Journal of Youth and Adolescence, 11,* 479–492.

Thornton, A. (1990). The courtship process and adolescent sexuality. *Journal of Family Issues, 11,* 239–273.

VanOss Marín, B., Coyle, K. K., Gómez, C. A., Carvajal, S. C., and Kirby, D. B. (2000). Older boyfriends and girlfriends increase risk of sexual initiation in young adolescents. *Journal of Adolescent Health, 27,* 409–418.

VanOss Marín, B., Kirby, D., Hudes, E., Coyle, K., and Gómez, C. (2006). Boyfriends, girlfriends and teenagers' risk of sexual involvement. *Perspectives on Sexual and Reproductive Health, 38,* 76–83.

Waldinger, R. J., Diguer, L., Guastella, F., Lefebvre, R., Allen, J. P., Luborsky, L., et al. (2002). The same old song? Stability and change in relationship schemas from adolescence to young adulthood. *Journal of Youth and Adolescence, 31,* 17–29.

Ward, L. M. (1995). Talking about sex: Common themes about sexuality in the prime-time programs children and adolescents view most. *Journal of Youth and Adolescence, 24,* 595–615.

Ward, L. M., and Friedman, K. (2006). Using TV as a guide: Associations between television viewing and adolescents' sexual attitudes and behavior. *Journal of Research on Adolescence, 16,* 133–156.

Ward, L. M., Hansbrough, E., and Walker, E. (2005). Contributions of music video exposure to Black adolescents' gender and sexual schemas. *Journal of Adolescent Research, 20,* 143–166.

Waters, E., Merrick, S., Treboux, D., Crowell, J., and Albersheim, L. (2000). Attachment security in infancy and early adulthood: A twenty-year longitudinal study. *Child Development, 71,* 684–689.

Weaver, J., Masland, J. L., and Zillman, D. (1984). Effect of erotica on young men's aesthetic perception of their female sexual partners. *Perceptual and Motor Skills, 58,* 929–930.

Weiss, F. L., and Nicholson, H. J. (1998). Friendly PEERsuasion against substance use: The Girls Incorporated model and evaluation. In J. Valentine, J. A. D. Jong, and N. J. Kennedy (eds.), *Substance Abuse Prevention in Multicultural Communities* (pp. 7–22). Binghamton, N.Y.: Haworth Press.

Weiss, R. L. (1980). Strategic behavioral marital therapy: Toward a model for assessment and intervention. In J. P. Vincent (ed.), *Advances in Family Intervention, Assessment, and Theory* (Vol. 1, pp. 229–271). Greenwich, Conn.: JAI Press.

Weiss, R. L. (1984). Cognitive and behavioral measures of marital interaction. In K. Hahlweg and N. S. Jacobson (eds.), *Marital Interaction: Analysis and Modification* (pp. 232–252). New York: Guilford Press.

Wekerle, C., and Avgoustis, E. (2003). Child maltreatment, adolescent dating, and adolescent dating violence. In P. Florsheim (ed.), *Adolescent Romantic Relations and Sexual Behavior: Theory, Research, and Practical Implications* (pp. 213–241). Mahwah, N.J.: Lawrence Erlbaum Associates.

Welsh, D. P., Grello, C. M., and Harper, M. S. (2003). When love hurts: Depression and adolescent romantic relationships. In P. Florsheim (ed.), *Adolescent Romantic Relations and Sexual Behavior: Theory, Research, and Practical Implications* (pp. 185–211). Mahwah, N.J.: Lawrence Erlbaum Associates.

Whitaker, D. J., Miller, K. S., and Clark, L. F. (2000). Reconceptualizing adolescent sexual behavior: Beyond did they or didn't they? *Family Planning Perspectives, 32,* 111–117.

White, K. M., Speisman, J. C., Costos, D., and Smith, A. (1987). Relationship maturity: A conceptual and empirical approach. *Contributions to Human Development, 18,* 81–101.

Whitehead, B. D., and Pearson, M. (2006). *Making a Love Connection: Teen Relationships, Pregnancy, and Marriage.* Washington, D.C.: National Campaign to Prevent Teen Pregnancy.

Williams, S., Connolly, J., and Segal, Z. V. (2001). Intimacy in relationships and cognitive vulnerability to depression in adolescent girls. *Cognitive Therapy and Research, 25,* 477–496.

Zani, B. (1993). Dating and interpersonal relationships in adolescence. In S. Jackson and H. Rodriguez-Tomé (eds.), *Adolescence and Its Social Worlds* (pp. 95–119). Hillsdale, N.J.: Lawrence Erlbaum Associates.

Zillman, D. (1994). Erotica and family values. In D. Zillman, J. Bryant, and A. C. Huston (eds.), *Media, Children and the Family: Social Scientific, Psychodynamic and Clinical Perspectives* (pp. 199–213). Hilllsdale, N.J.: Lawrence Erlbaum Associates.

Zillman, D., and Weaver, J. B. (1989). Pornography and men's sexual callousness toward women. In D. Zillman and J. Bryant (eds.), *Pornography: Research Advances and Policy Considerations* (pp. 95–125). Hillsdale, NJ.: Lawrence Erlbaum Associates.

Zimmer-Gembeck, M. J. (1999). Stability, change and individual differences in involvement with friends and romantic partners among adolescent females. *Journal of Youth and Adolescence, 28,* 419–438.

Zimmer-Gembeck, M. J., Siebenbruner, J., and Collins, W. A. (2004). A prospective study of intraindividual and peer influences on adolescents' heterosexual romantic and sexual behavior. *Archives of Sexual Behavior, 33,* 381–394.

Zoccolillo, M., Pickles, A., Quinton, D., and Rutter, M. (1992). The outcome of childhood conduct disorder: Implications for defining adult personality disorder and conduct disorder. *Psychological Medicine, 22,* 971–986.

Zubriggen, E. L., and Moregan, E. M. (2006). Who wants to marry a millionaire? Reality dating television programs, attitudes toward sex, and sexual behaviors. *Sex Roles, 54,* 1–17.